D1606584

Heroines of Comic Books
and Literature

Heroines of Comic Books and Literature

Portrayals in Popular Culture

Edited by
Maja Bajac-Carter, Norma Jones,
and Bob Batchelor

ROWMAN & LITTLEFIELD
Lanham • Boulder • New York • Toronto • Plymouth, UK

3/3/15
$ LB
75.00

Published by Rowman & Littlefield
4501 Forbes Boulevard, Suite 200, Lanham, Maryland 20706
www.rowman.com

10 Thornbury Road, Plymouth PL6 7PP, United Kingdom

Copyright © 2014 by Rowman & Littlefield

All rights reserved. No part of this book may be reproduced in any form or by any electronic or mechanical means, including information storage and retrieval systems, without written permission from the publisher, except by a reviewer who may quote passages in a review.

British Library Cataloguing in Publication Information Available

Library of Congress Cataloging-in-Publication Data
Heroines of Comic Books and Literature : Portrayals in Popular Culture / edited by Maja Bajac-Carter, Norma Jones, and Bob Batchelor.
pages cm
Includes index.
ISBN 978-1-4422-3147-4 (cloth : alk. paper) — ISBN 978-1-4422-3148-1 (electronic)
1. Women in literature. 2. Heroines in literature. 3. Women in popular culture. 4. Women in mass media. 5. Comic books, strips, etc.—History and criticism. I. Bajac-Carter, Maja, 1979– II. Jones, Norma, 1972– III. Batchelor, Bob.
PN56.5.W64H55 2014
809'.933522—dc23
2013040490

∞ ™ The paper used in this publication meets the minimum requirements of American National Standard for Information Sciences Permanence of Paper for Printed Library Materials, ANSI/NISO Z39.48-1992.

Printed in the United States of America

Contents

Acknowledgments

Heroines of Comic Books and Literature: Portrayals in Popular Culture would not have been possible without the support of Stephen Ryan at Rowman & Littlefield. As editors, we would also like to thank our contributors for being integral parts of this book. As a whole, your essays are creative and timely, and they allow for richer explorations of heroines in popular culture. We appreciate your works and contributions to further the understandings and readings of these heroic women.

Norma and Maja would like to thank Bob for giving us the encouragement and support to pursue this book project. We realize that as doctoral students, we are often more limited in our autonomy to initiate and then manage a book-length project such as this one. Bob, we would like to express our deep gratitude for your trust and guidance. You knew when to step in and when to let us go, and for this we thank you. We would also like to acknowledge our mutual advisor, George Cheney, in the College of Communication and Information at Kent State. We appreciate you trusting your advisees with the space to take on a book project while we were still in your classes. Thank you for being a fantastic mentor, teacher, and advisor.

Bob would like to acknowledge his colleagues at Thiel College, including department mates Victor Evans and Laurie Moroco. He would also like to thank Dean Lynn Franken and President Troy VanAken for their support and encouragement. Finally, it is a great honor to hold the James Pedas Professor of Communication position—many thanks to James Pedas and his family for their continued support of Thiel College, including providing the funding for the James Pedas Communication Center.

We also have some individual thanks as well.

Maja: I would like to thank my family, my mother Lidija who is an endless inspiration in my life, and my brother Vojislav. Also thanks to my friends, A and D, and Norma, my greatest friend and academic accomplice.

Norma: I would like to thank my family—the Chus, Murphrees, Joneses, Rayburns, Yaghmaeis, Yangs, Chens, and Lipscombs. To my wonderful Brent, I am deeply grateful for you, and everything I do is only possible with you. I also want to thank Maja who is my wonderfully awesome friend.

Bob: My family is incredibly supportive and kind, considering the fact that writing books necessitates long hours of writing and thinking time in virtual solitary. Thanks to my parents, Jon and Linda Bowen, for everything they do to make our lives infinitely better. My daughter Kassie's bright smile and the love in her eyes brings laughter and joy into every moment. My wife Kathy is my pillar of strength and soul mate.

Introduction

Heroines of Comic Books and Literature: Portrayals in Popular Culture is a unique anthology that updates existing books on action chicks, tough girls, damsels in distress, and sacrificial heroines by examining the portrayal of female characters in popular culture through a range of perspectives and theories about heroines from literature and printed visual media. It is important to offer more nuanced readings of heroines and understanding of existing critiques and move beyond theatrical versions of Ripley and Sarah Connor, toward heroines in contemporary literature and comics/graphic novels, which is precisely what the authors of this book bring to the discussion about female characters. But are these characters really different? Or do we still reiterate the same stereotypes?

Heroines of Comic Books and Literature: Portrayals in Popular Culture examines the changing role of female heroines in contemporary American culture. Analyzing depictions of female heroes, the authors demonstrate how critical these representations are for readers as they explore their worldviews, both from a critical and contextual perspective. Via exciting and sophisticated examination of heroines in print culture, the authors reveal how these portrayals influence American popular culture and the foundational notion of what it means to be a woman.

This engaging and important collection reconceptualizes the study of how women are and have been represented in print media into the twenty-first century. Essays in this book introduce a number of perhaps lesser-known printed media and ethnically diverse sources that have a profound impact on the ways we look at heroines. These essays are not part of a study nor do they deal with content analysis of mass media. They survey a wide range of different printed media texts, including American and Latino literature and graphic novels, contemporary letter writing, queer works, and classic Euro-

pean literature and offer an updated examination of female characters/hero-
ines who simultaneously challenge and perpetuate dominant gender and societal expectations. Award-winning contributors go beyond the expected accounts of women as mothers, wives, warriors, goddesses, and damsels in
distress to provide innovative analysis that situates heroines within cultural
contexts, revealing them as tough, self-sufficient, and breaking the bounds of
gender expectations in places readers may not have anticipated.

The opening section of the book contains essays that take on what we
may consider "traditional literature" forms: novels, memoirs, and letter writing. Lindow looks at contemporary women writers of fantasy and their depiction of the Heroine's Journey and how it is distinctive from the Hero's
Journey. In this exploration of traditional and contemporary urban settings,
the author examines diversity and multiculturalism in works of Robin
McKinley, Nedi Okorofor, Loren Beukes, Malinda Lo, and Nalo Hopkinson.
Clasen examines the traditional gender dynamic crafted throughout the Twilight series. This essay explores the ways in which Twilight shaped young
adult female heroines by embracing traditional feminine notions of care and
nurture. Lemley offers an interesting read of witches and their portrayal from
novels to television adaptations. Laity takes on the life of the twelfth-century
recluse Christina of Markyate in the context of both early medieval romances
like Marie de France's work and contemporary saints' lives and reveals a
woman who innovates both. Schneeweis explores the objectification and
commodification of Esmeralda, from Victor Hugo's celebrated novel *The
Hunchback of Notre-Dame* to recent popular-culture films and musicals. This
critical examination of artistic and mediated representations of "gypsies"
finds that the gypsy woman embodies characteristics consistent with historical stereotypes of the bohemian. Smith turns our attention to the status of
women in the armed forces and recent debates regarding the service of wom-
en soldiers in combat positions, as well as the dramatic rise of sexual violence against active-duty women, and examines how women communicate
their negotiation of these various challenges and violations.

In the next section of the book, the first two chapters may take up little
space, but they offer invaluable insight into culturally, ethnically, and religiously diverse literature. From the Americas through the Middle East, the
authors examine the construction and representation of lesser-known heroines, specifically less known to audiences in the United States. Espinoza
explores representations of various Latin American and U.S. Latina heroic
female figures in the late twentieth and early twenty-first centuries from a
"postcolonial feminism," or, more broadly speaking, "postcolonial gender
studies," perspective, as proposed by Gloria Anzaldúa in *Borderlands/La
Frontera*. Some of the heroines explored include La Malinche, the historical
translator of Hernán Cortez; Latina artist Laura Molina's comic superheroine
The Jaguar; and a look at Marvel's *Araña* and *Spider-Girl*.

Erhart and Eslen-Ziya take on Janissary, the only Turkish female superhero who lives in the DC Universe. Because of her representation as the veiled woman (marking other culture as foreign, exotic), she herself becomes a symbol for Islam, a barbaric and uncivilized culture. In this chapter, the authors focus on the representational strategies that offer an exotic heroine to a contemporary Western comic book fan.

Wagenheim and McDaniel offer an interesting reading of various editions and series of *X-Men* graphic novels regarding motherhood and marriage. Wagenheim establishes that the representation of mothers and mother figures within the foundational/origin story of the X-Men has remained static and problematic. He links the absence of mothers and their problematic representation to the psychoanalytic and sociological theories of mother-disidentification in regards to hegemonic male development and suggests that the *X-Men* franchise is, in part, teaching the mostly male comics consumer that separating themselves from their mother is an integral part of moving from boyhood to manhood. McDaniel compares the rhetorical space that Storm, a high-profile, black, female superhero, "claims" as a single, black woman and the rhetorical space that she has been "assigned" to as Panther's wife. This is further problematized as black and/or female characters often are marginalized in comic books; they are "assigned" the role of supporting/background personalities to male and/or other white characters.

Two chapters in one book about Wonder Woman may seem excessive, as much has been written about this quintessential character. However, these chapters offer a reading of Wonder Woman as a much more complex character than she appears: as an iconic image for young girls, she sets expectations for young female and male adults alike, as described in the Zechowski and Neumann chapter. Robbins, on the other hand, asks the question, are the Amazon princess Diana, her hometown Amazons, and her Holliday girl sidekicks lesbians? And is this a *bad* thing? Robbins argues that it will never be known if Wonder Woman's creator really intended any hidden lesbian agenda in his comics, or if suspicions of Sapphism were simply products of Wertham's McCarthyist mentality, but for over ten golden years, William Moulton Marston provided a haven for girls in the pages of his comics, away from Man's World. Next, Murphy examines the different ways that female comic heroines are defined by their creators and their readers and connects indie lesbian comic folk heroes of the past and present with their mainstream counterparts.

In the final section of the book, readers will encounter characters from contemporary American graphic novels. Miczo asks if a female superhero can stand alone, and reach her potential, without having her femininity become a liability by looking at Carol Danvers, aka Ms. Marvel. Cook takes on John Byrne's *Sensational She-Hulk* #40—the notorious "jump rope" issue which looms large in discussions of the objectification of the female body within superhero comics. His more nuanced reading provides a framework for understanding the jump-rope incident as part of an extended critique of the Comics Code and of the depiction of women in superhero comics. Darowski discusses the three female superheroes that were most prominent in this period—Invisible Girl, the Wasp, and Marvel Girl—and claims that only in the decades that followed were these problematically weak females transformed into independent women, team leaders, and powerful superheroes. On the other hand, Edmunds examines Marvel Comics' attempts to develop heroines, including the roles female characters have played in the major turning points in the Marvel Universe, and argues that there remains no true iconic Marvel superheroine. Pagnoni Berns reviews both Marvel and DC's characters, Spider-Woman and Wonder Woman. He calls them hesitant heroines, who seek dialogue and understanding in battle, heroines who continually seek to define their identity while questioning the violence around them. To close out the book, Kramer takes a feminist rhetorical perspective to analyze *The Evil That Men Do*, arguing that the book reinforces the no-win situation faced by many comic book heroines who often are punished for their power. Such depictions strengthen the status quo and further undermine the heroine's ability to deliver positive gender messages to society.

Part I

Literature

Chapter One

To Heck with the Village

Fantastic Heroines, Journey and Return

Sandra J. Lindow

In 1949, Joseph Campbell's groundbreaking book, *The Hero with a Thousand Faces*, described the man's hero journey as a "monomyth" that consisted of a call to adventure, separation from family and village, supernatural help which included initiation into secret knowledge, a magical boon, a series of trials, and eventually a triumphant return to the community.[1] Beginning in the 1960s, Second Wave feminists like Joanna Russ were, however, quick to note that Campbell excluded women from the hero journey except for stereotypical roles as virgins, temptresses, goddesses, earth mothers, and crones, and in 1971, Russ wrote, "Both men and women conceive our culture from a single point of view—the male."[2] Furthermore, folklorists were seeing a different pattern for women's journeys. Close reading of early versions of folktales with female protagonists such as "Cinderella," "Snow White," "Donkey Skin," and "Silver Hands"[3] revealed that young women did not hear the call to adventure and blithely leave their homes to seek their fortunes, but were driven out by extremes of drudgery, deprivation, neglect, and emotional and physical abuse. Stories like "Silver Hands"[4] included actual incest, rape, and maiming.[5] In most cases a triumphant homecoming was neither possible nor desirable. Rather, the goal of the heroine's journey involved a made-over, upwardly mobile, better-dressed[6] self finding a new home with less drudgery, more love and acceptance, and, for a while at least, a happily ever after. Initially, heroines tended to be innocent and weak, but their journeys taught them strategies, patience, networking, resilience, and wisdom—psychologically killing the dragons in their psyches and creating characters worthy of their new and better homes. Nevertheless, these tales of fantastic heroines continued to bother feminists like Russ who found them too limiting in their class and gender role restrictions.[7] Most of the tales reinforced a tyranny of standards for youth, beauty, and modesty that most women found impossible, what Carol Pearson calls the myths of virginity, romantic love, and maternal self-sacrifice.[8] Where were the stories about imperfect women (dare I say middle-aged and older women?) who transcended the feminine passivity and powerlessness inherent to a patriarchal society? Considering how few princess jobs are actually available, how can a heroine develop the agency to become a hero? This chapter will examine women's hero journeys written in the twenty-first century by women writers who transgress cultural norms, recreating what Russ called "workable myths" that interpret and reflect on women's actual life experience,[9] focusing on three critical times in women's lives: coming of age, creating mature sexual relationships, and coming to terms with aging.

Women, like men, attain heroism through the pursuit of truth.[10] Because the term *hero* implies greater agency than *heroine*, henceforth this chapter will use the term *hero journey* to describe this developmental process. In many cases, the true focus of the hero tale is not only on transforming the self but also on transforming "the monster of the status quo,"[11] that aspect of society that has become stagnated and dysfunctional. In 1981 Pearson[12] predicted that future work by feminists would attack the largely unconscious status quos regarding class, gender, and conventional feminine beauty, a direction first explored by writers like Ursula K. Le Guin in *The Left Hand of Darkness*, 1969; Joanna Russ in *The Female Man*, 1975; and Marge Piercy in *Woman on the Edge of Time*, 1976. Originally these novels were considered controversial and, to some, shocking, but the sea change of the late twentieth century, actively advocated and supported by feminist SF conferences such as WisCon[13] and the James Tiptree Award[14] for the exploration and expansion of gender initiated there, brought permissions for authors to write as gendered themselves, creating differently gendered characters with an increased acceptance of bodies, sexuality, and diversity.[15] By 2011, national polls have reflected that a majority of Americans accept same-sex unions; popular television programs like *Brothers and Sisters* and *Modern Family* have included gay characters who marry and adopt; and on May 9, 2012, Barack Obama became the first sitting U.S. president to publicly declare support for the legalization of same-sex marriage.[16] Many contemporary fantasy writers now premise their stories on gender, race, and class equality, a "Love will always prevail"[17] new romanticism. As Malinda Lo explains in her 2011 lesbian coming-of-age novel, *Huntress*, "Love knows no limits; it sees no distinctions based on birth or any other characteristic. A prince may love a seamstress as much as any princess."[18]

DARK BEGINNINGS, UNCONVENTIONAL CONNECTIONS

As in traditional fairy and folk tales, coming-of-age journeys by contemporary writers usually begin with something deeply amiss in the world, but they often follow a path where classism is subtly subverted and the realities of sexual attraction seem more important than the conventions of romance. Malinda Lo's *Huntress* follows a plotline that consciously redacts traditional fairy-tale tropes, beginning with a winter that will not end.[19] There is something unsettling the kingdom, an evil that evokes a "never-ending grayness, as if all the color had been leached from the world."[20] Crops won't grow, people are beginning to starve, and monsters have been coming out of the forest to attack unsuspecting travelers. Kaede and Taisin, two seventeen-year-old sages-in-training, accompany Con, the king's son, on a journey north to seek the help of the fairy queen. Although Taisin is gifted and conventionally feminine, Kaede has strength, assertiveness, skill, and compassion, an effective fusing of male and female qualities. Throughout their journey, verses from their *Tao*-like *Book of Changes* provide koans for the young women to interpret: "Those who seek to change . . . will be changed; / Those who grasp onto stones will find water."[21] As in traditional tales, the young women have been given boons to help them on their journey: Taisin, a magical medallion that enhances telepathic connection, and Kaede, a special dagger. The journey itself provides a postracial[22] melding of classes. Prince Con has cut his long black hair very short so that he will look "ordinary,"[23] and it is significant later that Shae, one of the guards on the trip, also wears her hair very short.[24] During the course of the journey, Kaede becomes a successful huntress,[25] and both Kaede and Taisin develop independence, stamina, and skill. The divergence from the old tales, however, is that neither falls in love with the prince: both are irrevocably drawn to each other despite the vows of chastity they have taken, while Con and the peasant-born Shae fall in love. In the end, Kaede saves the dying fairy queen through the blood of a unicorn, willingly sacrificed, an act that once again transcends barriers: "What difference there was between fay and human was erased because both understood the sorrow of loss."[26]

In *Chaos*, 2012, Caribbean Canadian writer Nalo Hopkinson interweaves various folktales, mythologies, and redactions to create a coming-of-age tale in a contemporary urban setting.[27] Her mixed-race sixteen-year-old protagonist, Scotch, whose given name Sojourner directly connects her to Civil War hero Sojourner Truth, has been forced to switch schools after repeatedly being bullied for sexually maturing earlier than other girls. Although Scotch has been given a new start in a new academic "village," she has developed a skin condition, a black stickiness she likens to the Tar Baby[28] that spreads slowly across her body, attaching her to an unruly magic let loose in contemporary Toronto. Moreover, nearly invisible, possibly hallucinatory creatures

called Horseless Head Men[29] follow her. Her brother disappears in an ex-
ploding bubble of light, a volcano emerges in Lake Ontario, Sasquatches
appear downtown, and Baba Yaga's[30] house begins attacking pedestrians.
All of this seems thematically tied, like poltergeist stories, to Scotch's cultural identity issues and her restless, burgeoning sexuality, a hormonal journey
that takes center stage early in the novel, with a level of frankness unseen in
mid-twentieth-century books intended for girls[31]:

> Me and Glory talked about it all the time. How would it be to sit on chubby
> Walter Herron's strong, sturdy lap? How would the plumpness of his skin feel
> under my hands? What does Sanjay Harsha's breath taste like? What would it
> feel like to run my hands through his hair? Ever since then, I'd been exploring.
> I wasn't the only one either.[32]

Eventually Scotch, aided by Baba Yaga's ambiguously moral witchery, is
able to save her brother and reset the out-of-whack balance of magic in the
world. It is clear here as it is in earlier works such as *Brown Girl in the Ring*,
1998; *Skin Folk*, 2001; *The Salt Roads*, 2003; and *The New Moon's Arms*,
2007,[33] that Hopkinson is consciously using and redacting folktale tropes to
confront repressive attitudes to developing young adult sexuality, remove the
blinders of heteronormativity, and create hero tales for a contemporary audience.

DANGEROUS BOYFRIENDS, CONNECTIONS TO THE EARTH

Increased acceptance of diversity should make finding a mate easier, but
there is a trend in the fantastic that increases the obstacles involved in finding
true love. It is the era of the dangerous boyfriend, typified by vampire romances, first popularized by novels like Anne Rice's *Interview with the
Vampire*, 1976; Tanith Lee's Dark Dance series, beginning 1992; and
Stephenie Meyer's hugely successful Twilight series, beginning 2005. Sex
with the Other has become acceptable, perhaps even preferable, to young
adult readers seeking to prepare for later real-life sexual journeys by first
experiencing passion on the page. Female protagonists rebelliously insist on
the right to follow their own paths to sexual satisfaction, and a sizeable
segment of young female fans are enticed by graphically depicted trysts
between hot-blooded young women and the chill, marble-white (possibly
perpetually erect) bodies of their vampire lovers. Here the hero journey requires extreme sacrifice, including a willingness to give up humanity itself
for the possibility of something colder but more enduring.[34]

Robin McKinley's *Sunshine*, 2003, is a vampire romance that redacts
Cinderella, and as its title suggests, it is less dark than many of its precursors.
Set in the city of New Arcadia, the story reflects a number of literary inspira-

tions including Sir Philip Sydney's[35] pastoral romance "Arcadia," 1590. In Greek mythology, Arcadia was the home of the Greek god Pan and Atalanta, the abandoned daughter of the king of Arcadia, but McKinley's New Arcadia is an alternate-history North American city besieged by vampires and "Other" magical creatures. The story evolves from the problematic romance between Sunshine, a sunlight-loving cinnamon roll baker, and Constantine,[36] her ethical vampire lover. Sunshine, whose birth name is Raven[37] (Rae) Blaise, is the daughter of divorced parents: a powerful sorcerer father and a working-class mother. She has inherited some of her father's gifts for magic, specifically transmutation, although as the story begins she has not seen him in years, and the gifts have lain dormant. Despite being humorously self-deprecating, Sunshine is not helpless when captured by vampires in the forest outside of town, forced to wear a scarlet ball gown, and offered as food to a shackled, starving vampire. She is a natural storyteller, whose favorite tale[38] is fittingly *Beauty and the Beast*,[39] and in a Scheherazade-like series of events, Sunshine is able to escape the ballroom of the abandoned mansion,[40] thereby saving the morose and suicidal vampire as well as herself, but since vampire relationships are taboo, she is deeply frightened, conflicted, and faced with a psychological need to keep her alliance with the vampire a secret as they are increasingly drawn together as allies in an ongoing war against evil.

Throughout her work, McKinley uses magic as a vehicle for harnessing the power of the unconscious through connection with nature. Sunshine channels sunlight and a tree to enhance her power, literally warming and shading her vampire. In McKinley's later novel *Chalice*[41], 2008, the danger is fire rather than ice. Mirosol, the protagonist, is a beekeeper and the newly chosen Chalice holder for the demesne. The Chalice is a magically endowed cup for creating healing and unity, and its power must be used wisely. Her love interest, the young Master, is literally too hot to touch. Before being called home by his brother's unexpected death, he was in the process of becoming a Priest of Fire, and now physical contact with him can burn human flesh to the bone. Not entirely human, he must wear heavy clothing to protect others from accidental touch. Like Sunshine's vampire, he is both compelling and revolting. Mirosol, however, is able to use her intuitive understanding of the connected powers of semiconscious earthlines in the demesne and honey's healing qualities to slowly reclaim the young Master's humanity. In both books, the female protagonists receive wounds that will not heal, requiring magical intervention by their love interests, a sharing that removes psychological barriers and strengthens emotional bonds. Although the male protagonists have magic, strength, compassion, moral development, and purpose, they are initially loveless and deeply damaged by what they have sacrificed to gain power. It is the female protagonists who have the intuitive intelligence, insight, and magic to unlock the door to a healthy, believable love.

After extensive analysis of folk and fairy tales, Jack Zipes has concluded that "magic . . . is nothing else but the realization of the divine creative powers one possesses within oneself," and for McKinley's characters, magic is channeled and learned through interaction with the divine Wild. Mirosol lives on the edge of the forest making her a kind of hedge witch, albeit a young one. Her paranormal connection to her bees is a powerful boon. Sunshine's alignment with sunlight can be used against creatures of the dark as well as to protect herself from being "turned." For Mirosol and Sunshine, the journey through the psychosexual forest is a process of coming to terms with their own magic and their possible dissatisfaction with the "normal" marital choices offered by their communities. As in traditional tales, McKinley's protagonists search for true love, and although their quests are informed by feminist sensibility,[42] resolution still reflects Sydney's Arcadian sonnet "My True-Love Hath My Heart":

> My true-love hath my heart, and I have his,
> By just exchange one for the other given:
> I hold his dear, and mine he cannot miss;
> There never was a bargain better driven.[43]

Together Sunshine and Constantine become very efficient vampire slayers, and their exchange of heart's blood is literal as well as figurative.

ANIMAL ALLIES, OVERCOMING ISOLATION AND ADDICTION

The course of the hero journey is, by definition, not easy; suffering is inevitable. Traditional folk and fairy tales do not spend much time on psychological pain and avoidance. Charles Perrault's Cinderella (1697) had good reason to be depressed, but Perrault was too busy painting her as demure and admirable. Nevertheless, fifteenth-century morality plays like *Everyman* did depict the depression that comes from purposelessness, and in 1678, Bunyan's *Pilgrim's Progress*[44] described the Slough of Despond, where humans get off course and are bogged down by a sense of hopelessness and a lack of spiritual/moral focus. One of the responses to the pain of despondency is addiction, which in itself creates a negative downward spiral that interferes with intimacy and stagnates further moral development. Lauren Beukes' 2011 Arthur C. Clarke Award–winning novel, *Zoo City*,[45] examines the fantastic consequences of addiction and recovery in a world where a plague of magically induced animal symbiots follows a trajectory similar to AIDS. These archetypal animals seem to be physical manifestations of psychological "shadow" issues their hosts must face in order to further their moral development. Since the animals appear after individuals have been responsible for a murder and must be in close proximity all the time, their existence works to physically and socially ghettoize their hosts; thus the title *Zoo City*. All is not entirely bleak, however, for each animal comes with a chance for redemption: a magical talent, a telepathic connection, and a forced intimacy that can work together to overcome the emotional isolation[46] that originally led to the death of another human being. Caring for the animal is parallel to caring for an infant, and, in a spiritual sense, caring for the lost soul of the one who died. As with fairy-tale boons, the gifts of being "animalled" can be used for good or for ill. The most evil and corrupt can corrupt their "aposymbiots"[47] as well, falling further into self-serving crime and addiction only to end up being torn to bits and dragged by a black cloud into "Hell's undertow" when their animal dies.[48] Set in a dismal alternate Johannesburg, the novel follows con woman Zinzi December[49] and her Sloth as she reclaims her moral focus after years of struggling to pay for her various substance and process addictions. By the end of the novel, Zinzi, whose addiction originally contributed to her brother's death, has overcome her dependency and avoidance, has killed a dragon in the form of a symbiot Crocodile, has identified a serial killer, and has set off on an altruistic road trip to save her lover's previously lost wife and children. Perrault's Cinderella would have had little chance against a semi-sentient Crocodile, but Zinzi has overcome sloth, learned agency, and prevailed.

EVERAFTERS

Traditional folk and fairy tales usually conclude when characters solve the developmental issues of young adulthood. The assumption is that after the hero journey, life achieves a more or less "happily ever after" norm, and the heroism of older individuals is ignored except as it functions to support the quests of the next generation. However, since the 1970s,[50] women writers and critics have been making active attempts to create and define hero journeys by older women who are able to transcend the remainder table and make a difference in their worlds. Le Guin was one of the first speculative writers to do so in stories like "The Day before the Revolution," 1974, and "Betrayals," 1994. Elizabeth Moon's 1996 novel, *Remnant Population*, is exemplary in its description of an older woman who makes a difference, as is Molly Gloss' *The Dazzle of Day*, 1998. None of these, however, explore older women in terms of folk and fairy tale tropes.

In 2010, however, veteran writers Jane Yolen and Midori Snyder published *Except the Queen*,[51] a collaborative novel that follows Meteora and Serana, two rather narcissistic fey who are banished from the Greenwood for revealing a secret about the Queen. As an effect of their banishment, the sisters must navigate a bafflingly complex contemporary world, having been suddenly thrust into the postmenopausal, overweight, arthritic bodies that they would have had without glamorous magical protection.[52] In Milwaukee, Meteora finds refuge in Baba Yaga's legendary house where she befriends Sparrow, a troubled young woman who is being stalked by an evil tattoo artist. Taken for a bag lady, Serana is rescued by a New York social worker and is given an apartment in a rundown neighborhood where she meets and adopts Robin, a feral, but extremely talented, musician. What is most interesting here is that the sisters' initial childlike frivolity and romantic preoccupation with "carnal play"[53] and other pleasures of the flesh are transformed by aging brains and blossoming moral maturity, creating the ability to delay gratification and to nurture others. Whereas other recent fantasy novels such as Larissa Lai's *When Fox Was a Thousand*, 2004, depict magical protagonists forever stuck in their moral development, Yolen and Snyder see value in wisdom and aging. Mortality and morality are linked through memory and narrative. Meteora explains, "When you live each day as we do, nearly immortal, there is no day that is unlike the other, . . . there is no memory of consequence. Each day is the same tale, so there is no need to remember it at all."[54] In late middle age, Meteora and Serana have learned consequence. Correspondingly, they are aged but not asexual; rather, they have gained the ability to create long-lasting relationships that are not ruled by transient lusts. Furthermore, their journey irrevocably changes their outlook. After helping to end a vitality-sapping war between Seelie and Unseelie courts, they do not choose to return to their previous selves. As Meteora explains, "There is nothing so beautiful to me now as a face that wears its history well."[55]

WITCHES AND CRONES IN WONDERLAND

Traditional folktales shy away from the heroism of old women perhaps because so few women actually lived long enough to be considered old. Today, although a majority of women live many years beyond retirement, the hero tales of old women continue to be neglected. Dubravka Ugresic's 2010 Tiptree Award–winning novel *Baba Yaga Laid an Egg*[56] begins with a quiet meditation on the marginalization of elderly women, a reprise of Tiptree's "The Women Men Don't See"[57]:

> Yes, at first they are invisible. They move past you, shadowlike, they peck at the air in front of them, tap, shuffle along the asphalt, mince in small mouse-like steps, pull a cart behind them, clutch at a walker, stand surrounded by a cluster of pointless sacks and bags, like a deserter from the army still decked out in full war gear.[58]

Do aging women lose vitality even as they gain baggage? Why are elderly women either invisible or terrible? Old age, in itself a battle that is ultimately lost, provides considerable opportunities for heroism. Ugresic's metafictional three-part novel, set in New Zagreb and an expensive Eastern European health spa, parallels the structure of Baba Yaga tales by depicting the interwoven lives of several older women as they seek to overcome emotional invisibility and find "treasure" in renewing relationships. Possible parallels are explained at the end in an over-the-top academic metacommentary, "If You Know Too Much, You Grow Old Too Soon,"[59] or "Baba Yaga for Beginners."[60]

It is not coincidence that Baba Yaga is an important character in both *Chaos*[61] and *Except the Queen*.[62] To enter Baba Yaga's forest is to face death's eventual inevitability whether it is in Milwaukee, Toronto, or Eastern Europe. She forces recognition of mortality when she threatens to eat protagonists,[63] reconsiders, and ends up saving them, thereby initiating essential passages in moral development.

Meeting the crone is an integral part of women's hero tales. Iron teeth and stringy hair aside, she is an archetypal trickster character, "an intermediary between worlds," a mediator between genders,[64] with power to overcome social invisibility and make a difference. She has an unapologetic agenda and the capacity to be rude as well as kind. She is, in *Huntress*, Mona, a white-haired woman limping slightly and leaning on a horned staff,[65] a greenwitch with an ambiguous past, who appears in a moment of desperate need and acts as a vigorous counterbalance to the dying fairy queen. She is a midwife[66] with a moral sword[67] who has learned the lessons of solitude.[68] In *Sunshine*, she appears both as Sunshine's landlady Yolande, a retired wardskeeper, who is older than she seems and knows more than she reveals, and as Maud, who appears pushing a two-wheeled shopping cart shortly after Sunshine muses that "good fairies don't exist." Maud offers a choice between fig carousel and chocolate pinwheel cookies,[69] possibly symbolizing a developmental fork in the road, a choice of directions, each valid but mutually exclusive, that will irrevocably influence the woman Sunshine will become.

REMAKING THE VILLAGE

In 1979 Susan K. Rowe wrote that "the female psyche has not matured with sufficient strength to sustain a radical assault on the patriarchal culture."[70] She concluded that "fairy tale visions of romance" continued to subordinate women and wondered if women had the "courageous vision and energy" to grow new fairy tales for the future.[71] Challenging the status quo is not in itself enough; there is a need to create acceptable alternatives. Beginning in the 1960s, angry Second Wave feminists like Joanna Russ, Doris Lessing, and Marge Piercy were adept at challenging the powers that be with their utopian and dystopian visions. Although changes in cultural acceptance of

diversity have occurred, the books discussed in this chapter present a continued need to challenge and transgress the status quo by re-visioning a better
"village" for the journey's end. Traditionally, folk and fairy tales were told as
a response to socioeconomic problems, and the same is true today. Contemporary women embark on heroic quests because power imbalances remain:
they continue to be marginalized especially if they are isolated, young, old,
gay, interracial, or poor. Correspondingly, woman authors clearly continue to
be dissatisfied by damaging sexual stereotypes and the appeasing myths of
folk and fairy tale traditions that still influence attitudes toward women.
There may be a little magic in the way human beings find, help, and learn to
love each other, but as McKinley's Sunshine explains,

> what this world doesn't have is the three-wishes-go-to-the ball-and-meet-your-
> prince, happily-ever-after kind of magic. We have all the mangling and malev-
> olent kinds. Who invented this system?[72]

Setting out to fight evil is, if anything, more complicated in the twenty-first
century than it was in the seventeenth. The protagonists of these tales are all
traumatized by encounters with embodiments of evil. The positive difference
today, however, is that during the course of the journey, moral decision
making is emphasized, and female protagonists are rewarded with certain
important freedoms; primary among them is the right to be angry, the right to
act assertively and fight for a cause, and the right to love dangerously and
boldly in a way that may conflict with community and family standards.
Certainly the women depicted in these tales do not wait to be rescued by the
prince. Furthermore, the value of becoming Mrs. Charming is significantly
downplayed. Protagonists are competent enough to live on their own and
brave and resourceful enough to rescue the prince as well as themselves
when rescuing is needed. The heroes of these contemporary tales achieve
their goals through intelligence, courage, and creativity, although not without
suffering loss and not without successful alliance. Rugged individuality is
out; networking is in. The old village is out; the new village is in.[73] Although
not entirely devoid of romantic ideals, their grasp of psychosexual reality
pushes female heroes into assertive action, and their newfound village supports this action. In several cases, especially *Chaos*, *Huntress*, and *Zoo City*,
the village is portable, a connection (via telepathy or cell phone) that is
powerful enough to withstand continued journey—the open road, reflecting
further moral development: to heck with the old village, onward with the
new.

NOTES

1. Joseph Campbell, *The Hero with a Thousand Faces* (Princeton, NJ: Princeton University Press, 1949), ix.

2. Joanna Russ, "What Can a Heroine Do? Or Why Women Can't Write," in *To Write Like a Woman: Essays in Feminism and Science Fiction* (Bloomington: Indiana University Press, 1995), 81.

3. In Jacob and Wilhelm Grimm's *Household Tales*, "The Girl without Hands" (http://www.pitt.edu/~dash/grimm031.html), the father makes a deal with the Devil and is "tricked" into cutting off his daughter's arms. In the Xhosa version of this tale, "A Father Cuts Off His Daughter's Arms," recounted by Midori Snyder, a young girl is raped by either her father or her brother, who takes her into the forest, cuts off her arms, and leaves her for dead.

4. Midori Snyder, "The Armless Maiden and the Hero's Journey," *Journal of Mythic Arts*, http://www.endicott-studio.com.

5. Midori Snyder, "The Armless Maiden," in *The Armless Maiden and Other Tales for Childhood's Survivors*, ed. Terri Windling (New York: Tor, 1995).

6. In the tale "Donkey Skin," a princess whose father either wants to marry her himself or marry her to an ogre asks for dresses "the color of the sun," "the color of the moon," and "the color of weather." In the prose poem "Donkeyskin," Terri Windling retells and adapts this story to a modern setting. Robin McKinley's novelized version is called *Deerskin*.

7. In 1978 Russ published a novella intended as a bildungsroman for girls, *Kittatinny: A Tale of Magic* (New York: Daughters, 1978). Kit, her protagonist, runs away from home to an imaginary world where, aided by a baby faun, she has adventures and learns how to handle her anger appropriately. Time passes. The story concludes when Kit returns home as a young adult only to find that a part of herself has been there all the time. Transcending heteronormativity, Kit then chooses Rose, her best friend, as her partner and traveling companion, and they go off together. See Sandra Lindow, "Kittens Who Run with Wolves: Healthy Girl Development in Joanna Russ's *Kittatinny*," in *On Joanna Russ*, ed. Farah Mendlesohn (Middletown, CT: Wesleyan University Press, 2009).

8. Carol Pearson and Katherine Pope, *The Female Hero in American and British Literature* (New York: Bowker, 1981), 18.

9. Russ, *Write Like a Woman*, 89.

10. Pearson, *Hero*, 8.

11. Ibid., 5.

12. Ibid.

13. WisCon, the first feminist science fiction conference, was held in February 1977 in Madison, Wisconsin. Jan Bogstad, one of the founders, has explained that it was intended as a free space for conversation about science fiction and gender, although it was a while before they called it a "feminist" science fiction convention (May 27, 2013).

14. The Tiptree Award was first announced by author Pat Murphy in her February 1991 guest of honor speech at WisCon. The first Tiptree Awards included a chocolate typewriter and were given in 1991 to Eleanor Arnason for *A Woman of the Iron People* and to Gwyneth Jones for *The White Queen*. Funding for the Tiptree continues to be largely supported by sales of items such as T-shirts, cookbooks, and baked goods.

15. Interracial marriages have been fully legal since 1967 when the Supreme Court deemed anti-miscegenation laws illegal.

16. "Obama Affirms Support for Same-Sex Marriage," *ABC News*, May 9, 2012 (retrieved March 20, 2013). It is common for politicians to maneuver to the front of a crowd when they realize its direction. On Monday, May 13, 2013, Minnesota became the twelfth state to support gay marriage.

17. Malinda Lo, *Huntress* (New York: Little, Brown, 2011), 115.

18. Ibid., 115.

19. Lo's previous novel, *Ash*, redacts the heteronormativity of the Cinderella tale.

20. Lo, *Huntress*, 358.

21. Ibid., 233.

22. Le Guin was one of the first to do this in her early novels such as *Planet of Exile* (1966) and the Earthsea series.

23. Lo, *Huntress*, 50.

24. Ibid., 62.

25. The choice of the term *huntress*, a romantic sexualizing *hunter-in-a-dress* connotative descriptor, is interesting considering the lack of sexual stereotyping elsewhere in the novel. It may be a marketing ploy to attract young female fantasy readers in a way *hunter* would not.

26. Ibid., 362.

27. Fellow Canadian writer Charles De Lint is also adept at creating strong female characters and interweaving folktales and mythology with an urban landscape.

28. The Tar Baby tale was told originally as an Anansi the Spider tale and later in America as a Brer Rabbit tale.

29. This is an obvious play on the headless horseman in Washington Irving's *The Legend of Sleepy Hollow*, but it also reflects voodoo mythology where a "possessed" individual is said to be a "horse" ridden by spirits or *loa*. Hopkinson has explored this in earlier work.

30. While Baba Yaga is simply identified as "the old lady," Hopkinson calls the house Izbouchka: an *izbushka* is a Russian cottage built on legs.

31. In *Childhood and Society*, Erik Erikson describes the goal of adolescence as being ego development: identity versus role confusion provides the developmental crisis. Successful negotiation of the crisis includes basic strengths of devotion and fidelity. This process is described in both *Huntress* and *Chaos*.

32. Nalo Hopkinson, *Chaos* (New York: Margaret K. McElderry Books), 15.

33. Hopkinson has won numerous awards for her work including the John W. Campbell Award, the Locus Award for Best New Writer, the World Fantasy Award, and the Gaylactic Spectrum Award. In 2008, *The New Moon's Arms*, a contemporary *selkie* tale, received the Prix Aurora Award (Canada's reader-voted award for science fiction and fantasy) and the Sunburst Award for Canadian Literature of the Fantastic, making her the first author to receive the Sunburst Award twice.

34. One of the most extreme of these "all for love" novels is Martine Leavitt's beautifully depicted YA novel *Keturah and Lord Death*. Here Keturah, the protagonist, gives up a village community typified by healthy relationships and human love in order to consciously choose and ride off with the personification of Death.

35. Sir Philip Sidney (November 30, 1554–October 17, 1586).

36. Constantine's name reflects loyalty, constancy, and reliability, but, like Prince Con in *Huntress*, there may be a reference to pro and con alternatives, the approach-avoidance conflict typical in romance.

37. The dark/light juxtaposition of her names has yin/yang appeal as well as indicating integral parts of the protagonist's personality. In Native American legends, Raven brought light to the world.

38. Sunshine's least favorite tales are Snow White and Cinderella, possibly because of the protagonists' passivity.

39. Robin McKinley, *Sunshine* (New York: Berkley, 2003), 42.

40. In a gritty nod at the Cinderella story, Sunshine has bare, bleeding feet when she leaves the ballroom, and the vampire must carry her. What she leaves behind is not so importantly her shoes but parts of her memory of the event, leaving her with posttraumatic stress disorder.

41. Robin McKinley, *Chalice* (New York: Ace, 2009).

42. Psychologist Erik Erikson's "stages of development" describe the goal of young adulthood as intimacy versus isolation.

43. Sydney, "My True Love Hath My Heart," in *Luminarium: Anthology of English Literature*, http://www.luminarium.org/renlit/truelove.html.

44. John Bunyan, *The Pilgrim's Progress*, retrieved from the Christian Classics' Ethereal Library, http://www.ccel.org/ccel/bunyan/pilgrim.html.

45. Lauren Beukes, *Zoo City* (orig. pub. South Africa: Jacana, 2010; Newcastle: Angry Robot, 2011).

46. In *Childhood and Society*, 1950, Erik Erikson writes that "when we don't find it easy to create satisfying relationships, our world can begin to shrink and, in defence, we can feel

superior to others." Successfully passing through this developmental crisis rewards us with love and affiliation.

47. The *apo* in *aposymbiot* is short for *apocalypse*, a reference to apocalyptic end times. Beukes, *Zoo City*, 83.

48. Ibid., 79, 191.

49. Zinzi's last name, December, may suggest that this is her last chance.

50. James Tiptree Jr. (Alice Bradley Sheldon) was one of the first to describe the social invisibility of older women in "The Women Men Don't See," 1973.

51. Jane Yolen and Midori Snyder, *Except the Queen* (New York: Penguin, 2010).

52. Ibid., 36.

53. Ibid., 4.

54. Ibid., 3.

55. Ibid., 369.

56. Dubravka Ugresic, *Baba Yaga Laid an Egg* (Edinburgh: Canongate, 2009).

57. James Tiptree Jr., "The Women Men Don't See," in *Her Smoke Rose Up Forever*, 2nd ed. (San Francisco: Tachyon Publications, 2004).

58. Ugresic, *Baba Yaga*, 1.

59. Ibid., 235.

60. Ibid., 243.

61. In *Chaos*, Baba Yaga was a poor old woman "with barely enough money to buy an egg for dinner" until she found Izbouchka wandering around without a Baba, 213.

62. "'Not small anymore.' She poked me hard in the ribs. 'But I would not eat you. You are not the sweet flesh and wine-blood of a man, which is what I crave.'" Yolen and Snyder, *Except the Queen*, 30–31.

63. Ugresic's fictional academic writes, "Psychoanalytically speaking . . . Baba Yaga's cannibalism may be a projection of a child's aggressive hunger. A hungry child wants to eat its mother. Conversely, the mother is a cannibal who wants to eat her own child." Ugresic, *Baba Yaga*, 172. I would suggest that every human being is eventually eaten by time, and facing that reality allows individuals to recover from loss and celebrate what remains, enabling an essential rite of passage.

64. Ibid., 273. The crone can mediate between the genders because she stands outside the reproductive cycle.

65. Lo, *Huntress*, 194.

66. *Babica* means midwife in Slavic languages. Ugresic, *Baba Yaga*, 243.

67. An important aspect of moral development is to be able to question authority. Mona tells Taisin, "Not everything they teach you is true," Lo, *Huntress*, 217.

68. Ibid., 195.

69. Ibid., 226.

70. Susan K. Rowe, "Feminism and Fairy Tales," *Don't Bet on the Prince* (New York: Routledge, 1987), 222–23.

71. Rowe, "Feminism and Fairy Tales," 223.

72. McKinley, *Sunshine*, 199.

73. Carol Pearson notes the "the true hero shatters the established order and creates the new community," *Hero*, 13.

Chapter Two

From Duckling to Swan

What Makes a Twilight Heroine Strong

Tricia Clasen

Enter "Bella Swan Heroine" into a Google search, and the first five results tell a powerful story: "Bella Swan as a heroine should be illegal," "A Feminist's Nightmare," "Five Heroines way better than Twilight's Bella Swan," "The Anti-Feminist Character of Bella Swan," and "Bella Swan versus Strong Heroines." It's painfully clear that readers and critics don't necessarily equate the widely popular Twilight series' female protagonist positively with the concept of a heroine. Certainly, connotations of a heroine vary. On one level, heroes/heroines are often placed in epic conditions, as a female who is brave and takes on challenges. A more generic definition of a heroine simply references the lead female character of a narrative. In the case of Bella Swan, the definitions are conflated. Twilight is classified as a young adult romance series. A female heroine in a paranormal romance novel is often considered a relatively passive figure. The series in which Edward Cullen, a vampire, and Bella Swan, a human, meet and fall in love demonstrates traditional gothic romance tropes such as a dark, distant male and a female character who lacks strength.[1] Because Bella is both the protagonist of a romance novel and the main character in a four-book epic arc, her journey as a heroine enlightens the reader about what it takes to achieve power as a woman in today's society.

LOVE TRANSFORMS WOMEN

In her research on romance novel readers, Radway claimed that the reading of romance novels provided an escape for many readers from a patriarchal, mundane existence.[2] In examining the reasons why women read romance novels and the meanings they glean, she argued romances follow a very tight structure in which the woman is "beautiful, defiant, and sexually immature" in contrast to a "brooding, handsome man who is also curiously capable of soft, gentle gestures."[3] Meeting these expectations proved successful for the series. With the book series selling over thirty million copies and movie profits over $2.5 billion, there can be no doubt that the formula worked.[4] Kokkola further contended that "much of the appeal of Meyer's 'Twilight' series arises from its conformity to the genre conventions of romance writing in general and teenage romances in particular; readers know what to expect and their expectations are satisfied."[5] Relying on these tropes of gothic romance, the Twilight series highlights relationships between characters who are "transformed" by love.

Because of the pervasive power of popular culture to influence our notions of both femininity and masculinity, Bella Swan is an important heroine for analysis. As Natalie Wilson argued in her book, an extensive cultural criticism of the messages in the Twilight series, "We need not deny our attraction to the saga . . . we should endeavor to become not sidekick Lois Lanes, but Super(wo)men, able to see through the illusions of our culture with a laser-like gaze."[6]

In previous research, I argued that four romantic myths permeated the Twilight series: love at first sight, love is forever, romantic love is the most important relationship, and love requires mind reading.[7] In this chapter, I propose that a fifth myth serves to define Bella Swan as a heroine: love transforms women. This chapter is primarily concerned about the ways in which the female heroine's path differs from that of a male hero. Bella Swan is painted as a broken female who ultimately finds her power by embracing traditional feminine qualities. In this chapter, I outline the basis of mythic analysis generally and the hero quest specifically. I identify the traditional gender dynamic crafted in the Twilight series which indicates Bella's brokenness. The story told is one in which women can only have power within the context of accepting societal definitions of femininity and family structure.

MYTHIC ANALYSIS

Myths are a powerful tool in literature. They are thought to establish a bridge between what "ought to be" rather than what actually "is."[8] Myths create and reveal the values and preferred actions of a society. Traditionally, myths are thought to guide cultural existence.[9] In fact, they shape and illustrate concepts of right and wrong. Fairy tales, for example, have been a key place for children to learn about family dynamics and positive behavior. Wicked stepmothers, lost children, and noble but misguided kings are symbolic representations of human existence. These stories both create and bear meaning. Told and retold, stories become encoded in icons, words, and clichés until they are socially remembered. [10]

According to Barthes, it's the fact that myths seem real that gives them their power. That's how they embed themselves into humans' collective consciousness and shape what we expect from our own realities. [11] The ideas are culturally and historically embedded in society in such a way that even when we learn that the myth is not entirely real, we still believe in it. Therefore, even if readers realize that the ideals of love presented in a story are meant as an escape and are not realistic, they influence cultural perceptions of what ought to be happening in relationships.

Barthes further argued that myths are messages. [12] Scholars then examine the symbolic evidence of those myths as well as the ideological and cultural implications which often foster traditional dominant culture perspectives. [13] As such, mythic analysis has unearthed ways in which women develop sexual and relational identities. For example, heterosexual women's happiness is generally determined by their relationships with men. [14] As Rose argued, a key cultural script in the United States is that "heterosexual romantic love will fulfill one's deepest needs." [15] Myths, then, offer stories of our existence; they create a vision that drives our sense of what it means to be a woman and how a woman can achieve power in society.

HEROINES AND THE MONOMYTH

In *The Hero with a Thousand Faces*, Joseph Campbell outlined the hero quest monomyth. He intended for this to be a gender-neutral approach to a hero's journey. The hero's quest involves several standard features including the introduction of the hero, a call to adventure, and often a reluctance to go. The hero will be faced with many tests, will have helpers along the way, and will ultimately face a final battle that will leave the hero near death.

Pearson and Pope detailed a more specific female-centric version of the hero quest. They identified particular social conventions which they claim are part of the challenge for the heroine. If she does overcome them, she cannot fulfill her quest. Myths of sex difference, virginity, romantic love, and maternal self-sacrifice all serve to prevent women from achieving power or recognizing her individual selfhood. Thus, unlike the male hero who is on an individual quest from the beginning, the female hero has an additional layer of challenges in addition to the specific quest at hand. For Pearson and Pope, this often results in failure for the heroine. Unfortunately, once the heroine "exits the garden" or the safety of the world she lives in upon introduction, she is still saddled with social constraints. [16]

Upon leaving the garden, or her uncomplicated surroundings, the heroine meets male counterparts who may serve as romantic and/or sexual interests. The suitor/seducer "awakens her to the possibilities of sexuality and love"; however, because she remains shackled by myths of romantic love and virginity, she cannot be satisfied by either separately.[17] Ultimately, this introduction prevents her from completing independent actions in her quest.

Further scholarship has indicated that in fantastical works, defeating gender myths is both possible and happens more readily.[18] Because the world created in a fantasy novel can deviate substantially from real social conditions, some constraints may be alleviated. Works of fantasy may employ a duomyth in addition to the well-known heroic monomyth. The male and the female heroes, then, embark on separate journeys, but the result is equal status. The appearance of two separate quests is really one goal split in two. The duomyth emphasizes a union of equals rather than the hierarchy of the monomyth. Bella Swan's quest sits at a unique intersection. The Twilight series is both fantasy and romance. As such, it embraces both the constraining gender myths and a potential duomyth.

BELLA'S HERO QUEST

As is true of the traditional male hero, the Twilight reader is first introduced to Bella Swan in mundane circumstances.[19] She's preparing to move from her home with her mother in Arizona to live with her father in Forks, Washington. However, in addition to the standard hero's introduction, the reader immediately understands that Bella is a broken heroine, setting up her need to be healed in some way throughout the narrative. There are numerous ways in which she demonstrates she is not a normal teen girl. Consistently, she references the ways in which she deviates from typical teenage girl behavior in terms of both age and gender.

THE BROKEN BEGINNING

Bella Swan is first and foremost a broken teenager. As she readies herself to leave Arizona, she's less concerned about her own ability to fit in and her own happiness with the move and more worried about how her mother will function after she leaves. "How could I leave my loving, erratic, harebrained mother to fend for herself?"[20] Rather than being cared for, Bella is painted as her mother's keeper. She ponders the sacrifice she is making for her mother. She does not want to move to Forks, but she believes this will help her mother.

Second, Bella sees herself as a broken female. When Bella describes herself, she says, "I should be tan, sporty, blond. . . . Instead, I was ivory-skinned, without even the excuse of blue eyes or red hair, despite the constant sunshine. I had always been slender, but soft somehow."[21] Interestingly, despite painting herself as broken because of her lack of athleticism and muscularity, Bella is giving the reader a first clue to the importance of traditional definitions of femininity, being weak and soft. Other clear marks of Bella's femininity include her ability to handle all domestic chores. As she unpacks and readies herself for the first day of school, she emphasizes activities like cooking, grocery shopping, and laundry. Despite these early references to Bella's femininity, as a heroine, both in her own eyes and to the reader, she is not only a broken teenager but a broken female.

While Bella is concerned about being the new girl, she is painted as a self-sufficient loner. She's uninterested in male attention and needs little help acclimating to her environment. As early as her second day of class, she is bothered by Mike, a classmate, showing too much interest in her. "It looked like I was going to have to do something about Mike, and it wouldn't be easy. . . . I had no practice dealing with overly friendly boys."[22] As the reader meets Bella, then, she has no interest in the normal activities of girls. She's neither highly social nor obsessed with boys.

As Bella's quest moves forward, I will focus primarily on only two of the four books in the series: *Twilight* and *Breaking Dawn*. Originally, Stephenie Meyer intended only to write the two novels. The quest, then, follows a more direct path when skipping *New Moon* and *Eclipse* in between, which were primarily added as layers of conflict.[23] There are details about characterization which apply to this discussion, but for the most part Bella's hero tale occurs in *Twilight* and *Breaking Dawn*. Additionally, as Bella's hero journey is a hybrid hero quest/healing myth, not all components of the traditional quest myth are as evident.

CHALLENGES AND TESTS

After introducing the broken heroine living in her ordinary surroundings, heroes are faced with an impetus or an invitation to the quest. Often, heroes are reluctant; however, Bella does not show much trepidation. The minute she sees Edward and his family of vampires, she is drawn to him. Even when he attempts to get her to stay away, she never feels uneasy in his presence. He tells her he's dangerous. She sees signs that something is not right with him, but she cannot stay away. The reader might believe that Edward is the prize, the quest, particularly if reading only the first novel. As per the earlier description of the heroine journey, Edward certainly serves as both the suitor and the seducer.[24] There is a second suitor, of course. The love triangle that ensues between Bella, Edward, and Jacob (the werewolf) establishes a unique relationship between the notion of sexual seduction and someone who seduces the hero in order to distract him or her from the task at hand. While the sexual attraction to Edward is substantial and becomes part of the tests and conflict in the middle two novels, to an extent, Jacob's role is to seduce Bella away from Edward who is integral to her ultimate quest, unlike a seducer who would want to take Bella's virginity, sullying her womanhood.

Once the heroine embarks on her quest, she leaves the tranquility of the garden. Then she faces many conflicts. The plot of *Twilight*, the first book in the series, introduces Bella to a paranormal world filled with vampires and werewolves. She's faced with very specific problems when human blood-drinking vampires want to kill her. The Cullens band together to protect Bella, but she, in turn, showcases in this first book that self-sacrifice is expected of her. She puts herself in the direct line of the evil vampire in order to save her human family and in hopes of protecting Edward. In this action, the reader glimpses Bella's actual quest.

Bella's quest has little to do with defeating bad vampires. At root, what she seeks is a traditional family structure.

> Although Edward and Bella are the center of the novel's narrative, the series is equally concerned with the contemporary American nuclear family, and a woman's role within that family. Identity, in the series, occurs within the context of group identity, particularly family. Bella's desire for eternal life as a vampire with Edward is closely connected with her longing for a stable family, which she has been denied after her parents' divorce, and which the archaic Cullen family offers. [25]

In analyzing her journey as a heroine, this is the ultimate aim. In order to become a member of that family and ultimately to have her own nuclear family, she must marry Edward.

THE JOURNEY TOWARD FAMILY

Bella's introduction as a broken woman is only one aspect of the healing narrative in the Twilight series. Throughout her journey, the reader meets several characters who affirm the notion that only by embracing her femininity can a woman be successful and whole. Of particular note is the role that motherhood plays in the lives of the female characters. In addition to Bella's own mother, unable to find happiness in her role as a wife and mother, four other female characters illustrate the complex gender dynamic, and again, all revolve around motherhood. In the Twilight world, all female vampires are infertile, so in the case of the three female vampires in the Cullen clan, the reader sees three unique models. First, Esme is the matriarch of the clan. She is the clearest representation of a traditional wife and mother, despite having "adopted" her adult children as vampires. Her primary role is nurturing and caring. Second, Alice is painted as a particularly petite girl, sweet and friend-ly. She's feminine but plays a more childlike role in the family. Finally, Rosalie, a woman who pre-transformation wanted nothing more than to be a wife and mother, has turned bitter and hateful as a result. A character who demonstrates a similar principle is Leah, a werewolf, who the reader also learns is infertile. In addition, she's a jilted lover, forced to be in a pack with her former fiancé. Again, she is angry and acts less feminine. Through these examples the reader comes to understand that being feminine means being happy and satisfied. Bella must learn to embrace these qualities before she can gain power.

Throughout the series, when Edward argues that Bella will eventually want children, Bella consistently dismisses it. She has never wanted children and sees no reason why this is a deal breaker. Her reaction, in part, causes Rosalie to dislike Bella. She cannot understand how anyone could give up those aspects of womanhood (though she refers to it as "life"). Bella's change of heart doesn't occur until she is already pregnant. Then the change is instantaneous. "I'd never understood Rosalie's pain and resentment before. I'd never imagined myself a mother, never wanted that. . . . This child, Edward's child, was a whole different story. I wanted him like I wanted air to breathe. Not a choice—a necessity."[26] When Edward, consumed only with Bella's safety, reveals his intention for her to have an abortion, Bella calls on Rosalie, the person with whom she has the poorest relationship, to assist her in protecting the child.

The dynamic that develops throughout Bella's pregnancy and into her transformation to a vampire is reminiscent of mother/monster dichotomies evident throughout media. Popular culture often looks to the mother/mother-hood as an indication of normality in female behavior. For example, the lack of morality and bad mothering are often the drive for murder in horror films. "Mothers who transgress their appointed maternal role therefore create de-formed offspring like Rosemary's baby."[27]

For Bella, the heroine, healing occurs both literally and figuratively. In Campbell's monomyth, heroes face a breaking point.[28] At that moment, he or she would be vulnerable, near death. All hope for the hero appears to be lost. There is no way he or she can reach the end goal. Pregnancy and birth are in many ways a low point for Bella as a heroine; her pregnancy is draining her. Because this section is told from Jacob's point of view, the reader only sees a woman wholeheartedly committed to her fetus, willing to sacrifice her own life for her baby. Other scholars have argued that this pregnancy and birth carry an underlying abstinence message, deterring teen pregnancy in the way it paints pregnancy and childbirth.[29] However, placed within the context of the hero quest, this period is a defining test of her strength as a woman willing to sacrifice. Bella's love for her child is so strong that even when her body is literally broken while giving birth, her only concern is for her baby's well-being. Because Edward injects her with his venom, this is where her healing and transformation begins.

FROM THE ASHES

Changing from a human to a vampire is a literal transformation process, known to take a few days. It involves extensive burning pain. Usually the person transforming writhes and screams; however, Bella undergoes her transformation silently, likely due to morphine which was given in advance. However, this once again indicates how she is atypical.

Upon waking, Bella continues to struggle with her identity, and Meyer provides a unique twist on the monster/mother dichotomy. Previously, the reader had witnessed women who were unable to have children in monster (vampire) form and a human mother who was somewhat inept; when Bella wakes, the concern is that she will not be capable of seeing her baby. Because her child is part human, and a newborn vampire is too immature to handle the smell of human blood without attacking, everyone wants to keep her from her daughter. "Right, I was the monster now. I had to keep away from scents that might trigger my wild side. From the people that I loved in particular. Even the ones I didn't really know yet."[30]

Quickly, Bella overcomes even this challenge. Despite actually becoming a monster, she reveals herself as the best model of motherhood almost instantly. She demonstrates a level of self-control that shocks and awes those around her. For vampires, hunting is a visceral process, one in which they give in completely to instinct. In her first hunting trip, Bella manages to stop herself from attacking a human she encounters. She says, "What else could I do? It might have been someone I know!"[31] At this point, Bella's control indicates two important elements of her journey: she is a good person, with strong morals with an incredibly powerful drive to protect her loved ones, and she is very good at being a vampire. A sense emerges that Bella's transformation had healed her sense of isolation and not fitting in anywhere.

> As a human, I'd never been best at anything. . . . After eighteen years of mediocrity, I was pretty used to being average. . . . I'd long ago given up any aspirations of shining at anything. So this was really different. I was amazing now—to them and to myself. It was like I had been born to be a vampire. The idea made me want to laugh, but it also made me want to sing. I had found my true place in the world, the place I fit, the place I shined.[32]

Bella's physical strength and appearance also undergoes a substantial metamorphosis, giving her a new element of power. As a human, she is consistently painted as weak, clumsy, and fragile. She's even seen as soft. Again, these do much to remind the reader that although Bella is broken, she is still female. When Bella becomes a vampire, she develops superhuman strength; in fact, as a newborn vampire she is stronger and faster than the male counterparts who have been protecting her for much of the series. However, through comments of others, it's clear that while Bella gained physical power, she also embodies a more dominant definition of beauty. Durham contents that "to be intelligible to contemporary viewers, the girl's body must be slender, small-boned, and curvaceous. The imperative of thinness works to counter and neutralize the threat of a physically strong teenage girl."[33] Bella fits this description well. Post-transformation, words like "supermodel" and "rocking body" describe her. When she first wakes, Bella believes she is still broken because she acts differently than other newborn vampires. She takes solace in her appearance. "Oh well," I said lightly, relieved that my thoughts were still my own. "I guess my brain will never work right. At least I'm pretty."[34]

Becoming a vampire is the easiest thing Bella has done. So, despite her transformation into adulthood (as a wife and mother) and becoming a vampire, "Bella seems remarkably untransformed by her transition into motherhood. In reality, sex is rarely transformational, but parenthood usually is. In undermining the transformational power of motherhood, Meyer draws on another well-established convention in children's literature: the fear of growing up.[35] In the end, the traditional gender dynamic was accentuated by the notion of protection. Throughout most of the series, Edward and Bella conflicted over his need to protect her. It was a constant battle and appeared indicative of him seeing her as weaker and less able to handle herself in dangerous situations. Once Bella became a vampire, she developed a power—the ability to shield or protect the ones she loves. The way this played out reflected a feminine notion of care. It was clearly in contrast to Edward's attempts to protect Bella through coercion, force, or manipulation.

> The shield blew out from me in a bubble of sheer energy, a mushroom cloud of liquid steel. . . . Everything underneath the flexible iron shield was suddenly a part of me—I could feel the life force of everything it covered like points of bright heat. . . . I thrust the shield forward . . . and exhaled in relief when I felt Edward's brilliant light within my protection.[36]

By being the nurturing protector, she won. Her family won. By transforming into a traditional family role and taking care of those around her, she demonstrated the "right" way to parent. "It felt like I had never wanted anything so badly before this: to be able to protect what I loved."[37]

By transforming into her role as a traditional wife and mother, Bella gains her superhuman "gift." As Silver wrote, "Meyer thus proposes that marriage and motherhood provide women with equality that they do not possess as single women. Motherhood becomes a location not only of pleasure and satisfaction but also of power."[38] Thus, Bella is healed, and her quest is complete. She gains the family she desperately sought, eternal life, love, and happiness.

CONCLUSION

Bella's transformation and source of power create an interesting dualism as an analysis of her as a heroine. Much like other fantasy heroines, Bella does actually succeed in her quest, and she gains equal status with her partner. Both Bella and Edward are transformed, as was true of the duomyth. They were on separate journeys of the same quest. "Bella's vampirism is as closely tied, symbolically, to motherhood as it is to her love for Edward. Once Bella becomes a vampire, Meyer repeatedly emphasizes that Bella and Edward are equals: sexually, in physical strength, as hunters, and in their psychic gifts."[39] Because Bella is less fragile as a vampire, Edward no longer holds back, and he trusts her more because she can take care of herself. She becomes his equal sexually and emotionally.

However, Bella's power comes only from embracing social norms regarding femininity. "Meyer depicts motherhood as a means of personal fulfillment and, more generally, underscores the series' persistent theme that identity comes from affiliation rather than individual accomplishment."[40] In other words, Bella does not succeed because of her individual strength but because of her connections to others. She is healed, and her quest complete, but the quest itself revolves around the very constraints that cause most heroines to fail in their quest.

NOTES

1. Kim Edwards, "Good Looks and Sex Symbols: The Power of the Gaze and the Displacement of the Erotic in Twilight," *Australian Screen Education* 53 (2009): 26–32; Laura Miller, "Real Men HAVE Fangs," *Wall Street Journal—Eastern Edition*, October 31, 2008, W1–W5.

2. Janice Radway, "Women Read the Romance: The Intersection of Text and Context," *Feminist Studies* 9, no. 1 (1983): 53–78.

3. Quoted in Radway, "Women Read the Romance," 55.

4. Barbara Vancheri, "Success of 'Twilight' a Mystery to Author," *Pittsburgh Post-Gazette*, November 16, 2012, http://www.post-gazette.com; David Konow, "Hunger Games Book Sales Rivaling Twilight," TGDaily, last modified July 29, 2013, http://www.tgdaily.com/games-and-entertainment-features/62415-hunger-games-book-sales-rivaling-twilight.

5. Quoted in Lydia Kokkola, "Virtuous Vampires and Voluptuous Vamps: Romance Conventions Reconsidered in Stephenie Meyer's 'Twilight' Series," *Children's Literature in Education* 42, no. 2 (2011): 179.

6. Quoted in Natalie Wilson, *Seduced by Twilight: The Allure and Contradictory Messages of the Popular Saga* (Jefferson, NC: McFarland, 2011), 7.

7. Tricia Clasen, "Taking a Bite out of Love: The Myth of Romantic Love in the Twilight Series," in *Bitten by Twilight*, ed. Melissa Click, Jennifer Stevens Aubrey, and Elizabeth Behm-Morawitz (New York: Peter Lang, 2010), 119.

8. David Hume, *Treatise of Human Nature*, ed. A Selby-Biggs (Oxford: Oxford University Press, 1960).

9. V. William Balthrop, "Culture, Myth, and Ideology as Public Argument: An Interpretation of the Ascent and Demise of 'Southern Culture,'" *Communication Monographs* 51, no. 4 (1984): 339–52.

10. Richard Slotkin, *The Gunfighter Nation: The Myth of the Frontier in Twentieth-Century America* (New York: Atheneum, 1992).

11. Roland Barthes, *Mythologies*, trans. Annette Lavers (London: Paladin, 1972), 155.

12. Barthes, *Mythologies*, 111.

13. Meenakshi Gigi Durham, "Dilemmas of Desire: Representations of Adolescent Sexuality in Two Teen Magazines," *Youth and Society* 29 (1998): 369–89.

14. Quoted in Suzanna Rose, "Heterosexism and the Study of Women's Romantic and Friend Relationships," *Journal of Social Issues* 56, no. 2 (200): 315.

15. Joseph Campbell, *The Hero with a Thousand Faces* (Princeton, NJ: Princeton University Press, 1968).

16. Carol Pearson and Katherine Pope, *The Female Hero in American and British Literature* (New York: R. R. Bowker, 1981).

17. Ibid., 68.

18. Christine Maines, "Having It All: The Female Hero's Quest for Love and Power in Patricia McKillip's Riddle-Master Trilogy," *Extrapolation* 46, no. 1 (2005): 23–25.

19. Stephenie Meyer, *Twilight* (New York: Little, Brown, 2005), 3.

20. Ibid., 4.

21. Ibid., 10.

22. Ibid., 31.

23. The official website of Stephenie Meyer, last modified July 19, 2013, http://www.stepheniemeyer.com.

24. Pearson and Pope, *The Female Hero*, 68.

25. Anna Silver, "'Twilight' Is Not Good for Maidens: Gender, Sexuality, and the Family in Stephenie Meyer's 'Twilight' Series," *Studies in the Novel* 42, nos. 1/2 (2010): 121–38.

26. Stephenie Meyer, *Breaking Dawn* (New York: Little, Brown, 2008), 132.

27. Edwards, "Good Looks," 94.

28. Campbell, *The Hero*, 138.

29. Kokkola, "Virtuous Vampires," 166.

30. Meyer, *Breaking Dawn*, 408.

31. Ibid., 419.

32. Ibid., 523–24.

33. Quoted in Meenakshi Gigi Durham, "The Girling of America: Critical Reflections on Gender and Popular Communication," *Popular Communication* 1, no. 1 (March 2003): 26.

34. Meyer, *Breaking Dawn*, 406.

35. Kokkola, "Virtuous Vampires," 176.

36. Meyer, *Breaking Dawn*, 690–91.

37. Ibid., 600.

38. Silver, "'Twilight' Is Not Good," 123.

39. Ibid., 130.

40. Ibid., 132.

Chapter Three

Salem's Daughters

Witchcraft, Justice, and the Heroine in Popular Culture

Lauren Lemley

> Their names are exposed to infamy and reproach, while their trial and condem-
> nation stands upon public record. We therefore humbly pray [to] this honored
> court, that something may be publicly done to take off infamy from the names
> and memory of those who have suffered as aforesaid, that none of their surviv-
> ing relations, nor their posterity may suffer reproach upon that account.
> —Petition of Francis Faulkner, March 2, 1703[1]

To shape the public's memory is to craft a narrative of immense power. It is a
truth the descendants of the victims of the Salem witchcraft crisis knew all
too well. For years after the conclusion of the infamous trials, surviving
family members of the more than 150 individuals who were charged with
witchcraft pleaded with the courts to not only supply them with financial
reparations for the money spent to care for their imprisoned loved ones, but
to also officially clear the names of those wrongfully tried, imprisoned, and
executed. It was only a fraction of the task facing a virtually destroyed town
attempting to rebuild some sense of order and community, and it was an
authentically *human* event, marked by a combination of emotion and mystery
that has captivated the imagination of writers, producers, and playwrights for
over three hundred years. But popular as it is, this story is only one brief
chapter in the history of the archetype of the witch that has been developing
for millennia.[2]

ARCHETYPICAL WITCHES

Although femininity has historically been a central component of the witch archetype, this characterization has also relied heavily on the idea that "in one way or the other, a witch was supposed to be different from others; a witch was a deviant, non-conformist and anything but a normal, ordinary person in her (his) neighbourhood."[3] Fear of such differences and their implications have long driven people, particularly members and leaders of religious groups, to seek out methods for identifying the witches whom they suspected of hiding in their towns and churches. Historian Richard Gordon claims that "from the very beginning, magic has been a term whose semantic implications can only be understood by close attention to context, to the values and claims that it is made to sustain."[4] Thus, it should not be surprising that as sweeping changes in politics, economics, gender status, and industry crossed the West in the early years of the twentieth century, the archetype of the witch underwent significant revision in literature and the young medium of film. This transition is perhaps most evident in L. Frank Baum's 1900 novel *The Wonderful Wizard of Oz* and the 1942 film *I Married a Witch*, adapted from Thorne Smith's 1941 novel *The Passionate Witch*, which each featured a new take on archetypical witchcraft—the witch-as-heroine. Indeed, these stories served as a turning point in the "the evolution of witch from satanic servant to the problematically empowered heroine of modern popular culture."[5] Both *Oz* and *I Married a Witch* highlighted the conflict between the previously dominant characterization of witchcraft as malevolent and the idea that some witches might use their power for benevolent ends. This tension was characteristic, as literature scholar Marion Gibson argues, "of the portrayal of witches in twentieth-century popular culture—as a transparent metaphor for debate over the role of women."[6]

As the twentieth century marched on and America's gender debate intensified, ABC returned to the premise behind Smith's book with *Bewitched*, a 1960s comedy "brave enough to suggest that witches might be both liberals and liberated . . . [arguing that] they did not have to be, or even begin as, bad women."[7] Their story of a loving, domesticated housewife and mother, who also happened to be a witch, paved the way for countless television and film incarnations of the witch-as-heroine who uses her supernatural abilities to fight evil and protect those she loves. Among these were other comedies, such as the 1990s television hit *Sabrina the Teenage Witch* and the 1987 film *The Witches of Eastwick*, and darker dramas, including *The Craft* (1996), *Buffy the Vampire Slayer* (1997–2003), and *Charmed* (1998–2006). But the widespread popularity garnered by these narratives was closely tied to the development of two key societal movements—feminism and Wicca.

Feminism

Arthur Miller's 1953 Broadway hit *The Crucible* is known for its use of the Salem witchcraft narrative to critique the highly controversial practices of American politicians at the height of the Red Scare, but Miller also inserted himself into the feminist conversation about gender and sexuality by inventing a love triangle involving John and Elizabeth Procter and Abigail Williams, one of the first girls to "cry witch" in 1692. This deviation from historical record merely served to further reaffirm the centuries-old link between witchcraft and sexuality, seeming to explain an instance of historical injustice as a consequence of unrequited love. A decade later, *Bewitched*'s Samantha served as a role model for the American housewife whose devotion to home and family argued that a woman's power and influence, whether mortal or supernatural, could be productively and benignly used in the domestic sphere. These two narratives communicated differing perspectives on feminine identity, but clearly defined women as driven by their sexuality and limited to the role of homemaker.

As ever-increasing numbers of women set their sights on careers outside the family in the run-up to the new millennium, pop culture's witch-heroines again changed with the times. Sociologists Berger and Ezzy contend that

> the positive representations of Witches in the mass media reflect attempts by television producers and filmmakers to continue to engage with the changing interests of young consumers. Inness (2004) argues that the emergence of "action chick," movies and television shows about tough, aggressive young women, reflects the influence of second-wave feminism on society. [8]

While these increasingly powerful representations of supernatural heroines signaled progress in societal perceptions of feminine agency, a significant gap still remained unaddressed by popular culture in the early years of the twenty-first century—a characterization of a witch who could be classified as "mainstream," someone who might break the centuries-old classification of witches as deviants, forced by society to hide their true identity from the world.

Wicca

As a religious movement, Wicca has seen significant gains in both popularity and legitimacy over the past quarter century. Some saw its influence reflected positively in contemporary mediated narratives, as they now tend to portray witches "as beautiful, youthful, and independent women who use their magical powers for the greater good . . . emphasizing respect for the strong, wise female protector figure, [which] is reflective of the Wiccan religion as well as of women's greater access to equality and power in the world."[9] But others, including the Pagan activist and author Starhawk, viewed the contemporary witch-as-heroine archetype prevalent at the dawn of the twenty-first century as limiting. In her landmark work, *The Spiral Dance*, Starhawk wrote that she was still "waiting for the TV witch who happens to be an auto mechanic, an engineer, or a molecular biologist."[10] Similarly, in her analysis of *Sabrina the Teenage Witch*, Gibson claims that "it is precisely 'girl power,' a media-friendly pseudo-feminism, that is the problem. Today's witches in popular culture are being denied the right to grow up."[11] Logan, a young adult practitioner of Wicca, provided his own assessment of this problem:

> I watched *Charmed* which amused me but also sort of made me angry . . . because it . . . only showed two versions [of witches], there is the old hag crone who is old and evil or there is the young beautiful half-dressed female. Like a sexual object as opposed to having anything in-between those two which is I think where most Witches actually fall.[12]

Sociologist Joke Hermes argues that the media's characterizations only truly become powerful when they are granted "reality status."[13] Thus, the desire for a more authentic, and necessarily more powerful archetypical witch-as-heroine lies at the heart of Starhawk's, Gibson's, and Logan's critiques. It is the same gap that I seek to answer in examining a new archetypical heroine that has recently emerged in vernacular public memory of the Salem witchcraft crisis.

PUBLIC MEMORY AND SALEM'S DAUGHTERS

In its most basic form, public memory scholarship explores the memories crafted by the public, or the collective, to discover the impact of such memorializing. By conceptualizing memory as a practice or a continuous work in progress, public memory scholars are able to address questions about how remembrance can be used, not only to consider the past, but to also contemplate how contemporary constructions of the past can have meaning for the present and even the future. Southgate articulates this argument in the following manner:

> For the past—or rather our memories of the past—is to be examined, not simply per se or "for its own sake," but in the light of our hopes for the future. Our revised narratives may, then, for example (if we so determine), prove to be less simplistic and more tolerant of unresolved complexities; and as such, they may enable the living of new and fuller lives, in what may then seem a more healthy, honest and open relationship with the past.[14]

Similarly, Bodnar argues that the educational function of scholarship on memory is essential because "public memory is produced from a political discussion that involves not so much specific economic or moral problems but rather fundamental issues about the entire existence of a society: its organization, structure of power, and the very meaning of its past and present."[15] My analysis in this chapter is grounded in these perspectives and, more specifically, in Schudson's call for memory studies to "try to understand not only how people may use the past but how the past confines the uses to which people may intentionally put it" through examining how public memories of the Salem crisis can be used to help modern audiences grapple with and understand current events.[16]

One of the unique features of Salem's witchcraft narrative is its abundance of female characters. Children, and particularly female children, held little to no status or power in colonial Puritan communities, yet preteen and teenage girls feature prominently in the historical record of this event. Historian Mary Beth Norton specifically notes that as the girls' accusations grew, "the male heads of their households and other adult men of their families gave them hours of concentrated attention, probably for the first time in their lives."[17] Because of this unique situation, Salem's female-dominated story has offered modern authors, screenwriters, and directors the opportunity to revise and remember the witchcraft crisis in a variety of different contexts and genres, each providing a new opportunity to consider the witch-as-heroine.

Throughout the twentieth century, virtually all American television shows, movies, and novels with witches as main characters relied on the Salem narrative in one way or another. In some cases the reference was as brief as the setting for an episode or mentioning one of the more infamous participants from the trials. But *Bewitched* and *Sabrina the Teenage Witch* stand out from the rest as texts whose rhetors engaged the Salem narrative in a deeper way by using it as the framework for the shows' heroines to seek justice. Although these plotlines played out on a relatively small, personal scale, Samantha's and Sabrina's insistence on justice as an anecdote to the injustice perpetrated at Salem contributed to the twentieth century's development of the heroine archetype beyond previous characterizations of leading women as damsels in distress, sidekicks for a central male hero, or merely sacrificial figures, resigned to be "distinguished from her heroic brothers and sisters by what are in effect *anti-heroic* qualities."[18] Yet, as I have already indicated, these pop-culture contributions to public memory of the Salem witchcraft crisis were still limiting, bound by the constraints of gender (*Bewitched*) and relegated to the realm of high school drama (*Sabrina*).

Fortunately, more recent contributions to American public memory of the Salem witchcraft crisis have graduated fictional retellings of the Salem narrative to the realm of adult literature, largely through the development of a new strain of feminine heroism—the witch-as-crusader. In the following analysis, I seek to understand how rhetors infuse female characters with the uniquely moral and emotional aspects of Americans' public memory of the Salem witchcraft crisis to develop compelling, believable heroines who take up issues of social justice in the space between history, myth, and contemporary social reality. To address this line of inquiry, I will specifically analyze how Deborah Harkness, author of *A Discovery of Witches*, used the themes of ancestry, the struggle for gender equality, and a crusade for social justice to forge a new supernatural heroine archetype, embodied by her main character, Diana Bishop.[19]

WITCH-AS-CRUSADER

The long, strange career of the Salem witches as an American cultural metaphor is an artifact of an equally long-held and complex collective memory of the trials of 1692. Always linked to cultural anxieties, the metaphor has meanings that shift to suit contemporary realities. . . . In raising the specter of Salem witchcraft in later centuries, Americans warned each other that there were limits both to liberty and to power.[20] —Gretchen A. Adams, *The Specter of Salem*

Adams' analysis of nineteenth-century American references to the Salem witch narrative offers an important starting point for understanding Harkness' construction of the witch-as-crusader archetype. Even before the trials were officially shut down in 1693, observers and participants had begun to critique the legal practices they rightly deemed unjust. The use of Salem as a metonymical representation of the dangers associated with unchecked power, rampant prejudice, and social tension has dominated American public memory of the trials ever since, and Harkness' novels are no exception to this norm.

Harkness begins *A Discovery of Witches* by introducing Diana Bishop, a well-respected historian of science at Yale, whom readers meet on the day she accidentally accessed her magical abilities, powers she has tried to keep locked away since her parents' death when she was only seven years old, to retrieve a book from a high shelf. As a descendant of Bridget Bishop and John Procter, both executed as witches in Salem, Diana is an exceptionally gifted witch, but she has always fought against her magic out of a desire to rely on "reason and scholarly abilities, not inexplicable hunches and spells."[21] But when she opens a manuscript known as Ashmole 782 in Oxford's Bodleian Library, Diana immediately recognizes it as bewitched—and damaged. Over the course of the novel, she discovers that the pages missing from this manuscript hold information central to the existence and survival of creatures—witches, vampires, and daemons. In Harkness' mythos, these three species of nonhuman beings coexist only through their avoidance of and prejudice toward one another, a reality that becomes highly problematic when Diana falls in love with a vampire, Matthew Clairmont. Together, Diana and Matthew must try to unite creatures in their fight to find Ashmole 782, help Diana learn to use her powerful abilities, and ultimately save witches, vampires, and daemons from allowing their prejudices to cause their own extinction.

ANCESTRY

A central theme of *A Discovery of Witches* is Diana's ancestral connection to the Salem witchcraft crisis. In his discussion of ancestry as a method of defining and understanding motives, Kenneth Burke argues that biological descent can create a context in which "motives would be situated in the individual, yet they would be motives common to the species, or tribe, of which it was a member."[22] By establishing such an ancestral link between past and present in her heroine, Harkness poises Diana to rely on her family's history as a believable rationale for embarking on a quest. This rationale is more powerful than that of previous heroines, such as Sabrina, who merely referred to Salem as an important historical event. For Diana, the legacy of the Salem trials is an integral part of who she is and the choices she makes.

Harkness explicitly connects Diana's quest to her heritage in the early chapters of the novel as her family continues to remind her that, no matter how hard she has tried to turn her back on her ancestry, "it is who you are. It's in your blood. It's in your bones. You were born a witch, just as you were born to have blond hair and blue eyes."[23] Eventually Diana realizes she must admit to herself that she had never successfully kept her witchcraft out of any part of her identity: "I've been using it in my work, without realizing it. It's in everything. I've been fooling myself for years."[24] This moment serves as an important turning point as Harkness slowly revels that Diana's ancestry and identity are not simply connected to her quest, but that her identity *is* her quest.

While the novel's characters learn more about the mysteries of Ashmole 782, they also discover that Diana and Matthew are featured in the manuscript that had been written more than five hundred years earlier. Creatures, including Diana's Salem ancestor, Bridget, begin to converge on the Bishop house in New York to deliver pieces of a centuries-old puzzle that countless generations had instructed their children and grandchildren to "give to the one who has need of it."[25] When these stories are read by a culture of readers who are constantly told they can and must "make a difference" and "leave their mark" on the world, this narrative of ancestral destiny reads like an episode of TLC's popular television show *Who Do You Think You Are?* or an

Ancestry.com commercial. Harkness uses echoes of Salem's story to effectively endow her heroine with an almost mythical power, granted by a magical sense of the past and made relevant by the broader cultural narratives of the present.

Diana's professional career also plays an integral role in her journey to truly understand her identity and heritage, so it is hardly coincidental that Harkness positioned her academically as a historian. But unlike previous incarnations of the witch-as-heroine, Diana does not have a merely passing interest in amateur family genealogy. In one episode of *Bewitched*, for example, Samantha learns that her mother had lived in Salem during 1692. But the reference is fleeting, presented more as an aside than a central plot element. In contrast, Diana is a scholar who spends a significant portion of her time in libraries and archives, not waiting for revelations to come from others, but investigating, interpreting, and unearthing her identity for herself. Yet as heroines of the past have illustrated, women have not always been granted the opportunities and independence to act on their ancestral destiny that are virtually unquestioned aspects of a hero's quest.

GENDER EQUALITY

Although an ancestry-bound quest is hardly uncharted territory for heroes and heroines, Diana embarks on her crusade in the midst of a personal fight to establish the norms for "acceptable" femininity that seem to be constraining her actions at every turn. In Harkness' narrative, Diana primarily struggles with gender equality on a personal rather than professional level, because she has been destined to fall in love with a vampire. While their choice to marry breaks centuries-old rules preventing cross-species relationships set by a supernatural governing council termed the "Congregation," it also becomes the center, literally and symbolically, of Diana's quest and opens the door for numerous challenges in her personal life.

Matthew, Diana's 1,500-year-old vampire husband, has spent a majority of his existence in time periods and societies where the man was generally accepted to be the head of family, home, and industry. Diana's fierce determination to defend herself, rather than remain in the shadows while someone else fights for her, challenges what he knows and believes about women. Of course, as the feminist movement has taught the modern American readers of Harkness' novel, Matthew's characterizations of femininity have historically been shared by many. To this end, Linaker writes that

> socially and historically accepted stereotypes of female characters in literature are projected as passive or active, frigid or lustful, selfish or generous. The sexist image of women has prevailed in myth and literature for so long that it seems inevitable and true in spite of the obvious logical impossibilities.[26]

As Matthew struggles to come to terms with breaking similar stereotypes he has carried for so long and to accept Diana's role as heroine and not damsel in distress, Harkness intentionally reveals his imperfections to her readers. Matthew makes demands of and decisions for Diana without consulting her. He acts irrationally without thinking and has to apologize for his aggressive behavior. He struggles with his desire to protect her from the magical world she has intentionally prevented herself from understanding. After a few days of observing her son and daughter-in-law's interactions with one another, Matthew's mother presents him with an accurate, yet critical assessment of his behavior: "This is why you are always losing at chess, Matthew. . . . Like Diana, the queen has almost unlimited power. Yet you insist on surrounding her and leaving yourself vulnerable."[27]

Whether reading Burke on identification or Fisher on the narrative paradigm, rhetoricians and literary theorists concur that stories and arguments can only achieve success when they connect with their audience's understanding of the world around them.[28] And as humans are not without their flaws, a rhetorician cannot hope to craft a persuasive narrative centered around characters who are devoid of flaws or vulnerability. To this end, Harkness allows Diana and Matthew to struggle and work through the question of gender equality as her plot evolves, culminating in the following demand that Diana makes of her husband: "Stop being all heroic and let me share your life. I don't want to be with Sir Lancelot. Be yourself—Matthew Clairmont."[29] Unlike other features of Diana's life, this statement is not magic, and it does not instantaneously prevent future problems in this aspect of their relationship. But it sets a goal of equality, of partnership, that becomes a permanent aspiration of their interactions with one another.

SOCIAL JUSTICE

The final element of the witch-as-crusader archetype is rooted in the heroine's ancestral quest, but is equally supported by her struggle to achieve gender equality. In 1965, *Bewitched* producer Danny Arnold argued that "fantasy can always be a jumping-off place for more sophisticated work. We can make it identifiable with people and relate to problems that are everyday. What we do in this series doesn't happen to witches; it happens to people."[30] Arnold's critique of the persuasive nature of fantasy is just as true today as it was almost four decades ago, and it is the element of relatability that both he and Starhawk addressed that is integral to Harkness' success in developing Diana's quest to transform a social system plagued by bigotry.

When Diana and Matthew travel to the Bishop house, Harkness frames Diana's aunts as witches who, rather than hiding their Pagan identity, show it off in the most ordinary of American ways, through "a new crop of bumper stickers [on the back of Sarah's car]. 'My other car is a broom,' a perennial favorite, was stuck next to 'I'm Pagan and I vote.' Another proclaimed 'Wiccan army: We will not go silently into the night.'"[31] After the American Revolution, the Bishop family had "set down roots in the community deep enough to withstand the inevitable outbreaks of superstition and human fear," and Diana's aunts, Sarah and Emily, are active members of their local coven.[32]

But resolving one form of discrimination typically gives other oppressed groups greater opportunity to advocate for their causes. In this case, Harkness presents the Bishops as a well-connected family, free from the typical oppression that history and fiction have associated with witchcraft, but sensitive to the cause of justice as a whole. As more people learn of Diana and Matthew's relationship, readers discover that the Congregation is willing to destroy anyone who stands against their desire to keep creatures segregated and blind to knowledge about their own history—a history that is detailed in Ashmole 782. Peter Knox, one of the three witches in the Congregation, tells Diana that she must find the manuscript for him because "we cannot let our history fall into the hands of animals like [Matthew]. Witches and vampires don't mix, Dr. Bishop. There are excellent reasons for it. Remember who you are. If you don't you will regret it."[33] But of course discrimination typically travels in multiple directions. When one of the Congregation's vampire members visits the couple, he presents Diana with a remarkably similar warning: "Relationships between witches and vampires are forbidden. You must leave this house and no longer associate with Matthew de Clermont or any of his family. If you don't, the Congregation will take whatever steps are necessary to preserve the covenant."[34]

Diana and Matthew, together with their families and friends, soon learn that the Congregation's prejudice and determination run far deeper than distaste for one relationship. A series of criminal acts—Diana's abduction and torture, Matthew's nearly fatal run-in with a former enemy, threats, burglaries, and a series of unexplained murders—convince everyone that the secrets hidden in Ashmole 782 are far more significant than they had first imagined. Hamish Osborne, one of Matthew's closest friends (and a daemon), summarized their cause succinctly toward the end of *A Discovery of Witches*:

> In this room we understand why such a war might be fought. It's about Diana and the appalling lengths the Congregation will go to in an effort to understand the power she's inherited. It's about the discovery of Ashmole 782 and our fear that the book's secrets might be lost forever if it falls into the witches' hands. And it's about our common belief that no one has the right to tell two creatures that they cannot love each other—no matter what their species.[35]

This is Diana's quest—to learn the powers she has inherited well enough that she might use them to find Ashmole 782, decipher its secrets, and find a way to free creatures from the Congregation's prejudice and oppression.

CONCLUSION

Agatha Wilson, a daemon who supports Diana's quest, tells her that "a little book can hold a big secret—one that might change the world. You're a witch. You know words have power."[36] Rhetoricians also understand the power of words, and in the case of Harkness' *Discovery of Witches*, one book has indeed made a significant impact on American public memory of the Salem witchcraft crisis. In his *Legal History* of the trials, Peter Charles Hoffer argues that rhetors responsible for pop-culture texts often tie their stories to Salem by following in the tradition of Miller's *Crucible*, which "is an inspiration to us, for it reminds us that we are not proof against the superstition and rumormongering that brought on the tragedy in Salem."[37]

Although Hoffer is not wrong in his assessment, the development of the witch-as-crusader heroine, a character who embarks on a quest to increase social justice that is deeply rooted in her own ancestry and fueled by her personal struggles for equality as a witch and as a woman, takes both the development of the heroine and the legacy of American public memory of the Salem narrative a step further. No longer does pop culture use Salem's story merely as a warning, but in the case of Harkness' novel, the Salem tragedy becomes a piece in a larger struggle for human rights and social justice. Perhaps Diana herself puts it best when she argues, "If we are at war, we're not fighting for a bewitched alchemical manuscript, or for my safety, or for our right to marry and have children. This is about the future of all of us."[38] It is a fight not so far removed from the struggles for freedom constantly unfolding around the world today, and that is a legacy truly worthy of a place within the collective's memory.

NOTES

1. "Petition of Francis Faulkner et al. to Clear the Records of Rebecca Nurse, Mary Esty, Abigail Faulkner Sr., Mary Parker, John Procter, Elizabeth Procter, Elizabeth How, Samuel Wardwell, & Sarah Wardwell," in *Records of the Salem Witch-Hunt*, ed. Bernard Rosenthal (New York: Cambridge University Press, 2009), 849.

2. Tracing the entire history of witches and witchcraft in the Western world lies far outside the scope of this chapter but has been the focus of many book projects. For several useful texts, see Julio Caro Baroja, *The World of the Witches*, trans. O. N. V. Glendinning (Chicago: University of Chicago Press, 1965); Brian P. Levack, *The Witch-Hunt in Early Modern Europe*, 3rd ed. (Harlow, UK: Pearson Education, 2006); Jeffrey B. Russell and Brooks Alexander, *A History of Witchcraft: Sorcerers, Heretics & Pagans*, 2nd ed. (New York: Thames and Hudson, 2007); Christina Larner, *Witchcraft and Religion: The Politics of Popular Belief* (Oxford: Basil

Blackwell, 1984); and Walter Stephens, *Demon Lovers: Witchcraft, Sex, and the Crisis of Belief* (Chicago: University of Chicago Press, 2002).

3. Nenonen, "Who Bears the Guilt for the Persecution of Witches?," *Studia Neophilologica* 84 (2012): 73.

4. Richard Gordon, "Imagining Greek and Roman Magic," in *Witchcraft and Magic in Europe: Ancient Greece and Rome*, eds. Bengt Ankarloo and Stuart Clark (Philadelphia: University of Pennsylvania Press, 1999), 162.

5. Marion Gibson, "Retelling Salem Stories: Gender Politics and Witches in American Culture," *European Journal of American Culture* 25, no. 2 (2006): 91.

6. Ibid., 92.

7. Ibid., 94.

8. Helen A. Berger and Douglas Ezzy, "Mass Media and Religious Identity: A Case Study of Young Witches," *Journal for the Scientific Study of Religion* 48, no. 3 (2009): 504.

9. Tanice G. Foltz, "The Commodification of Witchcraft," in *Witchcraft and Magic in Contemporary North America*, ed. Helen A. Berger (Philadelphia: University of Pennsylvania Press, 2005), 165–66.

10. Starhawk, *The Spiral Dance*, 3rd ed. (New York: HarperCollins, 1999), 269.

11. Ibid., 102.

12. Berger and Ezzy, "Mass Media and Religious Identity," 509.

13. Joke Hermes, "Media Figures in Identity Construction," in *Rethinking the Media Audience*, ed. Pertti Alasuutari (London: Sage, 1999), 74.

14. Beverley Southgate, "Memories into Something New: Histories for the Future," *Rethinking History* 11 (June 2007): 191.

15. John Bodnar, *Remaking America: Public Memory, Commemoration, and Patriotism in the Twentieth Century* (Princeton, NJ: Princeton University Press, 1992), 14.

16. Michael Schudson, "Lives, Laws, and Language: Commemorative versus Non-Commemorative Forms of Effective Public Memory," *Communication Review* 2 (1997): 5.

17. Mary Beth Norton, *In the Devil's Snare: The Salem Witchcraft Crisis of 1692* (New York: Knopf, 2002), 51.

18. Coline Covington, "In Search of the Heroine," *Journal of Analytical Psychology* 34 (1989): 243–44.

19. Harkness released the first book of her All Souls Trilogy, *A Discovery of Witches*, in 2011, the second, *Shadow of Night*, in 2012, and is currently working on the final installment. Although the story is unfinished, Harkness develops Diana's identity as heroine in great detail in the first book of the series, which will be the focus in this analysis.

20. Gretchen A. Adams, *The Specter of Salem: Remembering the Witch Trials in Nineteenth-Century America* (Chicago: University of Chicago Press, 2008), 157–58.

21. Deborah Harkness, *A Discovery of Witches* (New York: Penguin, 2011), 3.

22. Kenneth Burke, *A Grammar of Motives* (New York: Prentice Hall, 1945), 27.

23. Harkness, *A Discovery of Witches*, 86.

24. Ibid., 131.

25. Ibid., 529.

26. Tanya Linaker, "A Witch, a Bitch or a Goddess? Female Voices Transcending Gender as Heard and Recorded by Chekhov, Mansfield, and Nabokov," *Slovo* 17, no. 2 (Autumn 2005): 165.

27. Harkness, *A Discovery of Witches*, 331.

28. For more on Burke and identification, see Kenneth Burke, *Attitudes toward History*, 3rd ed. (Berkeley: University of California Press, 1984). For Fisher on his narrative paradigm, see Walter R. Fisher, "Narration as a Human Communication Paradigm: The Case of Public Moral Argument," *Communication Monographs* 51 (March 1984): 1–22.

29. Harkness, *A Discovery of Witches*, 351.

30. Joseph N. Bell, "A Witch to Watch," *Pageant*, April 1965.

31. Harkness, *A Discovery of Witches*, 409.

32. Ibid., 4.

33. Ibid., 188.

34. Ibid., 272.

35. Ibid., 554.

36. Ibid., 59.

37. Peter Charles Hoffer, *The Salem Witchcraft Trials: A Legal History* (Lawrence: University Press of Kansas, 1997), 8.

38. Harkness, *A Discovery of Witches*, 483–84.

Chapter Four

Heroine

Christina of Markyate

K. A. Laity

Christina of Markyate was a twelfth-century recluse. While the term *popular culture* should be used with caution when speaking of the Middle Ages, her life story proved popular reading in at least her region of England, modeled as it was on the most popular genre of the time, hagiography—the lives of saints. Hers is a fascinating story and an early biography of a woman in a time when few but kings and saints got their stories told. It is fortunate that someone important considered Christina close enough to the latter. We can tell the impact of her heroic example not only because we have her vita but because we have the *St. Albans Psalter* which "evidence from the text and illustrations suggests . . . was essentially created for Christina."[1] Such a time-consuming and valuable object would only be undertaken for a person of great importance to the spiritual community. Christina was their heroine.

To understand the scope of Christina's accomplishments, it may be helpful to say a few words about the context of the twelfth century. The knee-jerk association of "medieval" with "cruel and unusual" in current popular culture ignores the truth of the situation. Hideous torture and witch burnings, for example, were much more part of the so-called Renaissance, or Early Modern era as scholars now refer to the time. Women in Anglo-Saxon England had more rights and power than women in Victorian England. Although the effects of the Norman Invasion of 1066 reduced women's roles markedly, the process took time. The French nobles given position and land by the conquering king imposed a new culture.[2]

Christina was born "Theodora" in Huntingdon about three decades after the Norman Invasion. Her parents, Autti and Beatrix, were wealthy merchants; while her father's name suggests Norse origins, her mother's shows the Norman taste. Their concern with securing a position for their daughter in the midst of changing social circumstances provides a certain amount of anxiety to the young girl's life. Change was everywhere as the French-speaking nobles began to take precedence in the land, shifting the balance—and language—of power in England. The "ethnic tension" was plain: William the Conqueror's youngest son Henry, who took the throne around the time of Christina's birth, took a Saxon wife Ælfgifu, the great-great-grandniece of Edward the Confessor. She immediately changed her name to the more acceptably Norman Matilda, "but this did not stop the royal couple being mockingly referred to by the Anglo-Saxon names of Godric and Godgifu."[3]

THE RELIGIOUS VIRGIN

It's important, too, to understand the context of Christina's ambition to join the church. While we tend to think of the church as a repressive organization in the current age, for women in the Middle Ages it offered one of the few opportunities for independence and a little authority (assuming you weren't born to a royal family or likely to be married into one). As the lives of virgin saints demonstrate well, the best way for a woman to claim authority was to do it in God's name. The lives of early saints legends provided inspirational role models: a martyr like Catherine, Juliana, or Margaret could accomplish much with divine power on their side despite their inevitable beheading (like zombies, the only way to kill a martyr who could withstand any manner of torture unscathed.[4]

Religious communities flourished in twelfth-century England, when "eighty-five new communities for women were founded" in part due to the diversification of monastic orders; formerly the Benedictine order maintained a monopoly, but newer—and to their mind, "purer" and unsullied by centuries of corruption and reform—orders like the Cistercians and Gilbertines offered new options, including the revival of dual houses. Although Christina's initial entry into the religious life proves unconventional, that was certainly not her aim.[5]

Her spiritual interests manifested early on. The story is that a dove flew over to Christina's mother from the local monastery and nestled in her sleeve and stayed there a week while she was pregnant, demonstrating of course that the child was touched by the Holy Spirit. As a child, "she used to talk to [Christ] at night and on her bed as if he were a man whom she could see."[6] In the early Middle Ages, the primary image of Jesus was as a triumphant king. The modern imagination of "your own personal Jesus" was a long way off, yet there was a movement toward what came to be called "affective piety" which was thought to be particularly appropriate for women. It centered on how the sufferings of Christ on the cross affected the observer emotionally.

By the fourteenth and fifteenth century, this leads to figures like Margery Kempe, whose sobbing and wailing annoyed her fellow pilgrims.[7]

Our modern image of monasteries and convents tend to veer between seeing authoritarian organizations ruled by an iron fist or wild centers of debauchery and luxury as suggested by Chaucer's portrait of the monk in *The Canterbury Tales*. While both extremes certainly existed, the reality of course falls in between. Many young women from noble families were sent to convents to educate them in the necessary qualities for being a wife: mostly prayer and needlework. Some remained there if the family lacked sufficient dowry to arrange a suitable marriage. And many followed a genuine desire for spiritual connection.

Augustine's advice to women who wanted to devote their lives to Christ was to "unsex" themselves. Woman as "difference" was never so clear as in medieval theology. They had to remove that difference and become the original (male) in order to match God's perfection from which they were a deviation. Despite this removal, they were also seen as a phallic lack, but they could make up for that absence by employing the power of the divine.

We see this in the lives of the virgin saints, who wielded a borrowed power. Thus sweet maidens like Agnes, Judith, and Margaret were able to defend themselves against all onslaughts of force and secular power.[8] Divine grace gives Agnes a sudden abundance of hair to shield her modesty when stripped naked and thrust into a brothel. Judith, taken as a spoil of war, calls on her god to give her the strength to chop off the conquering army leader Holofernes' head—although in acknowledgment of her weaker female body, it takes her two strokes to do so.[9] Margaret is not only able to resist the charms of the governor Olibrius who would force her into marriage, but is also able to pop out of the belly of a dragon, who is of course really just a demon in disguise. Like a modern action hero, Margaret manages to throw him to the ground, put her foot on his throat, and demand that he give up all his secrets.

The distant past was not the only place for role models for Christina. She doubtless heard of extraordinary women in her own land like the abbess Hild, who brought together a great center of learning in Whitby.[10] She was not only responsible for discovering the first renowned native poet of these shores, Caedmon, but her prestige made Whitby the logical place for the great Synod that united the spiritual threads of the nation during the process of converting Anglo-Saxon England. When the Irish and Roman monks sat down to hash out a single religious identity for the land in 664, it was under Hild's roof.

Christina may not have been aware of the roughly contemporary role model of Hildegard of Bingen, but that nun was carving out a similar path. Hildegard's creativity encompassed music as well as healing and visions.[11] Often under fire for her unconventional approaches to faith, she made a habit of going over secular (and male) authority to claim her own—or at least that of the nearest archbishop, Henry of Mainz. Fortunately the highest authority approved of her mystic visions and the beautiful melodies she composed. Her visions were tested at the Synod of Trier, which led to Pope Eugenus giving them his approval, confirmation that they were divinely inspired.

Closer to home, Christina mostly found male role models, the first of these the monk Sueno. Even as a child he could see the spiritual potential in Christina. Like most heroines-in-the-making, Christina's potential manifested early on. While there was the dove that visited her mother before her birth and her childhood conversations with Christ, the first important milestone was her betrothal to her savior. Her goal was set.

Her family and the society around her didn't see it that way. Her parents had a fairly orthodox belief and sought to have her blessed by the church, but they had more worldly plans in mind.

THE ROMANCE HEROINE

Unearthly beauty is typical for romance heroines and gets carried over to sacred narratives as well. After all, they are also heroes, though of a specific type. In the Anglo-Saxon retelling of the story of Judith, the poet describes the young woman, favored by divine protection, as having "elfin beauty" too (in Christina's vision, Mary explicitly compares her with Judith). [12] The early virgin saints like Catherine and Margaret first get into trouble because their unearthly beauty attracts the attention of secular authorities who immediately fall in love with them. Christine has the beauty associated with good that remains the norm up through the twentieth century, and it attracts the wrong kind of attention.

The first uncomfortable encounter comes from the unlikely personage of Ranulf, the bishop of Durham. The spiritual advisor might be expected to help the young novice achieve her goal; instead "straightaway Satan, that songster of voluptuousness, put into his heart an evil desire for her." While a modern audience might be surprised by this, the medieval audience clearly expects these very physical failings in their leaders. Christina's aunt Ælfgifu had been his concubine and born him several children; "afterwards he gave Ælfgifu in marriage to one of the citizens of Huntingdon, and for her sake, he greatly esteemed the rest of her kin." [13]

This kind of sexual exchange proved to be the norm. Christina's refusal to comply with the demands of her parents marked her as a dangerous rebel. Her biographer makes the drama inherent in the situation even stronger with a vivid setting. While her parents get drunk with their friends, Ranulf commands the girl be brought to his chambers, "a room handsomely decorated with hangings." The description of his imprecations shows both restraint and loathing: "The shameless bishop indecently seized the maiden by one of the sleeves of her tunic, and with the mouth which he used to consecrate the holy sacrament he urged her to commit a wicked deed."[14] If the bishop had a moustache, he would be stroking it.

"Hear, then, how prudently she acted," the narrator tells us almost breathlessly. Our heroine sees that the door is closed but not bolted and suggests the danger of this to her would-be ravisher with an arch tone: "Allow me to fasten the bolt, for even if we do not fear God at least we ought to fear men."[15] After making her swear that she would do exactly that, the bishop releases her. Christina darts outside and bolts the door behind her, making her escape—the first of several.

While it might seem jarring to modern audiences, this depiction of a religious heroine as a kind of romance figure (romance in the original medieval sense of "adventure") fits into the storytelling traditions. Early saints behave more like the warrior heroes of poetry than like the pious ascetics modernity assumes. The culture that produced the epic *Beowulf* is keen to see saints like local son Guthlac battling demons and getting carried off to a hellmouth rather than simply living in quiet modesty.

Even the *Ancrene Wisse*, a thirteenth-century handbook for anchoresses, uses these familiar tropes. An anchoress was a woman walled into the side of a church in a small room. While she had a small window to communicate and receive food, she was meant to be dead to the world (sometimes to the extent of having the mass of the dead read over her as she was interred). In chapter 7 of the guide meant to ease the solitary hours, the wide book advises the anchoress to imagine herself as a noble but heartless heroine in a castle while a white knight, Christ, batters at the door to rescue her from indifference.

Christina's escape from her family into the (initially) secret life with a monk fits this romance mode perfectly. You'd think after such a clear sign as a dove nestling in her pregnant mother's sleeve her parents would resign themselves to offering her to the church, but no. They get her engaged to a rich young man, Beorhtred, despite her protests that she'd like to devote her life to quiet contemplation. But she, too, trusted that her link to the divine gave her all the authority she needed to flout convention.

The peer pressure was considerable. Her parents paid her friend Melisen for a year to chatter on about "the dignity and status of matrimony,"[16] though it fell on deaf ears and eventually led to her friend's corruption instead of Christina's own. Her parents refused to let her visit the monastery where she had her spiritual awakening, and alternately entreated and berated her for her stubbornness. A typical example came at the Gild merchant festival, where Christina's parents required her to be the cupbearer, putting the modest girl on display before the drunken crowd. They made sure to dress her in her best, "for indeed they hoped that the compliments paid to her by the onlookers and the accumulation of little sips of wine would break her spirit and prepare her body for the deed of corruption."[17]

Failing with this plan, they turn to an alternative: "They let her betrothed secretly into her bedroom so that, should he find the maiden asleep, he might suddenly violate her." The would-be attacker, however, was treated to a knowledgeable argument from Christina about the possibility of living without sin even within marriage as St. Cecilia and her husband Valerian had managed to do. He finally leaves in despair, only to have the waiting crowd disparage his masculinity and send him back for another attempt, vowing to help him violate her. Christina manages to conceal herself behind wall hangings, desperately holding to a peg in the wall with sudden strength while people search the room in vain.[18]

Her access to divine power gives her this strength. When Beorhtred next pursues her, Christina is able to leap a high fence. "For what woman do you suppose could avoid so many snares?"[19] Claiming always her previous betrothal to Christ, she refuses any attempt to wed her to her parents' chosen mate. People almost universally turn against her, including her original role model Sueno, who too easily believes in the frailty of a maiden. Though heartbroken by this betrayal, Christina is no less resolute. It is from this time that she truly earns her name reflecting Christ, although tellingly her family continues to refer to her as "Theodora" in their often heated exchanges. Her disputations with the prior Fredebert show that her intellectual development matches her spiritual course, her straightforward clarity overmatching his sophistry.

The first trial for many heroines is family life: Christina's parents were hell-bent on material success and thought their daughter the best way to assure it. The composer of her *Life* tells us that stubbornness runs in her family; we believe it when her mother beats the unbending girl such that "the scars on her back never faded as long as she lived."[20] Unable to change their minds and unwilling to consent to an impossible marriage, at last Christina endeavors, like so many a romance heroine, to escape. She gets a boost in belief with a vision of Mary, who offers the ultimate vote of confidence by allowing the young woman to gaze upon her face.

Having secured promises from a young servant, Loric, that he would procure horses for the escape, Christina made excuses to stay with her aunt whom she had bribed into laxity, unlike her ever-vigilant parents. She laid by men's clothes as a disguise, knowing that her female appearance would draw attention. But it was not simply masculine clothes that she had to acquire: Christina saw the active power she wished to assert over her own life as masculine, and leaping astride the horse, she had a moment of embarrassment at such an "unfeminine" position:

> Why delay, oh fugitive? Why respect your femininity? Put on manly courage and mount the horse like a man. So she put aside her fears, and jumped on the

horse as if she were a man, set spurs to its flanks, and said to the servant, "Follow me at a distance, for I fear that if you ride with me and we are caught, that they will kill you."[21]

Her words demonstrate how much of a transgression her flight was and how it flaunted every gender expectation. She first takes refuge with the recluse Ælfwynn, concealed from prying eyes, devoting her energies to finding joy in her savior. Her family sets out diligently to find her, turning first to the local monastery, then to anchorites, and finally to Roger the hermit, even bribing his disciples in hopes of revealing Christina's hiding place. When Beorhtred seeks his betrothed at Ælfwynn's, she turns him away with sophistry, saying, "It is not our custom to give shelter to wives who are running away from their husbands."[22]

THE RECLUSE

Roger the hermit feared the worst; having not offered help himself he assumed the young woman had been abducted and ruined, but one of his acolytes brought word that she was with Ælfwynn and he rejoiced. Nonetheless, it takes two years for him to finally offer her protection, while she is beset by visions of toads and demons who resent her purity. Although Ælfwynn objects to the unconventional arrangement, Roger brings the virgin to live in his cell:

> For the fire which had been kindled by the spirit of God which burned in each one of them cast its sparks into their hearts . . . and so, made one in heart and soul in chastity and charity in Christ, they were not afraid to dwell together under the same roof.[23]

Make no mistake: the contemporary audience would have found this part of Christina's story just as unbelievable as a modern reader would. A plank of wood concealed Christina's hidden nook, "no bigger than a span and a half," from which she could emerge only at night. Four years she remained there, and "O what trials she had to bear of cold and heat, hunger and thirst, daily fasting!"[24]

While we often think of holy people as being above the temptations of the flesh, it is their struggle against natural appetites that sets them up as role models for the medieval audience. Like many of her time, Christina engages in fasting and harsh scourging, especially when tempted by a "lewd cleric" who finds himself strangely "inspired" by her peerless example. He rewards her with the highest encomium, saying she was "more like a man than a woman" who behaves "manfully."[25] A vision of Christ as a child whom she clasps to her bosom for a whole day serves as her reward while, the biographer notes, the lust-filled bishop who persecuted her finally dies.

Christina's peerless conduct evokes envy in others and she frequently has to chastise her superiors because those men would rather wheel and deal wealth than praise God. Although she frequently assists women who have little access to power in the secular or religious spheres, it is her power among men that receives the most acclaim. Chief among the men she takes in hand is Abbot Geoffrey of St. Albans, the site that later produced the psalter for her. Geoffrey is a rather brash young abbot who brings a great deal of wealth to the abbey, but in the process he becomes arrogant and obstinate. When Christina first chastised him with information gleaned from a divinely inspired dream, the abbot dismissed the young woman and her "silly dream"; when she engaged in prayers and vigils, however, the abbot found himself surrounded by "many, black terrifying figures" that "struck him, suffocated him, and tortured him." It convinced the abbot that he ought to listen to the young woman after all, and so began the most unlikely of friendships. [26]

"Their affection was mutual but their sanctity took different forms. Geoffrey supported Christina in worldly matters; she commended him to God more earnestly in her holy prayers. . . . Nor did she make a secret of reproving him harshly in his presence whenever she knew that in his absence he had gravely sinned, thinking that the wounds of a friend are better than the flattery of an enemy." [27]

It was a relationship that brought much criticism, destabilizing the normal hierarchy of the church and upending the traditional gender roles as well. For a devoted partnership, Christina's biographer seems to lack any language but that of mundane love, describing her as "inflamed with desire," although making it clear that this was different from mere earthly love, for "his countenance transcend[ed] human beauty." Nonetheless, their obvious attachment gave rise to chatter, for the assumption persisted that a mere woman could not maintain a relationship with a man that was not fueled by carnality.

> From that time she became so attached to him that neither favour nor malice could prevent her from calling him her closest friend . . . nor did this happen without much spiteful gossip. For there were many people who wished to reach the same holiness of life and gain the same affection from Christina as the abbot enjoyed. But falling out of favour, they delighted in slander. [28]

Nonetheless, Christina receives frequent examples of the divine approval she maintains in the face of this earthly doubting, visited by visions of the divine in a wide variety for forms, often helping the abbot make difficult decisions and strengthening his resolve when he doubted, or when the men above him demanded actions that he was loath to commit. Inevitably things always came out in accordance with Christina's prayers. The abbot never regretted putting his life and decisions in her hands, even when her advice diverged from the instructions of the king.

Though in general the biographer upholds the gender biases of his time without questioning them, there are spaces within the narrative where he highlights the potential for female-positive interpretations of the Christian faith, for example, noting that "Beelzebub . . . despised the disciples of Christ because they took women about with them."[29] While on the whole the narrative emphasizes Christina's power among the hierarchies of men, her visions tend to be of Mary and such homely things as doves and herbs. Her reviled female difference nonetheless provides her a particular avenue to divinity, for it is Mary time and again who responds to her entreaties and offers her rewards.

So it's a busy life, fighting off demons and receiving prognostications from the Holy Spirit, and only a few recognized her for what she was. Most were ready to dismiss her with "gossip" or "poisonous slanders" or "barbed words" in an effort to defame her:

> Hence, some of them called her a dreamer, others a seducer of souls, others more moderately, just a worldly-wise business woman. . . . Others who could think of nothing better to say spread the rumour that she was attracted to the abbot by earthly love.[30]

It's fascinating that "business woman" could be such an insult, but the vow of poverty proves a double-edged sword. Responsible for a community of women, Christina did need to be sure to secure at least a minimal amount of food and fuel to keep them all alive, yet always remain alert to the judgmental eyes on earth and above measuring for any excess. It's a delicate balancing act, but Christina manages it.

While she and her convent continue to be tested by both men and demons, Christina offers a firm anchor which also receives the reward of divine guests, both as visions and, notably, as a pilgrim who arrives, charms and delights everyone, then disappears while locked inside the chapel.[31] While she did receive the church's ultimate approbation and become a saint, she was enough of a hero to her region to have the important investment of a recorded life (albeit incomplete in the only version that's come down to us) to give strength to men and women who sought to live a better life and overcome the struggles inherent in living according to an exacting spiritual path. For a modern audience, Christina shines even more magnificently. While readers may not be interested in pursuing the rigorous life she did, they will be amazed that a young woman so long ago found the courage to follow her dreams despite the disapproval of her family and her culture.

NOTES

1. University of Aberdeen, "Introduction," *St Albans Psalter* (2003), http://www.abdn.ac.uk/stalbanspsalter/english/essays/introduction.shtml (accessed July 28, 2013).

2. For a good overview of England after the Norman Invasion, see Hugh M. Thomas, *The English and the Normans* (Oxford: Oxford University Press, 2003).

3. C. H. Talbot, *The Life of Christina of Markyate* (Oxford: Oxford University Press, 2008), ix.

4. K. A. Laity, "False Positives: The Katherine-Group Saints as Ambiguous Role Models," *Magistra* 7, no. 2 (2001): 64–99.

5. Talbot, *Christina*, ix.

6. Ibid., 4.

7. See, for example, Sarah Beckwith, "A Very Material Mysticism: The Medieval Mysticism of Margery Kempe," *Medieval Literature* 4 (1986): 34–54.

8. Catherine Innes-Parker, "Sexual Violence and the Female Reader: Symbolic 'Rape' in the Saints' Lives of the Katherine Group," *Women's Studies: An Interdisciplinary Journal* 24, no. 3 (1995): 205–17.

9. Shari Horner, "Spiritual Truth and Sexual Violence: The Old English 'Juliana,' Anglo-Saxon Nuns, and the Discourse of Female Monastic Enclosure," *Signs* 19, no. 3 (1994): 658–75.

10. Nancy Bauer, "Abbess Hilda of Whitby: All Britain Was Lit by Her Splendor," *Medieval Women Monastics*, 1996, 13–31.

11. Constant J. Mews, "Hildegard of Bingen," in *Encyclopedia of Medieval Philosophy*, 476–78 (New York: Springer Netherlands, 2011).

12. Peter J. Lucas, "'Judith' and the Woman Hero," *Yearbook of English Studies* 22 (1992): 17–27.

13. Talbot, *Christina*, 7.

14. Ibid., 7.

15. Ibid., 7.

16. Ibid., 9.

17. Ibid., 11.

18. Ibid., 11.

19. Ibid., 13.

20. Ibid., 25.

21. Ibid., 34.

22. Ibid., 36.

23. Ibid., 39.

24. Ibid., 40.

25. Ibid., 46.

26. Ibid., 58.

27. Ibid., 60.

28. Ibid., 65.

29. Ibid., 78.

30. Ibid., 78.

31. Ibid., 86.

Chapter Five

The Bohemian Gypsy, Another Body to Sell

Deciphering Esmeralda in Popular Culture

Adina Schneeweis

From the first time I saw it, I easily fell in love with the musical *Notre-Dame de Paris*, for the enchanting voices, the beautiful tunes, the dancing, the contemporary décor, and the timely adaptation of a known story to current political issues like immigration, asylum, and diversity. What struck me, though, was my reaction to the beloved female lead Esmeralda; as much as the singer-actress played the role beautifully, the character seemed to repeat the familiar stereotype of the sexualized gypsy sorceress. I began to wonder about other adaptations of Esmeralda. This chapter examines the path of the heroine, from Victor Hugo's novel *The Hunchback of Notre-Dame* to recent popular-culture incarnations, which, I argue, continue to objectify and commodify a racialized, ethnic body.

I position my analysis of Esmeralda within the tradition of critical studies that have documented popular-culture and artistic representations of so-called gypsies (to refer to the Roma and other groups[1]). Most images are negative—stereotypically lazy, poor, dirty, unhealthy, genetically inclined to commit crime, unreliable, dangerous, dishonest, untrustworthy, irresponsible, promiscuous, having more children than they can afford to raise, immoral and amoral, with unstable lifestyles, marked by idleness, promiscuity and witchcraft, and, above all, unwanted and racially inferior—*an other*.[2] Some have noted "positive" representations—those of bohemian, romantic, nomadic, and artistic gypsies from Western popular culture, arts, and literature—which are also stereotypical and racist, despite their continued reproduction worldwide.[3] In this context, Esmeralda has seen a particularly stable trajectory, while other gypsy characters have shifted and adapted for contemporary audiences (bohemian guitar players or immigrants, for instance), and new ones have been added (reality TV stars, to name just one). Hugo's heroine is one of many feminine portrayals that have come under scrutiny for the fixed gender discourses they convey,[4] and one of several ethnic characters examined as overly sexualized and exoticized.[5] This chapter is thus relevant to present-day understanding of meanings associated with "gypsy" and with gypsy women, and contributes to the scholarship on feminist communication, feminist ethnic studies, and Romani studies. An analysis of Esmeralda as a heroine for young audiences, particularly girls, must be read alongside other work that calls for characters that defy stereotypes.[6] While scholars have documented discriminatory media practices, few focus on media representations of the gypsy woman in specific.[7] In this context, I argue that Esmeralda as a fictional gypsy embodies historic stereotypes that linger within present-day sociopolitical constructs of the European Roma. The character of Esmeralda and the accompanying memorabilia invoke tropes familiar to a European—and worldwide—audience of the enchanting, beautiful, racialized female body.

I began from Hugo's original description of the heroine. I also examined two graphic-novel adaptations,[8] marketed to China, Hong Kong, the Philippine Islands, Puerto Rico, and North America. Of the many theatre, opera, widescreen, and television adaptations, I chose to examine Maureen O'Hara's Esmeralda in the 1939 film; the 1956 Hollywood adaptation, starring Gina Lollobrigida as Esmeralda; the first Disney movie *The Hunchback of Notre Dame* (1996), with actress Demi Moore playing the heroine[9]; and the 1998 French-Canadian musical *Notre-Dame de Paris*. The latter has been translated and performed over three thousand times in France, Canada, Belgium, the United Kingdom, Russia, Poland, Switzerland, Spain, China, South Korea, the United States, Italy, Monaco, Taiwan, Singapore, and Lebanon, leading to international "stunning triumph" and arguably an "explosion of French musicals."[10] I used textual analysis to ground my discussion and employed various analytical tools in the process—semiotic, narrative, genre, and rhetorical.[11] I treated the selected texts not just as containers of content, but as complex sets of discursive strategies located in specific ideological and cultural assumptions. Although the list of texts is by no means exhaustive, and is limited to English-language adaptations, it offers variety across time periods and target audiences, thus offering a somewhat diverse repertoire of repackagings of Esmeralda. I assumed the collection of texts to play a critical part in creating a certain image of "the Esmeralda"—or "La Esmeralda," in Hugo's words—almost removed from any specific representation, but always connected to the concept of gypsy. I argue that the construct of the "beautiful gypsy Esmeralda" does not allow for much flexibility. I find such lack of character pliability problematic, given that historic discrimination and genocide against the gypsies have been possible because of immutable meanings and beliefs about one ethnic group's essential superiority over the other—in other words, because of fixed knowledge about otherness.

THE HEROINE ESMERALDA

The novel *The Hunchback of Notre-Dame* depicts the young gypsy on the streets of 1482 Paris, where she captures the attention of archdeacon of Notre Dame Claude Frollo, of Captain Phoebus de Châteaupers of the King's Archers, of poet Pierre Gringoire, and of Quasimodo, the hunchbacked bell ringer of the cathedral and Frollo's protégé. Esmeralda extends her kindness to Quasimodo, who falls in love with her, despite her revulsion for his appearance. She, in turn, is captivated by Phoebus, who is attracted to her as well. Following a romantic moment between Esmeralda and Phoebus, the gypsy is charged for attempting the murder of the latter, who is in fact stabbed by Frollo in a moment of jealousy. Esmeralda takes protection in the Cathedral, under law of sanctuary, but eventually is led to her hanging after she rejects Frollo's love. When the hunchback realizes Frollo's hand in the woman's death, he pushes the priest to his own end and then joins Esmeralda's body in the tombs, where he also dies.[12] Adaptations of Hugo's novel are expectedly shortened, simplified, and/or transformed.[13] For example, Esmeralda chooses to leave her sanctuary in order to join fellow persecuted gypsies in the musical *Notre-Dame de Paris*. Fitting for Disney's typical family audience, the 1996 rendition was adapted to a happy ending, with Phoebus as a hero ending up together with a living Esmeralda, and Quasimodo accepted by the city, thus allowing for a 2002 sequel featuring Quasimodo and some of the original cast. The 1939 film also closes with a living Esmeralda, this time in love and happily reunited with Gringoire. In the 1956 movie, she dies, shot by an arrow. Others leave out story lines about Esmeralda's mother and/or the goat Djali.

As a literary figure, Esmeralda belongs to a history of representations of "Spanish gypsies" like Preciosa, Carmen, Mignon, and others,[14] and as a popular-culture commodity, to the line of similar Disney figures including Mulan, Pocahontas, Jasmine, and other princesses. Like the latter, Esmeralda is nonwhite, beautiful, bright, kind, in love, and guided by inspiring hopes and good morals[15] —and also sexualized and exotic, particularly as a character of color.[16] Unlike other Disney heroines, however, Esmeralda is the most womanlike, mature, and voluptuous.[17] Aside from the Disney version where she exhibits the most daredevil and athletic traits,[18] Esmeralda is not particularly strong or adventurous; instead, she is dependent on the protection of Phoebus, Quasimodo, Clopin, and the Parisian gypsies; she is influenceable and impressionable (as we see in her learning to pray in the 1939 film, for instance); she is ultimately an eternal victim—of her status and of the system.

The appeal of the heroine's bohemian, exotic, and sexualized nature has contributed to her instant success, inspiring "Esmeralda dresses" in 1831 Parisian shops[19]; numerous works of art, including sculptures and paintings; and apparel and crafts following her debut on the commercial scene via Disney,[20] paraphernalia currently still for sale on websites like Amazon.com and eBay.com. Like other Disney princesses, Esmeralda was also made into a Mattel Barbie doll in 1995 and is a popular—and criticized[21]—Halloween costume. This commodification process recalls the construct of the *cipher*, defined as a container or "unwritten text" that can be filled with content and meanings and repackaged, marketed, and sold to global audiences.[22] Just as the cipher of Pocahontas was used to appropriate and commodify Native American cultures away from historical truths and into capitalist markets, Esmeralda also serves to translate "gypsy cultures," as defined in mediated landscapes, to global audiences. Although defenders of the commodification of Disney figures or popular-culture heroines may argue that memorabilia and marketing give audiences what they want and a product to relate to—after all, how not to love a pretty, dark-haired dancer and her cute, little goat?—through a feminist and critical lens, the argument seems self-serving and ignorant of the representational significance of the character.[23] In Marc DiPaolo's words,

> [I]t is one thing to provide products that cater to the interests of young . . . girls who love . . . gowns in the name of making a profit. It is another thing to bombard children with products that reinforce a narrowly defined definition of . . . femininity in our commodity culture.[24]

This is also problematic in the case of an ethnic, racialized character that communicates a fixed definition of the "gypsy woman."

The Gypsy Esmeralda

As a gypsy character, Esmeralda must be read among mediated and literary representations of singers living in colorful caravans, flamenco dancers, "dark-eyed" fortune-tellers, circus athletes, and horse traders, often in touch with nature, musical, artistic, free-spirited, romantic, and bohemian—and, at the same time, in the context of images of thieves and con men.[25] She follows the trajectory of other narratives attempting to explain the gypsies (like Bizet's *Carmen*), which offer "a unique, all-embracing, eternal—and practically archetypal" definition of gypsies.[26] First, the heroine is not white. Esmeralda first appears in the novel as "brown," and her name reminds the poet Gringoire of "Egyptian"; as Gringoire recognizes a small brass piece that drops from her hair, he labels her as other: "'Oh no!' said he; 'it's a gipsy.' All the illusion had disappeared."[27] Her "racialization"[28] is complete. Most popular-culture incarnations emphasize Esmeralda's dark skin, from graphic novel and Disney drawings, to dolls. Even when white actresses have played her role, the heroine's "gypsyness" is repeated as an appellative, as well as confirmed by her association with the Parisian homeless at the Court of Miracles. As such, the latter are, to Hugo, "people without letters, without religion," involved in sorcery, necromancy, wandering, rambling off, cunningness, and "close communication . . . with all the elemental agencies—with the winds and the waters, the light and the darkness, the mist and the sunshine, the lightning and the tempest," among beggars, thieves, pickpockets, charlatans, and "cripples"[29]—other castoffs, in other words. [30]

Second, and tied to Esmeralda's racial difference, the texts include attention to the stereotype of the fortune-teller/sorceress/witch, in both Esmeralda's and others' voices. The heroine emphasizes her own palm reading in the musical ("Who can tell what will come tomorrow. . . . It is written in the lines of my hand"[31]), recognizing "the mark of the devil" on Frollo's hands in the 1939 film,[32] or jokingly reading Quasimodo's palm. [33] Others' negative association with fortune reading is obvious in Frollo's repeated insults, calling her a "witch,"[34] "a foreigner . . . a bohemian, a sorceress . . . a bitch, an errant cat, an animal that lingers . . . a mortal danger."[35] Again, in the 1956 film, as Esmeralda is judged for stabbing Phoebus, the presiding priest shouts, "Silence! You are of the gypsy race, notorious for the practice of witchcraft. You're accused of consorting with the devil, in the guise of a tame goat."[36]

The musical is further suggestive of the overlap between different elements that come together to construct Esmeralda's otherness: she is a dangerous outsider, because of her homelessness (bohemian), but also because of her sexuality that "ravages the hearts and souls of those faithful to Notre Dame."[37] Others have commented on the overlap between sexuality and otherness, on the problems of defining women through their bodies, and the female body through sexuality[38]; the representation of Esmeralda follows this trajectory: the heroine is seductive, yet innocent (and manipulable by the other male characters); she is passionate, yet subdued; desirable, desired, and yet forbidden; in the musical, she is "Belle" (beautiful), but a "beautiful stranger"[39]; in a graphic novel, even to her fellow gypsies, to whom she is "our sister," she must be saved because she is "such a pretty girl. . . . We won't let them hang [her]."[40]

Hugo's Esmeralda turns out to not be a gypsy after all, but born Agnes to a Parisian prostitute; not all adaptations include this plotline, but all capitalize on her position as outsider and orphan. Some of the texts transform her orphan status to mean country-less, settled on the streets of Paris but dreaming of another land: "No one knows where my story begins. . . . I am daughter of meandering roads."[41] The evolution of the term "bohemian" is not of direct interest here, but it is significant to note that, as regards the gypsies, it has meant an outsider, one that is marginalized and outside mainstream conventions.[42]

More recently, as seen in the 1998 musical and the 1996 Disney cartoon, and different than in earlier Hollywood films, the female "bohemienne" is complete with character strength, pride, and feistiness, accompanying the more familiar earlier traits of hopefulness, wonder at life, innocence, and vulnerability. The blend of the characteristics of the femme fatale with innocence, sexuality, and a racialized body are not new, in the media or in art alike, and others have recognized the construction of the gypsy woman as "a symbol of freedom from mainstream conventions yet also . . . an unpleasant sense of assertive deviance."[43] As with other stereotypes, the perpetuation of this construction of the gypsy continues to dehumanize and limit the possibilities for real-world ethnic identity, and for its performance.

Esmeralda's Body

A significant aspect of the representation of Hugo's heroine is her body and its deployment to move the plot forward. Some have commented that texts visually depict Esmeralda as a "Spanish gypsy"—a common stereotype in literature and art. The image of a dark-haired girl, with flouncy long skirts, revealing cleavage, hand on hip, dancing with castanets or clapping her hands, portrays a carefree, promiscuous, and sexually available woman.[44] Esmeralda has been described to embody beauty and sin as a "naïve, almost savage young girl"[45] who captures the hearts of male protagonists. Hugo introduces her as adored and sought after; the poet Gringoire describes her to be fairy-like, angel-like, slender, with large eyes, black hair, dancing with parted lips, with bare shoulders and "fine formed legs."[46] Despite the fact that the novel is ultimately about the demise of the Gothic French cathedral Notre-Dame de Paris, and a critique to religion, tradition, and culture, adaptations of Esmeralda place the beautiful bohemienne at the forefront of readers' and viewers' focus.

Publicity materials used to promote the analyzed texts all give much attention to Esmeralda's body and beauty. She is always clad in long dresses that enhance a slender figure, sporting a generous cleavage, and lying or standing in positions meant to draw attention to her body and sexual appeal. For instance, the DVD cover of the 1939 film emphasizes Esmeralda's curvy (dead) body, with neck and breast line exposed. The 1956 DVD cover depicts Gina Lollobrigida in yet another sexually inviting pose, neck and cleavage exposed; from a visual design point of view, her figure is positioned in one of the key focal areas of a photographic image, and spaced neatly between the cover's text blocks to enhance viewer attention.[47] The Disney DVD cover displays bare shoulders and low neckline. The most advertised posters for the promotion of the 1998 musical depict the various Esmeralda artists to be wearing a shimmering green dress, with high cut on one leg that is always exposed; the DVD and soundtrack album covers display the profile of an overly sexualized cartoon figure, with a revealing red dress and a head scarf covering her black hair (not featured on the musical stage, but more in sync with the "Spanish gypsy" stereotype), and stretched-out body to display generous, pointed breasts. What emerges is that most, if not all, adaptations are *primarily* marketed as Esmeralda's story, the story of an attractive gypsy girl—and not that of Quasimodo, or of a religious critique. In the same vein, the "Making of" documentary of the French-Canadian musical production describes its success as a worldwide celebration of "the beauty of Esmeralda," returning the attention once again to the gypsy woman's centrality to the story, and to her physical appearance.

The 1956 Esmeralda played by Gina Lollobrigida and Disney's heroine seem to be the most sexualized. In 1956, Esmeralda's wording and acting are more enticing, sensual, and flirty than in other adaptations, and the plot shows her leading Quasimodo on (consistent, certainly, with other Lollobrigida roles). The Disney film shows a sexually appealing Esmeralda as well, despite its family-friendly target audience. Others have noted the increased sexualization and exoticization of Disney heroines, particularly of ethnic female characters, and culminating with Esmeralda.[48] Her dress in the Disney cartoon has been called "the epitome of the exotic/sexual" and suggestive of her ethnicity[49] (like Lollobrigida's dresses). Her flirty dancing concludes with spinning around a pole, a daring move for Disney and a most explicit sexual representation. The heroine is also a clear object of the male gaze (Frollo's, Phoebus', Quasimodo's, and even Gringoire's in some texts), as suggested by intentional shots and acting techniques.[50] In the musical, for example, the three lead men, Quasimodo, Frollo, and Phoebus, sing the famous "Belle" (sold as a single in more than 2.5 million copies and nominated song of the century in France[51]) as they gaze with passion over Esmeralda's stretched-out body. The men sing their lust for her body, "O Lucifer! . . . Allow me only once to slip my fingers through Esmeralda's hair. . . . O Notre Dame! . . . Allow me only once to push the gate to Esmeralda's garden. . . . I will go pick the flower of Esmeralda's love." Later, Quasimodo deplores the gypsy's death and sings "Dance, My Esmeralda" over her listless body, as three other women's "corpses" float in the background, bodies hanging limp, swung and held by hooded male figures.[52]

CONCLUSION

I have shown in this chapter how Esmeralda's representations in popular culture have been remarkably consistent across texts and time periods. Her various incarnations embody characteristics consistent with well-established stereotypes of the romantic bohemian—nomadic, seductive, forbidden, inno-cent, and a victim, all at the same time. Her character has been framed as an other, both as an exotic, sexualized object of adoration, and as a dangerous sorceress. Esmeralda's character thus appeals through her gendered body, as well as through her country-less spirit that invokes a longing for community and belonging.[53] An examination of Esmeralda from a Hugonian character to a mediated popular-culture scene entails seeing her as the cipher she has been transformed into, defining a young gypsy girl in the imagination of nongypsy cultures as a racialized brown body to admire, desire, and eventually dis-card—and sell, as we see with Disney's commodified Esmeralda, which cannot die in the story for this very reason. The goal of the cipher is thus achieved, as Esmeralda fulfills the function of conveying an idealized ab-straction of a gypsy girl. As a popular-culture commodity, she also rips the body of the gypsy woman of any real-world meanings[54] and transforms it exclusively into an object of gaze. The construction of Esmeralda thus gives life to a body, to be desired, fought over, and ultimately thrown away as a dead corpse. Her body, race, ethnicity, sex, and gendered roles are fetish-ized—like Pocahontas' construction[55]—and allowed to float in thin air, as if at a tasting where guests can come to pick their flavor.

It is expected for adaptations to respect but also rework an author's vision of a character.[56] The character's stability in itself is not a concern as much as perhaps a mark of a lack of artistic creativity; what is problematic, however, is how easily Esmeralda as a heroine lends herself to a critical and feminist critique. "The Esmeralda" from Hollywood films and other popular-culture texts has become iconic in her naiveté, innocence, and dependence on men at the same time, defining a fixed construct of "the gypsy woman." She is no longer a French text about a French orphan in the fifteenth century, but an international representation of "gypsy womanhood"—which serves as a plat-form for contemporary objectifications of gypsy bodies in, for instance, real-ity television that overfocuses on otherness and sexual appeal.[57]

At the same time that I examined the selected texts as different locations, I do not mean to suggest their independence from one another. The interplay between the different Esmeraldas outside of any one media platform—liter-ary, artistic, or contemporary popular media renditions—recalls Kathryn Grossman's use of "hypertextual ambiguity."[58] Although new audiences emerge to old texts as they are adapted and reinterpreted, there is always a back-and-forth between them, as they reference, and build upon, each other. Future texts cannot reinvent Esmeralda outside the tradition established by earlier popular-culture texts, especially Disney's, which has rendered the heroine an international celebrity. One can look at the interactive meaning-making process with an optimistic look toward increasingly mobile audi-ences. Yet one must remember that such commodified and heavily marketed products constitute nearly entirely different constructions than the people that they supposedly represent. The process of de-ciphering and unpacking the gypsy character becomes necessary, therefore, recognizing the commodification of "the Esmeralda" (as a body to conquer and consume), to be followed by a significant rethinking of our own relationship to it. Glossing over the social and moral implications of representation only further traps the gypsy and limits interethnic living.

NOTES

1. In this chapter, I use the lowercase term *gypsy* to refer to the ethnic group, because this is how Esmeralda is referenced in most translations of Hugo's text. Although I recognize its stereotyping connotation and potential homogenizing implications—as well as the recent move to *Roma* in political language and advocacy circles—my use of *gypsy* is a rhetorical strategy to be consistent with Esmeralda's appellative in the analyzed texts.

2. Werner Cohn, *The Gypsies* (Reading, MS: Addison-Wesley, 1973); György Csepeli and Dávid Simon, "Construction of Roma Identity in Eastern and Central Europe: Perception and Self-Identification," *Journal of Ethnic and Migration Studies* 30 (2004): 129–50; Karmen Erjavec, "Media Representation of the Discrimination against the Roma in Eastern Europe: The Case of Slovenia," *Discourse & Society* 12 (2001): 699–727; Ian Hancock, "Non-Gypsy Attitudes towards Rom: The Gypsy Stereotype," *Roma* 9 (1985): 50–65; Ian Hancock, *The Pariah Syndrome: An Account of Gypsy Slavery and Persecution* (Ann Arbor, MI: Karoma Publishers, 1987); Alaina Lemon, *Between Two Fires: Gypsy Performance and Romani Memory from Pushkin to Post-socialism* (Durham, NC: Duke University Press); Adina Schneeweis, "If They Really Wanted To, They Would: The Press Discourse of Integration of the European Roma, 1990–2006," *International Communication Gazette* 74 (2012): 673–89, doi: 10.1177/1748048512458561.

3. For example, Brian Belton, *Questioning Gypsy Identity: Ethnic Narratives in Britain and America* (Walnut Creek, CA: AltaMira, 2005); Lemon, *Between Two Fires*; Joanna Richardson, "Talking about Gypsies: The Notion of Discourse as Control," *Housing Studies* 21 (2006): 77–96; Schneeweis, "If They Really Wanted To."

4. Marc DiPaolo, "Mass-Marketing 'Beauty': How a Feminist Heroine Became an Insipid Disney Princess," in *Beyond Adaptation: Essays on Radical Transformations of Original Works*, ed. Phyllis Frus and Christy Williams (Jefferson, NC: McFarland, 2010), 168–80; Rebecca-Anne C. Do Rozario, "The French Musicals: The Dramatic Impulse of *Spectacle*," *Journal of Dramatic Theory and Criticism* 19, no. 1 (2004): 125–42; Lan Dong, "*Mulan*: Disney's Hybrid Heroine," in *Beyond Adaptation: Essays on Radical Transformations of Original Works*, ed. Phyllis Frus and Christy Williams (Jefferson, NC: McFarland, 2010), 156–67; Lauren Dundes, "Disney's Modern Heroine Pocahontas: Revealing Age-Old Gender Stereotypes and Role Discontinuity under a Façade of Liberation," *Social Science Journal* 38 (2001): 353–65.

5. Celeste Lacroix, "Images of Animated Others: The Orientalization of Disney's Cartoon Heroines from *Little Mermaid* to *The Hunchback of Notre Dame*," *Popular Communication* 2 (2004): 213–29.

6. See, for instance, Dundes, "Disney's Modern Heroine"; Rebecca C. Hains, *Growing Up with Girl Power* (New York: Peter Lang, 2012).

7. Peter Gross, "A Prolegomena to the Study of the Romani Media in Eastern Europe," *European Journal of Communication* 21 (2006): 477–97.

8. Tim A. Conrad, *The Hunchback of Notre Dame* (Milwaukie, OR: Dark Horse Books, 2012); Michael Ford, *The Hunchback of Notre Dame* (Hauppauge, NY: Salariya Book Company, 2007).

9. The Disney version of the story has been deemed to be a *transformation* of the original text and not an *adaptation* per se; while relevant, the argument is not of import to this chapter; see Phyllis Frus and Christy Williams, "Introduction: Making the Case for Transformation," in

Beyond Adaptation: Essays on Radical Transformations of Original Works, ed. Phyllis Frus and Christy Williams (Jefferson, NC: McFarland, 2010), 1–18.

10. Do Rozario, "French Musicals"; Thomas P. Finn, "Incorporating the *comédie-musicale* in the College French Classroom," *French Review* 77 (2003): 303; Lira Nassiboullina, "Comparative Analysis of the French, English, and Russian Versions of the Musical *Notre-Dame de Paris*" (MA thesis, Concordia University, Montreal, Canada, 2011), http://spectrum.library.concordia.ca/7512; also see Luigi Pestalozza, "Italie 1945–2003: Une histoire de la musique, mais pas seulement," *Raisons politiques* 14 (2004): 125–41, doi: 10.3917/rai.014.0125.

11. Elfriede Fürsich, "In Defense of Textual Analysis: Restoring a Challenged Method for Journalism and Media Studies," *Journalism Studies* 10 (2009): 238–52; Paula Saukko, *Doing Research in Cultural Studies: An Introduction to Classical and New Methodological Approaches* (London: Sage, 2003).

12. Victor Hugo, *The Hunchback of Notre-Dame* (orig. pub. 1831, *Notre-Dame de Paris, 1482*; New York: Knopf, 2012).

13. Frus and Williams, "Introduction."

14. Lou Charnon-Deutsch, "Travels of the Imaginary Spanish Gypsy," in *Constructing Identity in Contemporary Spain*, ed. Jo Labanyi (New York: Oxford University Press, 2002), 26–27.

15. Dong, "*Mulan*," 158.

16. Lacroix, "Animated Others."

17. Ibid.

18. Ibid.

19. Jean-Marc Hovasse, introduction to *The Hunchback of Notre-Dame*, by Victor Hugo (orig. pub. 1831, *Notre-Dame de Paris, 1482*; New York: Knopf, 2012), xviii.

20. Stewart Dearing, "Painting the Other Within: Gypsies According to the Bohemian Artist in the Nineteenth and Early Twentieth Centuries," *Romani Studies* 20 (2010): 161–201.

21. Lynn Hooker, "Gypsiness and Gender in the Hungarian Folkdance Revival," *Anthropology of East Europe Review* 23 (2011): 52–62; Carol Miller, *The Church of Cheese: Gypsy Ritual in the American Heyday* (Boston, MA: Gemma Media, 2010).

22. Kent A. Ono and Derek T. Buescher, "*Deciphering Pocahontas*: Unpackaging the Commodification of a Native American Woman," *Critical Studies in Media Communication* 18 (2001): 25.

23. DiPaolo, "Mass-Marketing 'Beauty,'" 172.

24. Ibid.

25. Charnon-Deutsch, "Imaginary Spanish Gypsy"; also see Cohn, *The Gypsies*; Lemon, *Between Two Fires*.

26. Goran Gocic, *The Cinema of Emir Kusturica: Notes from the Underground* (London: Wallflower Press, 2001), 98.

27. Hugo, *Hunchback of Notre-Dame*, 59–60.

28. Eva Woods Peiró, *White Gypsies: Race and Stardom in Spanish Musicals* (Minneapolis: University of Minnesota Press, 2012).

29. Hugo, *Hunchback of Notre-Dame*, 66–70.

30. The recent musical *Notre-Dame de Paris* transforms the gypsy crowd somewhat; although they retain stereotypical traits, living in the gallows, racially different, and outside the norm, Esmeralda's cohort has now become the "sans-papiers" ("those without papers," verbatim, or "refugees"), a covert statement about French immigration—and, as the musical travels across cultures, about seeking asylum worldwide.

31. *Notre-Dame de Paris*.

32. *Hunchback of Notre Dame* (1939).

33. *Hunchback of Notre Dame* (1996).

34. *Hunchback of Notre Dame* (1939).

35. *Notre-Dame de Paris*.

36. *Hunchback of Notre Dame* (1956).

37. *Notre-Dame de Paris*.

38. Michel Foucault, *The History of Sexuality: An Introduction*, vol. 1 (New York: Vintage, 1990); David Spurr, *The Rhetoric of Empire: Colonial Discourse in Journalism, Travel Writing, and Imperial Administration* (Durham, NC: Duke University Press, 1999).

39. *Notre-Dame de Paris.*

40. Conrad, *Hunchback*, 36.

41. *Notre-Dame de Paris.*

42. Dearing, "Painting the Other"; such idealizations are part of how gypsy migration has been represented in fiction, as seen in Tony Gatlif's 1993 musical documentary *Latcho Drom*; also see Belton, *Questioning Gypsy Identity.*

43. Dearing, "Painting the Other," 165.

44. Ian Hancock, "The 'Gypsy' Stereotype and the Sexualization of Romani Women," in *"Gypsies" in European Literature and Culture*, ed. Valentina Glajar and Domnica Radulescu (New York: Palgrave Macmillan, 2008), 181–91; Judith Okely, "Gypsy Women: Models in Conflict," in *Perceiving Women*, ed. Shirley Ardener (London: Malaby Press, 1975), 55–86.

45. Hovasse, introduction, xvii.

46. Hugo, *Hunchback of Notre-Dame*, 59–60.

47. See Kenneth Kobré, *Photojournalism: The Professionals' Approach*, 6th ed. (Oxford: Focal Press, 2008).

48. For instance, Lacroix, "Animated Others."

49. Ibid., 222.

50. For instance, the 1939 film, the Disney animation, the musical, or Tim Conrad's graphic novel; also see Lacroix, "Animated Others."

51. Do Rozario, "French Musicals"; Finn, "College French Classroom"; Nassiboullina, "Comparative Analysis."

52. *Notre-Dame de Paris.*

53. Belton, *Questioning Gypsy Identity.*

54. This, in the context where privacy around the female body has been a tenet of traditional cultures; see Dearing, "Painting the Other"; Okely, "Gypsy Women."

55. Ono and Buescher, "*Deciphering Pocahontas.*"

56. DiPaolo, "Mass-Marketing 'Beauty'"; I also show elsewhere that the 1998 musical makes contemporary claims in the construction of asylum seekers in a way that it does not with Esmeralda; see Adina Schneeweis, "Just Another Gypsy Dancer, Just Another Refugee: Constructions of Gypsies in Musical and World Publications" (paper presented at the annual meeting for the International Communication Association Conference, London, United Kingdom, June 17–22, 2013).

57. See Adina Schneeweis and Katie Foss, "We Are Rom. We Are Gypsies: Constructions of Gypsies in American Reality Television" (paper presented at the annual meeting for the Association for Education in Journalism and Mass Communication Conference, Washington, DC, August 8–11, 2013).

58. Kathryn M. Grossman, "From Classic to Pop Icon: Popularizing Hugo," *French Review* 74 (2001): 492.

Chapter Six

Writing Women in War

Speaking through, about, and for Female Soldiers in Iraq

Christina M. Smith

Journalist David Carr called the War in Iraq the most "ferociously documented" military engagement in history.[1] The rise of digital media in the form of video cameras, YouTube, Facebook, and blogs allowed soldiers serving on the front lines to communicate their firsthand experiences to audiences in the United States and internationally. A variety of blogs were created and updated by independent media professionals, civilians, and members of the military. These authors wanted to give audiences an eyewitness account in order to supplement limited or biased mainstream media coverage.[2] Moreover, the milblogs of soldiers and military personnel such as L. T. Smash, Matthew Burden, and Colby Buzzell provided the public with information and imagery originating from those engaged in battle. As Burden described in his memoir, milblogs served as the contemporary letter home, though they circulated more rapidly. He pointed out that soldiers used milblogs to share their views, provide family and friends with a means of communication, and give additional information and insight into the War on Terror.[3] Like Burden, upon returning home from battle, many soldiers expanded their blogs into memoirs, some of which were quite popular and others of which received critical acclaim.

Yet female soldiers authored very few of these popular memoirs. This is notable considering the increased attention focused by the media and military establishment on the status of women in the armed forces. Particularly important are recent debates regarding the service of women soldiers in combat positions and the dramatic rise of sexual violence against active-duty women. According to the Pentagon, in 2011 there were 22,800 violent sex crimes in the U.S. military, the majority of which were committed against women. At least 20 percent of women soldiers are sexually assaulted, and 70 percent indicate they were sexually harassed at some point during their service. The Department of Veterans Affairs is also having a difficult time assisting female veterans who say they were sexually assaulted or raped while serving. As pointed out by author Helen Benedict, the VA lacks specialized facilities to treat women, with only twenty-two women's clinics offering medical and/ or psychological services targeted toward female veterans. [4]

This chapter investigates how women communicate their negotiation of these various challenges and violations in four literary works. As Harari points out, there is a growing cultural interest in memoirs by "common" soldiers, and a slew of soldier-authored memoirs about the Iraq War began to surface in 2007. [5] The *New York Review of Books* overviewed several, focusing on common themes such as the distrust of leadership, the boredom and monotony of war, and the mental drain resulting from frequent IED and mortar attacks. Of the four books under investigation here, female soldiers wrote two, and renowned journalists wrote two. *Love My Rifle More than You: Young and Female in the U.S. Army* (2005) was written by Arabic linguist and former Army intelligence specialist Kayla Williams, who participated in the early 2003 invasion of Iraq. Former Marine Corps officer and current Middle Eastern Affairs officer Jane Blair authored the newest memoir, *Hesitation Kills: A Female Officer's Combat Experience in Iraq* (2011), which chronicles her experience in an aerial reconnaissance unit in Iraq. *Band of Sisters: American Women at War* (2007) was authored by journalist Kirsten Holmstedt and contains a moving foreword by Major Tammy Duckworth—former Army soldier, double-amputee, and current Illinois representative. Professor of journalism at Columbia University Helen Benedict wrote *The Lonely Soldier: The Private War of Women Serving in Iraq* (2009) as a series of portraits. The latter book led to the production of a highly acclaimed documentary called "The Invisible War," which chronicles the widespread problem of sexual assault and violence in the military.

Each novel poses intriguing questions about authorship, authenticity, and the reporting of personal experience. For example, Williams' and Blair's memoirs are written by former soldiers. Holmstedt's book is a collection of intertwined stories about different military women, all of which address issues of relevance to female soldiers. Benedict chooses to compose her chapters based on the experience of one specific woman. However, the latter two authors have never served in the military. As a result, they are largely speaking on behalf of their subjects, raising questions about the accuracy and symbolic import of their representation. Thus, the four novels are examined for the ways in which they portray contemporary female soldiers and the wider sociopolitical and cultural environment in which they perform their service.

Ultimately, I argue that the two memoirs focus more on the author's individual struggle to negotiate the long-standing "female soldier paradox." As such, they provide an authentic, firsthand narrative of military service. The two collections are less authentic in their accounting of personal experience but nevertheless offer readers valuable context for the sexism and sexual assault faced by female soldiers. In this case, the profiled women serve as a synecdoche for the problems faced by all female military personnel. Read together, these literary works offer two contradictory representations of female soldiers: they are presented as both occupationally capable and vulnerable. That is, both the memoirs and the accounts attempt to subvert the patriarchal military establishment by portraying women in the armed forces as successful in executing their assigned duties and mission. However, in discussing the rampant culture of sexual assault in the military, the works implicitly suggest that women are unfit to serve in combat as a result of their perceived sexual vulnerability. This case study illustrates the challenge of disentangling these simultaneous but oppositional notions surrounding contemporary representations of female soldiers.

THE IRAQ WAR AND THE REPORTING OF LIFE EXPERIENCE

Memoirs, autobiography, life-writing, and personal narrative have been widely explored in the fields of communication, performance studies, and cultural theory.[6] Scholars have established that autobiography and memoir serves as a form of identity creation and contestation that is influenced by the institutional, social, cultural, and political norms from which they pull.[7] These works are a combination of one's personal memory and imagination. Such writing is also inherently connected with collective memory, as well as the reading practices of audiences who consume such material. Chawla maintains that autobiographies tell the reader about the sociocultural worlds that the author inhabits, while also helping the audience form a stronger self-perception. Thus, autobiography functions as a "cultural document." This is particularly important when memoirs deal with notable geopolitical events like war and conflict. Studies have established the common themes that compose a successful memoir, including the writer's understanding and connection of self and others, called "autobiographical reasoning," and a clear sense of temporality.[8] Brockmeier notes that "autobiographical time" (which can be either static or fragmentary) plays a particularly important role in memoir.[9]

Memoirs engage the reader of the text in meaningful ways. Chawla identifies the centrality of the reader in memoir by describing two moments of reading. First, the memoirist reads her own life, potentially engaging in self-reflexivity while doing so. Indeed, Williams' memoir is critiqued for its lack of awareness and reflection, instead choosing to focus on a superficial retelling of personal characteristics and specific events. Next, Chawla notes that the reader consumes the memoir by relating it to her own life, producing a collaborative experience in the autobiographical act.[10] This mutually influential relationship creates a "pact" between writer and audience.[11] In the case of Iraq War memoirs, the relationship involves a firsthand glimpse into the challenges facing female soldiers to American audiences, many of whom are unfamiliar with, or not directly impacted by, war.

Finally, much work in autobiography focuses on the construction and understanding of self. Luca suggests the writing process serves as a beneficial mechanism for sense making and self-understanding. The successful crafting and communication of an identity from a multiplicity of sources, such as people, locations, and related cultural texts, is central to the construction of a memoir.[12] The notion of identity relates to all the texts under investigation here, as the women authors or subjects attempt to form and sustain a sense of womanhood within a patriarchal and sexist institution. Studies have identified this "female soldier paradox," and it becomes central to a woman's experience in the military. Williams' memoir updates this dichotomy with the labels of "slut" (women that are outgoing) or "bitch" (those that are more reserved) when she states, "If you're a woman and a soldier, those are the choices you get."[13] In this sense, many enact what Shane Moreman calls a performance of hybrid identity—performing both the masculine values long esteemed by the military establishment while maintaining their own unique feminine traits and values. Their memoirs and stories thus become a performance that allows audiences to bear witness to this negotiation of identity, which involves multiple and potentially contradictory roles within the space of their experience.[14]

Notably, there are few existing studies of female heroine memoirs, though Humbert's investigation of Lucie Aubrac provides one example. Aubrac's memoir, *Outwitting the Gestapo*, overviews her life and struggle as a member of the French resistance during World War II, as well as the daring rescue of her captured husband. Humbert examines the narrative's structural use of flashback to chronicle Aubrac's life, beginning with her pregnancy and the couple's escape to London days before the baby's birth. Humbert notes how the memoir was criticized for its flexibility with style and the "invention" of life facts.[15] Similarly, substance and style are critiqued in all the literary works under investigation here.

As journalist Anne Kingston pointed out, even though women serve in the military in increasing numbers, existing images of the female soldier tend to be polarized between masculine and feminine norms. She contends that this is "evident in the readiness to create one-dimensional depictions of Jessica Lynch and Lynndie England."[16] Indeed, during the War in Iraq, Americans were offered two opposing images of female soldiers: one was heroine Jessica Lynch, who was supposedly rescued in a military operation to free her in a dramatic media event. It was later revealed that Lynch's rescue was largely exaggerated and staged to gain public support. As noted by Howard and Prividera in their study of Jessica Lynch, media representations of Lynch and other captured or killed female soldiers perpetuated the "female soldier paradox." Such a paradox positions women soldiers within existing social constructions of femininity and motherhood and functions to reinforce patriarchal roles for all soldiers. In fact, the authors contended that Jessica Lynch received extensive media coverage because she successfully fulfilled the role of submissive female in need of rescue. News coverage often focused on her "cute" appearance, sexual vulnerability, and victimization while in enemy hands. The authors maintained that her rescue ultimately demonstrated U.S. military prowess and reinforced long-standing masculinist constructions of "warrior heroes."[17]

On the other hand, Americans saw images of Lynndie England engaging in degrading physical and sexual treatment of detainees at Abu Ghraib prison. Due to her presence in many images, England became the "face" of abuse at the prison, for which she was dishonorably discharged and jailed for three years. Howard and Prividera's examination of media framing found that England was represented as out of line with existing conceptions of the warrior hero. Media coverage framed her as an embarrassment and sexual deviant, focusing on her personal and professional shortcomings. The authors suggest that this framing helped preserve the subordination of women in the military.[18]

While these were the dominant images of heroines to emerge from the War in Iraq, the memoirs of Williams and Blair, as well as the stories offered by Benedict and Holmstedt, offer a nuanced alternative. In the prologue to her memoir, Williams tells readers that she wanted to share "what life is like for the 15 percent. Don't count Jessica Lynch. Her story meant nothing to us. The same goes for Lynndie England. I'm not either of them, and neither are any of the real women I know in the service."[19] These novels provide readers with the opportunity to explore how female soldiers communicate and negotiate the specific challenges encountered in their daily lives, combat operations, sexism and patriarchy in the military, sexual assault and violence, and occupational/organizational challenges.[20] Due to the varied subjectivities of the writers, the books also raise issues of authorship, such as the reporting of personal experience and the authenticity of women's voices, the reception of such material by critics and audiences, and narrative structure. Thus, the following analysis examines the construction and portrayal of the contemporary female soldier in these books, focusing on the critical reception of the novels' style and substantive commentary that explores the sociopolitical and cultural context in which such women serve.

CRITICAL CONSUMPTION OF THE IRAQ WAR MEMOIRS

The four novels examined all provide readers with similar themes: the struggle to negotiate the physical and mental demands of warfare, the entrenchment of military structure and hierarchy, and the constant forms of sexual harassment faced by female soldiers, though some focus attention more heavily on various components. Many accounts discuss the physical challenges and difficulties faced by women in the military. In one of Holmstedt's stories, Gunnery Sergeant Yolanda Mayo described how she was "trespassing into male territory" via her assignment to a Marine Corps gunnery unit. Fellow soldiers were surprised that she chose to carry a heavier pack (though one preferred by "old-timers") despite the availability of smaller, lighter options. She also details how even the most basic of bodily functions like going to the bathroom are more challenging for women.[21] Similarly, Williams and Blair both discuss the various physical capabilities of female soldiers during training and while deployed. The books also address a theme that is common to many war memoirs: the military organizational structure and hierarchy. Stories in all the works mock incompetent commanders, many of whom issue contradictory orders in an effort to outdo one another. Interviewee Terris Dewalt-Johnson described such "chickenshit" as "small-minded and ignoble and takes the trivial seriously. [It] can be recognized instantly because it never has anything to do with winning the war."[22] In one chapter, Blair discusses the total lack of postinvasion Iraq War planning on the part of military and civilian leadership. However, the most prominent theme in all the books dealt with issues of acceptance in a male-dominated institution.

As Helen Benedict pointed out in a letter to the *New York Times*, women make up only 10 percent of troops in Iraq and are therefore outnumbered and often resented—a theme that is common throughout many of the stories under investigation here. In addition to the struggle for recognition and/or advancement, numerous stories detail varying levels of sexual harassment or assault. Blair seems to have experienced the least of it, but still describes an incident where a subordinate refused to salute her because she was female.[23] In her memoir, Williams highlights a situation where she and fellow soldiers were stationed along the Syrian border and they offered her money and candy in exchange for showing off her breasts, as well as another incident where a fellow soldier attempted to sexually assault her.[24] In Holmstedt's collection, Polly Montgomery recalls a story of how a sexual harassment claim against her senior master sergeant divided her company and led to internal strife.

Benedict reported how many female soldiers feared the men in their unit more than the enemy. Several stories recall how female soldiers were instructed to take a "battle buddy" with them to the restroom or mess hall while deployed. In Benedict's book, Mickiela Montoya describes a situation where she was traveling with her buddy (because there were so few women in her unit, it was a man) and he made a joke about raping her. Several additional interviewees recount stories of harassment and assault. Jennifer Spranger details how she was harassed at all levels of service—from recruitment to deployment. Eli Painted Crow notes that two majors and a lieutenant all assaulted her while serving in Honduras. While she was able to fend off two with verbal threats, one required physical resistance. Unfortunately, she ends her story by saying, "I never reported them because nobody believes you."[25] A superior officer assaulted Abbie Pickett shortly after she left basic training. She remembers hearing other women report victimization at the hands of the same man. Moreover, she reports the difficulty of obtaining assistance at the VA for the assault.[26] These are just a few examples of the many stories recounted by both the former soldiers in the memoirs and by those interviewed by the journalist authors.

In addition to the prominent themes present in these novels, it is useful to explore the variety of critical attention they received upon their release. Between the two authored by former soldiers, Williams' received the most coverage.[27] Critics were divided on her memoir's style and voice. Some suggested that the voice was irritating and distracting, arguing that it "sounds something like the staccato of an M-16 automatic rifle." Others contended that it was "terse," contained "showy, rough language," and was "self-consciously ragged writing."[28] One critic maintained that the memoir swings from "insightful to banal . . . from literary to pedestrian." Another negative reviewer contended that it is "written with all the grace and panache of a poorly worded postcard."[29] While the language utilized in the memoir is at times rough and explicit, I maintain that this prose provides an authenticity that is lacking in the works composed by journalists and more effectively facilitates the "pact" between author and reader.

Indeed, other reviewers praised the book's language and tone, calling it "chick-lit meets battlefield memoir."[30] Williams' style was celebrated as providing readers with a "raw unadulterated look at war and what it does to people." Echoing the idea of authentic communication, critics suggested that it was an "honest, clear-headed, uncompromising memoir."[31] Still others noted that the memoir "sets the right tone—blunt, post-feminist and gutsy," ultimately offering a "sharp insider account of military life."[32] Notably, reviewers recognized that the occasional awkwardness of the memoir's composition was likely due to the use of a ghostwriter (Michael Staub), who was Williams' former professor. Reviewers pointed out how such "collaborative" memoirs challenge notions of voice and content. One reviewer specifically mentioned that the "cheap" writing was likely due to the collaboration, highlighting issues of voice and authenticity in forms of life-writing.[33]

One review authored by a female soldier is particularly important. Former military linguist Debra Dickerson was highly critical of what she called an "insufferably self-absorbed memoir" written by a "lost girl playing GI Jane dress-up." In it, she chided Williams for her insubordination and laziness, suggesting that the memoir never performs any meaningful analysis or reflection on the experience of Iraq. While this critique is accurate in the memoir's reporting of the overall war effort, Williams does engage in reflection about her role in interrogations of Iraqi prisoners. Ultimately, Dickerson pointed out that the memoir's worth lies not in its content, but in the fact that it was written by a woman and therefore gives a marginalized perspective on the war.[34]

Though smaller in number, reviews for Blair's *Hesitation Kills* were more positive, with one reviewer arguing that the author "ably depicts the chaotic and often disillusioning experiences of modern warfare," providing readers with "eloquence in examining the grim emotional costs of military service."[35] Notably, Blair's memoir is structured, composed, and executed with great literary skill. She provides readers with a striking combination of strategic information, personal experience, military history, and engaging dialogue. The level of detail likely stems from her primary sources: her own journals in combination with her platoon commander's notebooks. In 2005, Blair attended a National Endowment for the Arts–sponsored workshop titled "Writing the Wartime Experience," where she began work on the book.[36] Despite the variance in critical reception, both memoirs offer a firsthand accounting of how individual women perceive their wartime experience and negotiate the challenges of a fundamentally sexist military establishment.

Due to the authors' training as academics and journalists, reviews of the styles in *Lonely Soldier* and *Band of Sisters* were more positive. One critic noted that the latter offered a "powerful message . . . written in a compelling style" of five women that "reflect the ethnic and socioeconomic composition of women in the contemporary US military." Another suggested that *Band of Sisters* was "well-organized and easy-to-read" and the author "masterfully captivates and holds the attention of readers with her word choice and vivid imagery."[37] Nevertheless, issues of authenticity and representation were also raised in the reviews. Some critics suggested that the authors represented their subjects in ways that were inappropriate. One contended that Benedict "makes some choices that are less than illuminating. No one wants to hear soldiers whining about rough conditions." Still another emphasized that Holmstedt wrote *Band of Sisters* to be creative and not controversial. As a result, "readers are essentially left with self-serving stories of women's perceptions of successful integration into the non-existent front lines."[38] Finally, one female soldier reviewer suggested that "one annoying distraction is when Holmstedt offers her own thoughts on what the combatant was feeling at the time, trying to explain their situation or thought process."[39] The collections do contain a blend of the author's commentary, narrative details provided by interviewees, and recreated dialogue. At times, the balance is disparate, posing a challenge to the reader in terms of engagement and identification. The above reviews underscore the journalist authors' struggle to replicate and communicate the lived experience of their subjects.

While critics and reviewers disagreed about the stylistic elements of each author's writing and organizational style, all supported the topic of the books as timely and relevant. The books were praised for the important connections they made with the wider cultural, social, and sexual issues faced by women in the military. Critics noted that the addition of women's voices to the public debate regarding women in the military was highly valuable (and heretofore largely absent). Of note was the discussion of detainee mistreatment outlined in *Love My Rifle*. In one section, Williams recounts a story where she was asked to assist in the interrogation of a prisoner. Though she initially thought it was due to her Arabic-language ability, it ultimately was a situation whereby her gender was used to humiliate the uncooperative prisoner. Reviewers praised her view as "particularly critical of the military" and its treatment of prisoners. Critic Lucy Clark noted that "Kayla Williams tells of the enormous disillusionment she feels at being involved in a war based on lies, the guilt about not speaking up against the torture of Iraqi prisoners, [and] the confusion about her country's ongoing role in Iraq."[40] Similarly, one reviewer emphasized Williams' memoir as indicative of "what these messed-up men and women are actually doing in or for Iraq."[41] The analysis of Williams' prisoner abuse story was a focus of many reviews and provides one example of her self-reflexivity in crafting the narrative.

However, the most important function of all the books was providing a woman's viewpoint on war in relation to sex and gender issues. This is crucial because women's war stories are fundamentally different from men's, and, as Alison Rowat suggested, existing "war literature dwells on the absence of women, their nurturing, civilizing presence."[42] As demonstrated, women soldiers operate within an "institution that is founded on and perpetuates certain ideals of maleness and masculinity."[43] Thus, all authors were praised for their critique of the sexual politics of war. Critics argued that Williams' memoir shows that "the sex war is still being fought at every level" and gave readers numerous "dismal examples of ingrained sexism" in the military. Another pointed out that the novels clearly illustrate that "no woman can escape sexism" and they are subject to "a continual barrage of misogynist slang and jokes."[44] Indeed, one reviewer claimed that Benedict's book ultimately illustrates that the "dangers military service poses to women far outweigh the benefits. Most of these dangers come not from the enemy but from the male soldiers in the women's own units."[45] Taken together, the books clearly demonstrate that the "female soldier paradox" continues to flourish.

In summary, critics were divided in their reception of the novels' stylistic elements and narrative structure. Widespread agreement and celebration of the books centered on their ability to emphasize that sexual harassment and violence occur across military locations, ranks, and soldier race and ethnicity, and it is present throughout training, deployment, and discharge. What is moving about the diversity of the women represented in the novels is the similarity of their experience in relation to these issues, suggesting that the ingrained sexism and patriarchy in the military establishment will be difficult to change. At the same time, the women presented in the novels clearly model the values upon which the military establishment is built: strength, courage, loyalty, and, above all, professionalism. Therefore, these literary works complement existing conceptions of "warrior heroes" and "warrior women" in popular culture. [46]

CONCLUSION AND IMPLICATIONS

As indicated, the four literary works under investigation received a variety of criticism about their substance and style. In particular, Williams' book received the majority of criticism for its focus on her personal traits and crude descriptions of everyday life during deployment. While it received less coverage due to its recent release, Blair's memoir similarly chronicled her daily experience, using an approach that provided a solid balance between rich description and meaningful analysis. Thus, the two memoirs serve as a useful mechanism for tracing the "female soldier paradox" through the authentic, firsthand account of the authors. Since both address the gendered experience of only a single person, these memoirs potentially downplay the important connections to broader sociocultural issues that surround female soldiers. On the other hand, journalists authored the other two collections, choosing to chronicle and present the experiences of female soldiers as a single chapter (Benedict) or as a collection of intertwined narratives (Holmstedt). These novels lack the authenticity of the memoirs and at times seem disconnected and disingenuous; however, they do an excellent job of situating the stories of the profiled women within broader discourses of patriarchy, sexism, and sexual violence. In the end, the four literary works illustrate the contradictory representations of contemporary female soldiers as simultaneously capable and vulnerable.

Scholars in the field of communication note that memoir and autobiographical writing helps to foster both personal and political transformation. [47] Importantly, such forms can serve as a tool for identifying and disrupting dominant ideological discourses, cultural practices, and stereotyped representations. [48] This could be particularly impactful when applied to the military establishment, where notions of masculinity are deeply embedded within the organizational structure and cultural values. Indeed, recent debates surrounding the integration of women into combat roles have highlighted the status of women in the military. In an interview, Helen Benedict described how female soldiers are seen as "second class" and feel a lack of respect. Benedict suggests that when respect is lacking, it opens the door to harassment.[49] Chairman of the Joint Chiefs of Staff General Martin E. Dempsey seemed to agree when he said that officially allowing women in combat might alleviate some problems of sexual harassment and assault that have plagued the armed forces. In an interview with the *New York Times*, Dempsey said, "We've had separate classes of military personnel. . . . When you have one part of the population that is designated as warriors and another part that's designated as something else, I think that disparity begins to establish a psychology."[50] The acknowledgment of the problem by a respected military leader is significant.

Yet other lawmakers and military leaders simultaneously reinforced existing patriarchal discourse. Senator Saxby Chambliss suggested that allowing women to enter combat roles would function to increase the incidents of violence, while the Army's director of force management for special operations, Major General Bennet Sacolick, expressed concern over whether newly integrated women could overcome "cultural, social, [and] behavioral issues" in order to be accepted by their male comrades.[51] Here are the same patterns described by nearly every woman in the memoirs or collected stories. Each recalled their struggle to be accepted by fellow soldiers, despite executing their assignment to near perfection. Many recounted being the victim of sexual harassment or violence, the result of an institutional inequality that privileges masculine values. Thus, the long-standing dichotomy, or the "female soldier paradox," is reinforced by the aforementioned attitudes and policy making of military leadership. It seems that Williams' description of the two roles available to women soldiers continues to be perpetuated by the media and military establishment: you're either a slut or a bitch.

NOTES

1. He was quoted in G. Kaufman, producer, *Iraq Uploaded: The War Network Television Won't Show You, Shot by Soldiers and Posted Online*, television episode, *MTV News* (New York: Music Television, 2006), http://www.mtv.com/news/articles/1536780/20060720/index.jhtml.

2. For a discussion of milblogs and their impact, see Stuart Allan, "The Culture of Distance: Online Reporting of the Iraq War," in *Reporting War: Journalism in Wartime*, ed. Stuart Allan and Barbie Zelizer (London: Routledge, 2004), 359; and Melissa Wall, "Blogs of War," *Journalism* 6 (2005):153–72.

3. Matthew C. Burden, *The Blogs of War: Front-line Dispatches from Soldiers in Iraq and Afghanistan* (New York: Simon & Schuster, 2006), 4.

4. Helen Benedict, "For Women Warriors, Deep Wounds, Little Care," *New York Times*, May 26, 2008, 15.

5. Yuval Noah Harari, "Military Memoirs: A Historical Overview of the Genre from the Middle Ages to the Late Modern Era," *War in History* 14 (2007): 297.

6. For the purposes of this chapter, these terms are used interchangeably to refer to a general body of work involving the description of life experience.

7. Paul J. Eakin, *Fictions in Autobiography: Studies in the Art of Self-Invention* (Princeton, NJ: Princeton University Press, 1985), 5.

8. Devika Chawla, "The Writerly Reader in Memoir: Inter/subjectivity and Joan Didion's *The Year of Magical Thinking*," *Review of Communication* 8 (2008): 379.

9. Jens Brockmeier, "Autobiographical Time," *Narrative Inquiry* 10 (2000): 51–73.

10. Chawla, "Writerly Reader," 387.

11. Sidonie Smith and Julia Watson, *Reading Autobiography: A Guide for Interpreting Life Narratives* (Minneapolis: University of Minnesota Press, 2001).

12. Ioana Luca, "Edward Said's Lieux de Memoire: Out of Place and the Politics of Autobiography," *Social Text* 24 (2006): 125–44.

13. Kayla Williams, *Love My Rifle More than You: Young and Female in the U.S. Army* (New York: Norton, 2005), 13.

14. Shane Moreman, "Memoir as Performance: Strategies of Hybrid Ethnic Identity," *Text and Performance Quarterly* 4 (2009): 349.

15. Brigitte E. Humbert, "Lucie Aubrac: A Resistance Heroine from Page to Screen Text," *Literature Film Quarterly* 40 (2012): 109–26.

16. Anne Kingston, "There's No Life Like It: Women Go to War," *National Post*, August 27, 2005, WP2.

17. John W. Howard and Laura C. Prividera, "Rescuing Patriarchy or Saving Jessica Lynch: The Rhetorical Construction of the American Woman Soldier," *Women and Language* 27 (2004): 89–97. See also Deepa Kumar, "War Propaganda and the (Ab)uses of Women," *Feminist Media Studies* 4 (2004): 297–313.

18. John W. Howard and Laura C. Prividera, "The Fallen Woman Archetype: Media Representations of Lynndie England, Gender, and the Abuses of U.S. Female Soldiers," *Women's Studies in Communication* 31 (2008): 287–311.

19. Williams, *Love My Rifle*, 15.

20. Cynthia Enloe, *Maneuvers: The International Politics of Militarizing Women's Lives* (Berkeley: University of California Press, 2000).

21. Kirsten Holmstedt, *Band of Sisters: American Women at War in Iraq* (Mechanicsburg, PA: Stackpole Books, 2007), 221–23.

22. Helen Benedict, *The Lonely Soldier: The Private War of Women Serving in Iraq* (Boston: Beacon Press, 2009), 76.

23. Jane Blair, *Hesitation Kills: A Female Marine Officer's Combat Experience in Iraq* (Lanham, MD: Rowman & Littlefield, 2011), 16.

24. Williams, *Love My Rifle*, 23, 207–8.

25. Benedict, *The Lonely Soldier*, 81.

26. Ibid., 68.

27. This is likely due to the recent release of Blair's novel in late 2011.

28. Dianne Dempsey, "Love My Rifle More Than; Off the Shelf," *The Age*, January 20, 2007, 26. Also cited is Tina Giannoukos, "The Women Who Go Off to War," *Herald Sun*, April 15, 2006, W27; and Giles Whittell, "A Bigger Battle than the Sex War," *Times*, January 21, 2006, 12.

29. Kaye Lorien, "Memoir: Love My Rifle More than You; Off the Shelf," *The Age*, March 4, 2006, 32; Carole Cadwalladr, "Women at War: My Life as a Bitch," *The Observer*, January 29, 2006, 22.

30. Philip Sherwell, "Author Is First Female Soldier to Publish a Frank Account of What It Was Like to Serve in Iraq," *Sunday Telegraph*, August 28, 2005, 028.

31. John Riddick, "The Meaning of War," *Library Journal*, September 1, 2005, 159. Also cited is Harry Thomas, "Trapped by War in a Male Combat Zone: Books," *Sun Herald*, February 26, 2006, 73; and Jonathan Beckman, "Review: *Love My Rifle More than You*," *The Observer*, November 19, 2006, 27.

32. Book Reviews, "Paperbacks," *Sunday Times*, November 5, 2006, 56; and Aimee Shalan, "Review: Paperbacks," *Guardian*, November 4, 2006, 18.

33. Kaye Lorien, "Memoir," 32. Also cited is Carol Burke, "One of the Boys," *Women's Review of Books*, March 2006, 3–5; Janet Maslin, "Books: Nonfiction," *New York Times*, September 7, 2005, 10.

34. Debra Dickerson, "Chicks with Guns," Salon.com, October 24, 2005, http://www.salon.com/2005/10/24/williams_20.

35. Ingrid Levin, "Biography," *Library Journal*, June 15, 2011, 95.

36. Linda McIntosh, "Woman Marine Writes Book on Combat Experiences," *San Diego Union Tribune*, September 7, 2011, http://www.utsandiego.com/news/2011/sep/07/woman-marine-writes-book-combat-experiences.

37. Jennifer G. Mathers, "I Am Not the Wonderful Person I Was," *Women's Review of Books* 27 (2010): 8. Also cited is Kelly Twedell, "Women's Combat Roles: Author Depicts Lives, Ordeals of Female Fighters in Iraq War," *Washington Times*, September 3, 2009, 2.

38. Neil Genzlinger, "The Feminine, Touched: War as Women's Work," *New York Times*, March 10, 2009, 4. Also cited is Major Tyesha E. Lowery, "Book Reviews: *Band of Sisters*," *Army Lawyer*, 2008, 46 and 50.

39. Major Laura E. Johnson, "Review," *Air Power History*, Winter 2008, 62.

40. Dianne Dempsey, "Memoir," 26. Also cited is Elisabeth Bumiller, "War in Well-Written Glimpses," *International Herald Tribune*, February 2, 2010, 2; and Lucy Clark, "The U.S. War on Its Own Recruits," *Sunday Telegraph*, February 12, 2006, 94.

41. Natasha Walter, "Saturday Review: Still One of the Guys: When Will Women Be Free to Play up to Their Own Fantasies, Not Men's," *Guardian*, February 18, 2006, 9.

42. Alison Rowat, "The Women Who Love Their Rifles More than Men," *Herald*, September 3, 2005, 5.

43. Jennifer G. Mathers, "I Am Not," 8.

44. Olivia Ward, "Ex-General's Toughest Battle," *Toronto Star*, April 15, 2006, A19; Kate Saunders, "Scenes from the Sex War," *Sunday Times*, February 5, 2006, 59; Giles Whittell, "A Bigger Battle than the Sex War," *Times*, January 21, 2006, 12; and Carol Burke, "One of the Boys," 3–5.

45. Mathers, "I Am Not," 8.

46. For a discussion of the warrior hero, see John W. Howard and Laura C. Prividera, "Rescuing Patriarchy," 90–91. For a discussion of the warrior woman, see Frances Early and Kathleen Kennedy, *Athena's Daughters: Television's New Women Warriors* (Syracuse, NY: Syracuse University Press, 2003).

47. Linda M. Park-Fuller, "Performing Absence: The Staged Personal Narrative as Testimony," *Text and Performance Quarterly* 20 (2000): 20–42; and Elizabeth Bell, "Sex Acts beyond Boundaries and Binaries: A Feminist Challenge for Self Care in Performance Studies," *Text and Performance Quarterly* 25 (2005): 187–219.

48. Naida Zukic, "Webbing Sexual/Textual Agency in Autobiographical Narratives of Pleasure," *Text and Performance Quarterly* 28 (2008): 396–414.

49. Edward Colimore, "Female Soldiers Say Combat Decision a Positive Recognition of Proven Courage," *Philadelphia Inquirer*, January 27, 2013, A01.

50. Jennifer Steinhauer, "Elite Units in Military to Admit Women," *New York Times*, June 18, 2013, 11.

51. Craig Whitlock, "Lawmakers Demand Crackdown on Sex Assault in Military," *Washington Post*, June 4, 2013; and "Military Plans to Open More Combat Jobs to Women by 2016," *Washington Post*, June 18, 2013.

Part II

Exotic, Foreign, Familiar, and Queer

Chapter Seven

The Borderland Construction of Latin American and Latina Heroines in Contemporary Visual Media

Mauricio Espinoza

"*¡Watchate!* I resist!"[1] yells Linda Rivera, a young East Los Angeles Latina law student who transforms herself into the Aztec-powered superheroine the Jaguar in Laura Molina's 1996 comic *Cihualyaomiquiz: The Jaguar*. Her Indigenous-derived identity, her use of Spanglish (in this case meaning "Watch yourself!"), and the statement of resistance she utters as she fights institutionalized racism in the comic's story world make the Jaguar a perfect example of the hybridity and political contestation that underlie the construction of contemporary Latin American and U.S. Latina heroines in art and popular culture. Using hybridity and political contestation as conceptual blueprints, this chapter explores the construction and representation of various Latin American and Latina heroic female figures in the twentieth and twenty-first centuries, who are representative of the larger process of mythologization of female power throughout the Americas. This analysis focuses on visual and hybrid visual/textual representations, including film, comics, photography, art, and public-space imagery such as murals and graffiti. This choice is not arbitrary. While Latin American and Latina heroines also appear in contemporary literature and other texts, I am interested in investigating the power and limitations that images have on the cultural construction of strong female figures and their potentially contestatory discourses—operating as *oppositional gaze* and "as a site of resistance [against] the imposition of dominant (male and European) ways of knowing and looking."[2]

Because the heroines explored in this chapter tend to incarnate resistance against gender but also ethnic, racial, and cultural oppression, I have chosen to employ a critical framework referred to as "postcolonial feminism," or, more broadly speaking, "postcolonial gender studies." Specifically, I am interested in the approach proposed by Gloria Anzaldúa in *Borderlands/La Frontera*, which incorporates both the concepts of hybridity and political contestation that are central to this study. In this groundbreaking book, Anzaldúa argues that Latinas can resist the myth of patriarchy and the legacies of colonial domination by developing a subversive "mestiza consciousness" that acknowledges and draws from their mixed cultural heritage and hybrid constitution as women of color. This new consciousness would allow for a plurality of identities, or what Anzaldúa terms "divergent thinking," which is characterized "by a movement away from set patterns and goals and toward a more whole perspective, one that includes rather than excludes."[3] Anzaldúa proposes applicable metaphors for and constructions of resistant identity politics via alternative myth building. One of those metaphors is the "borderland," conceptualized by Anzaldúa not as a line of division but rather as a space of confluence, where differences and ambiguity are embraced in order to disrupt the oppressive Western system of binary logic—that is, Mexican/Anglo, Indigenous/European, legal/illegal, native/alien, virgin/ whore. While Anzaldúa's book deals specifically with the physical U.S.-Mexico borderland, her conceptualization is much broader, as she includes the "psychological borderlands, the sexual borderlands and the spiritual borderlands" that are present "wherever two or more cultures edge each other, where people of different races occupy the same territory, where under, lower, middle and upper classes touch."[4] Thus, the borderland operates as a fluid space in which hybrid identities, competing representations, and ideological wrangling take place, as it encompasses a plurality of histories, perspectives, and human experiences inevitably imbued with power relations.

With this theoretical foundation in mind, I posit that contemporary Latin American and Latina heroines are essentially "borderland heroines," as their construction and representation break away (sometimes abruptly, sometimes subtly) from rigid identity categories and traditional gender roles. I focus my study on four heroines, two historical and two fictional, whose portrayal in popular culture exemplifies the alternative borderland myth-building advanced by Anzaldúa. The first is Eva Duarte de Perón, better known as Evita, the mid-twentieth-century Argentine First Lady who is still revered as a heroine of the working classes for championing social justice and women's rights. Evita's conflicting legacy as whore/mother of the Argentine nation has been copiously reimagined in government building murals, street art, musicals, and films, transcending the borders of her home country. Another iconic figure with transnational appeal is La Malinche, the sixteenth-century translator of Spanish conquistador Hernán Cortés. La Malinche has been historically regarded as a cultural traitor and the "fucked" mother of the Mexican nation, but in recent decades she has been reinterpreted by Chicana artists in the United States as a heroic mestiza mother figure who embodies resistance against both the Spanish invaders and Mexican/Chicano patriarchal culture. The last two heroines come from the world of comic books. Molina's aforementioned superheroine the Jaguar channels her inner Mesoamerican feline spirit to protect her people in an alternate timeline in which Proposition 187 has turned California into a police state ruled by right-wing fundamentalists. Finally, I will look at Marvel's *Araña* (2004) and *Spider-Girl* (2010) comics, both of which feature New York City teenager Anya Corazón, who is of Puerto Rican and Mexican descent.

While iconic figures such as Evita, La Malinche, or the *soldaderas* who played an important role in the Mexican Revolution have received scholarly attention in Latin America and the United States, seldom have these women been studied within the framework of heroism or given the label of heroes. Scholarly works about Latina heroines are also scarce. For example, the 2006 collection *Heroes and Hero Cults in Latin America* (edited by Samuel Brunk and Ben Fallaw) includes only two women, Frida Kahlo and Evita, among the ten notable heroic figures that it selected for analysis. Meanwhile, Mike Madrid's *The Supergirls: Fashion, Feminism, Fantasy, and the History of Comic Book Heroines* (2009), fails to include a single Latina superheroine. Some recent contributions to the study of Latin American and Latina heroic figures are helping to reverse this trend, including Robert McKee Irwin's *Bandits, Captives, Heroines, and Saints: Cultural Icons of Mexico's Northwest Borderlands* (2007); Guisela Latorre's *Walls of Empowerment: Chicana/o Indigenist Murals of California* (2008); Frederick Aldama's *Your Brain on Latino Comics* (2009); and Lee Bebout's *Mythohistorical Interventions: The Chicano Movement and Its Legacies* (2011). This chapter seeks to advance the study of visual representations of heroines in Latin American and Latina art and popular culture, as well as to contribute to fill one of the many voids still present in the scholarship of postcolonial gender studies.

EVITA: THE HEROINE AS MOTHER/WHORE OF THE NATION

Although her life was very short, Eva Duarte de Perón (1919–1952) has become one of the most influential women in Latin American history, who "established her heroism . . . in behalf of the weak against the powerful" and whose image "has proved resistant to promiscuous political use, either positive or negative."[5] Her many names and epithets (Eva Duarte, Eva Perón, "the mother of the shirtless," or Evita) correspond, as Lidia Santos posits, "to the different facets of the myth that transformed her into an icon whose reach extends beyond the borders of Argentina."[6] These facets, which reveal a hybrid existence and multiplicity of representational possibilities, include her humble upbringing; her life as an actress and claims that she was a prostitute; her marriage to future president Juan Perón; her influential work as First

Lady and other political posts, in which she identified with the laborers and
the poor; and her internationalization thanks to mass media and the global-
ized circuits of the postmodern popular-culture industry. Underscoring the
intimate connections that exist between gender, power, and nation formation
in Latin America, the hybrid nature of Evita's myth appears to be the result
of "manipulation of different traditional symbols,"[7] as the two main ways in
which she has been represented derive from highly gendered and sexualized
roles typical of Western patriarchal societies: Evita is either the caring mother of the dispossessed, who represent the "new" Argentine nation in the mid-
twentieth century, or she is a whore, a fake, a marketing construct tied to
fascism, authoritarianism, and paternalistic populism.

For many Argentines then and today, Eva Duarte de Perón is simply
"Evita," an endearing term for their symbolic "mother," a heroine "capable
of giving her life for her shirtless ones."[8] As such, she appealed mostly to the
impoverished masses, playing a decidedly "feminine" role in the construction of the Argentine nation. Evita's maternal and caring persona is clearly
captured in some of her most popular and highly reproduced images. Her
official portrait, in particular, reinforces her role as a mother by showing an
elegant but conservative-looking Evita. The choice of clothing, hairstyle, and
background make her look much older than a woman in her late twenties,
which contributes to the creation of a more "traditional" maternal image;
additionally, there appears to be a saintly aura around her head, further emphasizing her virtuous public image. This representation of Evita has remained ingrained in the Argentine consciousness, as evidenced by the 2011
unveiling of two giant iron mural depictions of Evita on a Buenos Aires
government building, one of which is based on the official portrait. The
second mural reproduces another popular representation of Evita that shows
her passionately delivering a speech in front of a microphone, and which has
come to symbolize her commitment to speaking out on behalf of the masses.
These images further reinforce her maternal role and populist discourse that
was common of the Peronist regime and which still resonates among the
disenfranchised in Argentina. Moreover, Evita's monumental depictions are
modeled after a similar iron mural of famed guerrilla fighter Che Guevara in
Havana, effectively linking her legacy to discourses of revolution and sacrifice.

In stark contrast to her almost saintly heroization as the caring mother of
the Argentine nation, other texts have helped to create and reproduce a different, less flattering portrayal of Evita—which is also suffused with politics,
and politics of gender. Evita's "bastard children" (as Santos calls those who
have challenged her "official" history and representation) "deny her ability to
generate and unify a nation, underscoring, instead, her capacity to fragment
it."[9] One example of this phenomenon is Néstor Perlongher's 1975 short
story "Evita Lives (in Every Brothel)." Banished from her public, political

space, Evita finds herself in a bordello, which inverts her political myth and denies her political agency. Santos posits that in this fictionalization Evita is still a "saint," but of a different kind and to a different group of people, representing a different concept of nation: they are not the masses of political rallies supporting Perón that "contributed to the development of the image of a national subject," but the lumpen, the dwellers of the bottom of society excluded from socially acceptable categories.[10] This negation of Evita as motherly heroine and powerful national symbol can be found in a variety of images. For example, tabloids published photographs of her "life as an artist" that show a young Eva Duarte in provocative poses, billing them as "forbidden by the dictatorship." Contemporary street artists in Buenos Aires have appropriated her official portrait via stencils to protest her legacy, also playing with the spelling of her name to tell fellow Argentines to "Evitá" (Avoid) Evita.

Evita's appeal and visual reinventions would not end there. Andrew Lloyd Webber's musical based on her life and a 1996 filmic version of the musical would help take Evita from national myth to global popular-culture icon. This reinterpretation, however, has been highly criticized by both ordinary Argentines and scholars. Marta Savigliano sees the Hollywood film as a "downsizing" of the historical/mythical character of Evita "to situate spectators comfortably, to help them take a look at a tamed Eva, an Eva made familiar."[11] The film strips Evita of her female agency and contributions to the politics of her country, privileging instead a male character—the hybrid Che Guevara/narrator, played by Spanish actor Antonio Banderas, who embodies several characters from Argentine society, speaks authoritatively from all possible class positions, and puts Evita in her "womanly place."[12] Her diminished representational power is enacted in one particular scene, where Che and Evita dance the tango and she appears behind him, holding on to him, thus visually and discursively subordinated to the male figure. More patriarchal constructs appear during the scene of Evita's funeral, where Che defiantly places a last kiss on the body as Perón looks on. The two powerful men exchange menacing looks as the movie ends, as if trying to stake a claim to property over the woman and her legacy. Savigliano also discusses the choice of U.S. pop singer Madonna to play Evita, a decision that was highly controversial in Argentina. Because, as a superstar, Madonna "appropriates" rather than inhabits the characters she plays, she "dissipates Evita's national and historical specificity and she renders visible a transcultural Evita in terms of universal woman-ness."[13] As a result, Evita's own image "as a strong, foul-mouthed, independent woman is subdued in Madonna's representation, offering spectators a softened Evita" that takes on the "conservative femininity of her times."[14] The famous depiction of Evita delivering a speech in front of a microphone is reproduced in the movie, but the passion and power of the "original" is lost, replaced by a melancholy-looking, "subdued" Madonna—the impact of her clenched fists negated by her passive gaze and attitude.

As a mythologized historical figure with a multiplicity of identities and conflicting representations that show her at once as a saintly mother figure, a treacherous whore, and a revolutionary fighting for the poor and disenfranchised, Evita inhabits and negotiates the borderlands of gender and politics like no other contemporary Latin American heroine. Evita stands as a uniquely enduring heroic figure in the region because, as Julie M. Taylor claims, she was able to personify femininity, spirituality, and revolutionary leadership—and "only a woman can embody all three elements of this power."[15]

ALWAYS IN BETWEEN: LA MALINCHE AS TRAITOR, VICTIM, AND FEMINIST ICON

La Malinche—also known as Malintzin and many other names—has been called the "bad mother of Mexico," a treacherous, Indigenous woman traitor who not only assisted Cortés in the overtaking of the Aztec Empire by serving as his translator, but who also bore him a child: symbolically the first mestizo, the firstborn of the Mexican nation. Over the centuries, La Malinche's legacy has been constantly reinterpreted and represented in a variety of often-conflicting ways in written, visual, and other cultural texts. More recently, scholars and artists (particularly U.S. Chicanas) have sought to vindicate her image through new resemantizations, portraying her as either a victim of patriarchy, a survivor full of agency, or a "good," heroic mother figure. Visual depictions of La Malinche appear as early as the mid-sixteenth century, but here I focus on representations made after the Mexican Revolution, when the country underwent a profound social and political transformation and endeavored to build a new national identity.

After the revolution, Mexican muralist painters attempted to find the "essence" of their nation's history and a new vision for the republic anchored in ancient Indigenous culture. Such a project entailed including Aztec figures and motifs as the main elements in monumental works, while portraying the Spanish conquistadors and anyone associated with them (including La Malinche) as enemies of the nation. La Malinche, specifically, was regarded as a traitor. José Clemente Orozco portrays Cortés and La Malinche together, naked, standing over the corpses of Indians. Diego Rivera's Malinche rendition, meanwhile, presents Cortés in armor and La Malinche in a sleazy outfit. According to María Herrera-Sobek, "the painting projects Rivera's view of her as a sell-out, a whore to the Spanish soldiers" and "projects the contempt and disrespect many contemporary Mexicans have for the couple."[16] These images helped to create the concept of "malinchismo" as synonymous with

treason in Mexico. According to Norma Alarcón, La Malinche "was transformed into Guadalupe's monstrous other,"[17] with the hybrid icon of the
Virgin of Guadalupe/Tonantzin taking on the role of "good mother" of the
Mexican nation (a mother who is silent and self-sacrificing), in clear contrast
with the "bad mother" who speaks as a sexual being, independently of her
maternal role.

Once the revolutionary nation was consolidated, other perspectives
(slightly less negative but equally gendered and sexualized) were formulated
regarding the role of La Malinche in Mexican history and culture. In his 1950
book *The Labyrinth of Solitude*, Mexican poet and critic Octavio Paz associated La Malinche with "La Chingada," the violated woman whose rape
gave birth to an "impure," mestizo nation, and in doing so he helped desa-
cralize Mexico's supposed origins "by shifting the founding moment from
Guadalupe to Malintzin."[18] While this ideological shift helped to propel a
revisionist approach to regarding La Malinche's role in Mexican history and
culture, her characterization as "the fucked one" still emphasized the sexual
implications of being conquered: both the rape of women and the emasculation of men. The sexualized ways in which Paz and other scholars have
portrayed La Malinche also underscore misogynistic attitudes present in mid-
twentieth-century Mexican nationalist discourses, which still viewed sexuality and female agency as dangerous—the monstrous double of the "asexual
and virginal feminine" represented by Guadalupe.[19]

La Malinche's transgressive role, which relegated her to marginality and
exclusion in the predominantly patriarchal processes of Mexican nation-formation, would nonetheless allow her to be rediscovered and heroicized after
the 1960s as an icon of female empowerment and criticism against that same
patriarchal order. The Chicana movement in the United States, in particular,
was fundamental in this resemantization, as its members identified with La
Malinche for having, just like them, an "individualized nonmaternal voice"
that earned them the label of "malinches" or "*vendidas*" (sold out).[20] As a
result, La Malinche became a transnational icon, straddling the physical and
cultural U.S.-Mexico borderlands. In this context, La Malinche is portrayed
as a *mestiza*, not as an Indian, representing Mexico's mixed, hybrid heritage.
Chicana artists and writers contend that La Malinche was not a traitor, but a
woman who was victimized by patriarchal culture and who "took charge of
her own destiny."[21] In this new light, she had agency—the same thing that
Chicana activists were attempting to achieve as part of the larger Chicano
movement, which itself was highly *machista* and either denied women positions of leadership or ridiculed the few female leaders that existed as "unfeminine, sexually perverse, promiscuous, and all too often, taunted as lesbians."[22] During this time, La Malinche's critique as a traitor to her race is
also revisited from a feminist perspective, portraying her instead as a "survivor" who endured having been given as a slave to the Mayas and then to the

Spaniards. In addition to La Malinche's legacy, the Chicana movement also reinterpreted the myths of Aztec goddesses who had previously been associated with treachery. As Guisela Latorre explains, "Chicanas, like these indigenous women in Mexican history and myth, had felt the stigma of being labeled *traidoras* for having strayed away from the Chicano nationalist cause," which was not concerned with issues of gender. [23]

One reformulation of La Malinche that is representative of this period is Santa Barraza's painting *La Malinche*, which depicts her "as the mother of the new mestizo race." Her new role is that of fertility goddess. Cortés is present in the painting, but he stands behind her, marginalized. While the image points toward rebirth (perhaps of a more inclusive or even matriarchal Mexican/Chicana society), the past is not forgotten: a corpse hangs from a tree in the background, reminding us about the destruction of the Indigenous people. Despite its progressive, feminist orientation, this recasting of La Malinche also has its limitations. The Barraza painting, for example, still links the power of *mestiza* women with their reproductive power as mothers. Meanwhile, other representations of La Malinche that depict her as a romanticized lover of Cortés or as a seductive ethnic "other" abound in different types of media even today. It appears as though the myth of La Malinche will continue to be redrawn and restaged for years to come, just as competing visions of gender, ethnicity, power, and nation continue to operate and evolve in Mexican and Chicano/a societies.

FORGING NEW IDENTITIES IN A NEW AMERICA: COMICS AND LATINA GIRL POWER

Since the appearance of Superman in 1938, superheroes have been a fixture of U.S. comic books. For the longest time, however, the role of comic book superheroes was solely occupied by white, hypermasculine figures, while women and ethnic/racial minorities were either excluded or relegated to playing villains or, at best, sidekicks. As Frederick Aldama notes, the world of U.S. comic books was ripe with "ethnic and gendered representational distortions—superhero as Anglo versus supervillain as dark, disfigured, effeminate, 'alien' Other."[24] By the early 1970s, an alternative comics movement burst onto the scene, offering new types of stories and exploring the hot-button social and political issues of the time, including gender, race, and ethnic relations. This decade saw the emergence of the first Latino comic book superhero (Relampago, 1977) created by a Latino (Texas judge Margarito Garza). Around the same time, mainstream comic book publishers such as Marvel and DC began introducing a few Latino/a characters, including White Tiger (1975) and El Dorado (1977). In 1981, Marvel introduced its first Latina superheroine, Firebird. Generally, mainstream Latino/a superheroes created during the 1980s and 1990s played minor roles and relied on stereotypes.[25] Latino/a artists sought to address this representational imbalance by publishing their own comics and creating complicated characters whose Latino/a culture was central to their heroic personas, and who engaged in protecting their ethnically diverse communities. Examples of this trend include Richard Dominguez's *El Gato Negro* (1993) and Javier Hernandez's *El Muerto* (1998). In the 2000s, mainstream publishers found a renewed interest in Latino/a superheroes, creating characters and story lines that complicated Latino/a identity and experience and even turning Latinos/as into main protagonists. Eleggua and the Santerians (Marvel, 2005) and Blue Beetle as Jaime Reyes (DC, 2006) are among this new generation of Latino/a superheroes. While portrayals of Latinas as superheroines are still few and far between, the ones who have been able to break the glass ceiling have much to tell us about U.S. Latina self-determination and America's growing multicultural complexity. *The Jaguar* and the Anya Corazón character are perfect representatives of these phenomena.

In 1996, the Jaguar became the first Latina comic book superheroine created by a Latina artist. In introducing her politically aware, culturally proud, and feisty character, Laura Molina didn't mince words with regard to her ideological motivation. In what is most likely a jab at the giant comic book publishers, Molina writes that her self-published book (only one issue of the comic has appeared) "is no corporate sell-out."[26] The book's cover immediately establishes the heroine's heritage and her mission: "Out of Aztlán [what Chicanos/as call the U.S. Southwest] into the new age, comes a woman warrior dedicated to the struggle for social justice, human rights, and Mother Earth."[27] This inscription is complemented by the defiant and confident figure of the Jaguar, who warns "right-wing fundamentalists, racist bigots and white supremacists" that "I resist!" and a sidebar that invites readers to look inside for "more feminist-Chicana anarchy."[28] With the economy of words and images that characterizes comic book art, Molina manages, in just one page, to locate her character in a discursive, multifaceted borderland: the physical U.S.-Mexico borderland; a cultural borderland in which U.S. (through the use of English), Mexican, Chicana, and Mesoamerican cultural influences converge; a political borderland infused with ethnic and power struggle; and a gender borderland in which resistance and agency are clearly configured as female based. The cover also establishes the comic as a work of hybridity—English, Spanish, Spanglish, and Nahuatl are used throughout, while the Jaguar's outfit combines the skintight, full-body spandex suit traditionally worn by superheroes with elements from ancient Aztec warriors such as a feather headdress, gold jewelry, and, of course, jaguar prints.

The Jaguar is an activist superheroine, spurred to action by new legislation and political leadership that led to the rise of hate groups, police brutality against minorities, and a myriad of discriminatory policies and practices in California. Law student Linda Rivera employs her education to do "what is necessary to see that justice is done"[29] for the people of East Los Angeles. But when the legal system is not sufficient to achieve results, she engages in vigilante justice by invoking the powers of Huitzilopochtli, Aztec god of war, and her animal spirit, the jaguar. In one such mission as the Jaguar, Linda encounters a pair of neo-Nazi men who accuse her of "destroying white people's property."[30] The superheroine easily defeats the skinheads, telling them that they were lucky this time because "my ancestors used to eat their enemies."[31] The Jaguar's Chicana feminist identity is reflected in the comic's fight scene, which challenges the historical oppression and discrimination of Mexican Americans and of women in the United States by staging the superiority of a woman of color over white, racist men. Stylistically, the Jaguar's physical and moral predominance is evidenced through the way Molina draws her characters: the heroine is athletic, with chiseled muscles, and her facial expressions are depicted in great detail, while the villains are shown as weak and their faces are generically drawn, signifying anonymity and lack of representational importance. The Jaguar continues a long-standing tradition of Latino/a cultural heroes (Gregorio Cortez and César Chavez among them) rising up to defend their communities from Anglo oppression. However, this heroine rejects her ethnic group's social normativity by standing up as a strong female hero in a cultural tradition marked by patriarchy and predominantly male leadership. As Molina has said, "I wanted to create a strong, nonstereotypical Chicana character who would appeal to girls like myself when I was twelve years old. She wouldn't be subservient or passive. . . . She would inspire confidence in young Chicanas."[32] The Jaguar does live up to this expectation.

Eight years after the appearance of *The Jaguar*, mainstream publishers would finally take a chance on giving a Latina superheroine her own comic book. Marvel's *Araña* ran for twelve issues between 2004 and 2005 and introduced Brooklyn teenager Anya Corazón, who is of mixed Latino/a descent and who acquires special powers when chosen by the ancient Spider Society to battle the Sisterhood of the Wasp. Unlike previous Latina heroines created by Marvel and DC, Araña is a fully fleshed-out character, and her story reflects the complexities of being an adolescent, a female, and a minority in a highly diverse environment where racial, ethnic, gender, and religious lines are constantly crossed. Anya's character is also firmly grounded on her cultural heritage and her family through her Puerto Rican father, an investigative reporter, and the memory of her Mexican mother, who made her promise she would "always be brave."[33] Additionally, the use of Spanish for the heroine's and the comic's name (*araña* means "spider") is significant, as it validates the presence of alternative cultural and linguistic codes in a popular-culture genre that is slowly trying to catch up with the diversity of the American experience. Matthew Smith has analyzed the process of cultural assimilation many immigrant and ethnic superheroes (particularly Wonder Woman) have gone through, as these characters have been molded to "fulfill expectations associated with the melting pot metaphor."[34] *Araña*, however, challenges this drive toward complete assimilation by leaving intact Anya's hybrid identity. This new approach by comic book publishers is most likely due to the rise of multiculturalism, the new U.S. demographic landscape, and the resulting change in the consumer base. According to Aldama, with the creation of *Araña*, Marvel "aimed to appeal to a fast-rising middle-class Latino demographic."[35] This move seemingly paid off, as Araña was named "woman of the year" by *Latina* magazine in 2004.

While the *Araña* series was discontinued in 2005, Marvel decided to bring back Anya Corazón in 2010, but this time she "took on a new moniker, Spider-Girl, wanting to stay true to the same principles that drove her hero, the Amazing Spider-Man."[36] The character's second iteration represented a sort of "promotion" in the sense that she would now be fighting alongside heavyweight Marvel superheroes such as Spider-Man and could potentially reach a larger, more mainstream audience. However, such changes came at a representational cost to the character's ethnic identity and female agency. First, the Spanish name Araña was dropped and replaced with an English name that would be more familiar to non-Latino/a readers. This is an example of the process of cultural assimilation that Smith has referred to, as indicated above. Second, Anya's outfit and appearance were significantly "feminized" in the second comic: Araña's baggy street wear, boots, backpack, wild hair, and spider exoskeleton gave way to Spider-Girl's tight jeans and tops, skirts, open-toed heels, ponytail, and the traditional, curve-hugging spandex suit. Finally, while Anya stood out as the main heroic figure in *Araña* (she appears alone on the cover), she is joined by a number of other, mostly male heroes in *Spider-Girl*, which undermines her role as protagonist (on the cover of *Family Values* she appears with Spider-Man, who is obviously the most recognizable of the two figures). Despite these issues, Anya is represented in both comics as a strong, smart, determined, independent, feisty, fearless young woman and superheroine—an excellent role model for Latinas and non-Latinas alike.

*   *   *

While scholars tend to shy away from the concepts of "heroism" and "hero" because they are incredibly broad and are used indiscriminately in the media and in everyday parlance, they can be very helpful and powerful for analyzing cultural representation and discourses associated with power structures, social imaginaries, and gender, among others. After all, the figure of the hero and the heroic narrative are among the most universal and enduring myths and forms of storytelling developed by humans.[37] Heroes are fluid cultural texts that change over time as societies transform themselves. Consequently, the appearance, disappearance, reformulation, and appropriation of heroes can allow for nuanced and insightful readings of those societies. As we have seen in this analysis, the construction of female heroic figures in Latin American and Latino/a art and popular culture is intimately connected with highly contested efforts to define the nation, the role of women in society, and the representation of ethnic minorities. Latin American and Latina heroines also tend to be portrayed as hybrid characters who inhabit a multiplicity of physical, psychological, social, and cultural borderlands, and who engage in various forms of political contestation. There is still much to be learned from and about them.

NOTES

1. Laura Molina, *Cihualyaomiquiz: The Jaguar* (Arcadia, CA: Insurgent Comix, 1996), cover.
2. bell hooks, *Reel to Real: Race, Sex, and Class at the Movies* (New York: Routledge, 1996), 210.
3. Gloria Anzaldúa, *Borderlands/La Frontera* (San Francisco: Aunt Lute Books, 1987), 79.
4. Anzaldúa, *Borderlands/La Frontera*, preface.
5. Linda B. Hall, "Evita Perón: Beauty, Resonance, and Heroism," in *Heroes and Hero Cults in Latin America*, ed. Samuel Brunk and Ben Fallaw (Austin: University of Texas Press, 2006), 229–30.
6. Lidia Santos, "Eva Perón: One Woman, Several Masks," in *Contemporary Latin American Cultural Studies*, ed. Stephen Hart and Richard Young (London: Oxford University Press, 2003), 102.
7. Santos, "Eva Perón," 102.
8. Ibid., 105.
9. Ibid., 105.
10. Ibid., 106.
11. Marta E. Savigliano, "Evita: The Globalization of a National Myth," *Latin American Perspectives* 24, no. 6 (1997): 156.
12. Savigliano, "Evita," 157.
13. Ibid., 158.
14. Ibid., 159.
15. Julie M. Taylor, *Eva Perón: The Myths of a Woman* (Chicago: University of Chicago Press, 1979), 147.
16. María Herrera-Sobek, "In Search of La Malinche: Pictorial Representations of a Mytho-Historical Figure," in *Feminism, Nation and Myth: La Malinche*, ed. Rolando Romero and Amanda Nolacea Harris (Houston: Arte Público Press, 2005), 127.
17. Norma Alarcón, "Traddutora, Traditora: A Paradigmatic Figure of Chicana Feminism," *Cultural Critique* 13 (1989): 58.
18. Alarcón, "Traddutora, Traditora," 65.
19. Ibid., 68–69.
20. Ibid., 63.
21. Herrera-Sobek, "In Search of La Malinche," 130.
22. Ramón Gutiérrez, "Community, Patriarchy and Individualism: The Politics of Chicano History and the Dream of Equality," *American Quarterly* 45, no. 1 (1993): 47.
23. Guisela Latorre, *Walls of Empowerment: Chicana/o Indigenist Murals of California* (Austin: University of Texas Press, 2008), 203.
24. Frederick Aldama, *Your Brain on Latino Comics: From Gus Arriola to Los Bros Hernandez* (Austin: University of Texas Press, 2009), 2.
25. Aldama, *Your Brain on Latino Comics*, 31–38.

26. Molina, *The Jaguar*, preface.

27. Ibid., cover.

28. Ibid., cover.

29. Ibid., 4.

30. Ibid., 8.

31. Ibid., 9.

32. Quoted in Aldama, *Your Brain on Latino Comics*, 213.

33. Fiona Avery, *Araña: Heart of the Spider* (New York: Marvel, 2005), 9.

34. Matthew Smith, "The Tyranny of the Melting Pot Metaphor: Wonder Woman as the Americanized Immigrant," in *Comics and Ideology*, ed. Matthew McAllister, Edward Sewell, and Ian Gordon (New York: Peter Lang, 2001), 130.

35. Aldama, *Your Brain on Latino Comics*, 38.

36. Paul Tobin, *Spider-Girl: Family Values* (New York: Marvel, 2011), 10.

37. Patrick Colm Hogan, *Affective Narratology: The Emotional Structure of Stories* (Lincoln: University of Nebraska Press, 2011), 129.

Chapter Eight

Janissary

*An Orientalist Heroine or a
Role Model for Muslim Women?*

Itir Erhart and Hande Eslen-Ziya

Since its establishment in 1923, the Republic of Turkey went through several *laicité* reforms whose main objective was to displace the sacred order and establish a new system of politics in Turkey based on secularism. In 1934, certain women's rights were granted, such as the right to vote and to be elected to parliament. Women were further given the opportunity for education in secular public schools, and they were given access to employment. Women were further encouraged to unveil. Moghadam refers to this nation-formation model in Turkey as the "women's emancipation model of revolution" or "the modernizing model."[1]

Ninety years after the Republic's foundation, we observe divergence among different feminist groups: liberal, republican, and Islamist. Such divergence is due to the strong secular tradition of the republican movement and the religious tradition of their rival Islamists. Most of the leading republican feminists have been secular-oriented Kemalists[2] who view themselves as the guardians of the Turkish secular regime. As argued by Eslen-Ziya and Korkut, their differences "become more acute when the perspectives of Islamist women's groups are considered."[3] While the liberal and republican feminist groups and their ideology are influenced by Western discourses and concepts of modernity, the Islamist feminists, on the other hand, subscribe to a more limited version of women's rights. The divergence among republican and Islamist women's groups become more apparent especially around the issue of the headscarf in Turkish politics:

The liberal group is able to reconcile its goals with the Islamist feminist groups when it comes to the topic of the headscarf in Turkish politics, unlike the republican women's group, who subscribe to a more limited version of modernity relative to their liberal peers. [4]

Though the divergence among women's groups due to their positioning on the headscarf issue can be observed in many areas of Turkish daily life, its emergence in comic books is a novel one. In this respect this chapter is an attempt to analyze a Muslim female character in DC Comics, Janissary, and her representation. She is a woman who has declared war against evil forces who want to take "modern" Turkey back into its Ottoman past. [5] However, since "the veiled woman" is a highly symbolic representation that marks the other culture as both foreign and irrational, [6] she herself becomes a symbol for Islam, a barbaric and uncivilized culture. She is an exotic woman, and her values are culturally incompatible with the values, norms, and interests of the West. [7] She is Islamic but, at the same time, by fighting back to protect the Turkish Republic, represents the republican women. Therefore she, in one body, becomes the symbol of the two different positionings of women's groups in Turkey, Islamic and republican.

Selma Tolon, aka Janissary, [8] is the only Turkish female superheroine who lives in the DC Universe. After studying medicine in the United States, she returns home to work for the Turkish Red Crescent—a humanitarian aid organization that operates in Muslim countries. During earthquake relief she finds herself in an underground cavern where she discovers the mystical scimitar of the Ottoman Empire sultan Suleiman the Magnificent and a book of spells by the wizard Merlin. She uses her powers to defend Turkey against a general who, in partnership with Iblis—the devil in Muslim mythology—is planning to overthrow the government with an Islamist revolution. Her task is to "defeat the magical menace before the Ottoman Empire rises again to claim the land where East meets West." [9] The chapter, in this respect, is an attempt to focus on the exoticist representation [10] of Janissary, the representational strategies that offer an exotic heroine to a contemporary Western comic book fan. It will further elaborate on the reactions of the Turkish secularist and political elite to the introduction of a veiled Turkish superheroine.

The chapter proceeds in the following order: In the first section, we provide a brief discussion of the different positionings of feminist groups over the ban of the headscarf. The section will be concluded with our research question: how can this dilemma be applied to the heroine Janissary? The second section focuses on the analysis of Janissary, first as a superheroine, then as an embodiment of two different positionings of women in Turkey, a secular daughter of the republic and a Muslim Other. The last section will include the reactions of the political elite to the introduction of Janissary and bring forth the concluding remarks for the chapter.

FEMINIST POLARIZATION: THE REPUBLICAN AND ISLAMIST WOMEN ON THE HEADSCARF

In Turkey, with the establishment of the secular Turkish Republic in 1923, the Sharia codes of the Ottoman Empire were replaced with secular laws. Thereafter women gained certain rights, and the introduction of gender equality policies became a fundamental aspect of the process of eliminating the Islamic political order in Turkey.[11] Hence, with the establishment of the Turkish Republic, women became part and symbol of the nationalist movement where women were seen as the "mothers of the next generation," and "care-giving, marriage and motherhood, nurturing, and self-sacrificing roles of women" were seen as the ultimate path that would secure the Turkish Republic.[12] The reforms that replaced the old Ottoman Sharia codes abolished Islamic laws and outlawed polygamy. Women gained the "right to vote and to be elected and also enhanced rights of divorce and inheritance. The use of the headscarf, *hijab* and veiling in general was discouraged by the state."[13] Hence the republic "not only stipulated the rights and obligations of Turkish women, but also what it expected from the Turkish woman subject in terms of her behavior and, specifically, her dress."[14] While the Western dress code represented the civilized world (Europe), it saved the whole nation from being subject to an Orientalist discourse.

> Our republican era provided freedom to Turkish women in terms of her dress. Among many revolutions which challenged the conservative frame of mind [of the ancien régime], was the introduction of the dress code, which was prevalent in the civilized world [Europe] for both men and women. It saved the Turks from being in a separate Oriental universe. . . . The frame of mind which demanded *hijab* from cultured women has been eliminated. . . . Racially, the Turkish women are not different from the Westerners, and there should be no means to differentiate them in their dress either.[15]

In this respect, such bans of the headscarf, *hijab*, or the veil in public spaces and the encouragement of Western dress codes represent a deeper goal for the Kemalists: being a European forward-looking nation.

The rights that were encouraged during this modernization process according to Turam are unique not only in the kind of secularism that they promoted but also in the form of feminism they represented, which can be referred to as "state feminism."[16] These state feminists—which we will refer to as republican feminists—see the secular state as the key protector of women's rights and gender equality and give great importance to Western dress codes and the "modernization" they represent. According to some critics like Arat, Turkish women were treated not as equal partners of men but instead as symbols of modernization and Westernization, a key to becoming European.[17]

In the late 1960s and early 1970s the discouragement of the headscarf in the public sphere and its ban in state institutions brought about a certain polarization of religion. These policies were contested primarily by preaching and attempting to attend state schools without removing the Islamic headscarf.[18] In the early 1980s the movement got wider and more influential and made the ban of the headscarf in state institutions and schools an issue. In the late 1980s, this opposition grew, and Islamist women mobilized street and university protests to draw attention to the headscarf issue. This ban, which is the major source of conflict among two major feminist groups in Turkey—republican and Islamist—continues to this day. While for the republican women the headscarf is the symbol of a backward social order, for the Islamist women, as Kandiyoti[19] argues, it is a "discourse of injury and a posture of marginalization vis-à-vis the assumed hegemony of state secularism." Islamist women argue that they are marginalized and oppressed by the secular regime. This in return results in a discourse which, according to Marshall, is oppositional to the secular feminist one. She further argues that

> there are some Islamist women who selectively use feminist assertions to develop arguments that mesh with Islamist ideology. A small group of these women openly identify themselves as feminists, but with the qualification that they are Islamist, not secular.[20]

These two groups lean on separate ideologies, and their answer to the "woman question" remains different. These differences, in fact, reflect modern Turkey's bigger dilemma: the secular versus Islamist dichotomy. For this very reason, the use of such a dichotomy by DC Comics via Janissary, as we argue and try to portray, may bear a deeper meaning. In this respect this chapter aims to explore where one can position Janissary: Does she belong with the Islamic or republican woman's groups, or is she the embodiment of this duality? For this reason, primarily *JLA Annual #4: On Call* written by Brian K. Vaughan,[21] where Janissary makes her first appearance and was the center of the story, was analyzed. Issues of *Day of Vengeance: Infinite Crisis Special*,[22] *Birds of Prey*,[23] and *Shadowpact*,[24] where she was part of the background story, were also utilized in our research. We analyzed the comic books independently for recurring themes and images. Those that emerged in the process were then compiled and discussed until consensus was achieved. This was followed by a reexamination of the comic books according to these themes and images. The findings are discussed in the following sections.

INTRODUCING JANISSARY

Janissary's introduction to the DC Universe was a very exciting development for Turkish comic book fans. The long-expected Turkish female superheroine had finally arrived. Furthermore, she seemed to incorporate several positive traits: she was attractive, secular, educated, strong, idealist, modern, Muslim, nationalist, patriotic, selfless, and successful. She was a Stanford graduate humanitarian aid worker who also was good with her scimitar. However, a closer look into her story and a deeper character analysis frustrated many of these fans as well as the Turkish political elite. This section will first analyze Janissary as a superheroine and discuss her strengths and weaknesses. It will then explore where she falls in the secular–Islamic dichotomy. The representational strategies that offer an exotic heroine to a contemporary Western comic book fan will also be examined.

Janissary as a Superheroine: Strengths and Weaknesses

Like all super heroes and heroines Janissary has strengths and weaknesses. She is depicted as strong willed. When Iblis notices her on TV, he asks, "Who is this magnificent creature? With her body as my temple, I would be unstoppable." Kazim's response is clear: "Your host had to be willing. This woman fancies herself a do-gooder. She would never allow herself to be possessed."[25]

She is strong, but since she is a medical doctor who took the Hippocratic oath,[26] Selma will never take a life or harm a living creature. On page 24, she says, "I won't kill and I won't turn my back on Turkey." Her patriotism surfaces even in her defense of her weapon: "Turkish scimitar is sharper and sleeker than your [Aquaman's] unwieldy blade."[27] Hence, her patriotism and faith could also be listed among her weaknesses: "As a very observant Muslim, Dr. Tolon is committed to praying five times a day [*salat*], giving alms to the poor [*zakat*] and fasting during the month of Ramadan [*sawm*]."[28] She criticizes Kazim for hiding in a crystal mosque: "You hide your sins at the mosque? You are a disgrace to our country and faith Kazim."[29]

Also her inexperience in fighting evil is noteworthy. She has trouble performing the spells in her book. When not the skeleton but only his sword bursts into flames, she admits, "I'm afraid I have yet to master any of the spells in my Eternity Book."[30] According to Sébastien Andrivet, "she lacks control over her spells" and "big supernatural menaces, burning giant demons and zombie hordes were a tad above her weight class, but with advice from more experienced heroes such as Batman she rose to the occasion just fine."[31]

Although the Justice League enlisted her aid to defeat Kazim, and she made a good impression on them—was even invited to join them—it can be observed that she is not in the same league as American super heroes and heroines. She is passive and secondary. This becomes more evident when she appears in stories other than her own. For instance, in *Birds of Prey* she gets a letter from Oracle: "You have three minutes to read this."[32] The illustration depicts her in Bursa. She is seen from behind, covered. In *Day of Vengeance* she stands still, again covered, and does not speak a word. At the Oblivion Bar, she hangs out with the rest of the gang without being bothered by "normals,"[33] but we do not see her participating in any of the conversations. She is in the back row, silent. Her presence in the "background" will be discussed in the following sections where it will be argued that she actually embodies the secular versus Islamist dichotomy in Turkey.

The Janissary as a Daughter of the Republic

Selma Tolon, aka Janissary, is a devout Muslim. She first defines herself as a subject and humble servant of Allah. She is ready to accept whatever challenges he sends her,[34] and she claims to get her strength from the Prophet Mohammed's bones.[35]

Her second commitment is to the "modern" Turkish Republic and its values. She could be considered as one of the "Daughters of the Republic" who defended the borders during the Independence War[36] which narrowed the physical gap between men and women.[37] After the Republic was founded in 1923, these women became the protectors of the newly founded state, its commitment to the principles of secularism, and the legal, institutional, and structural reforms which brought Turkey closer to the West. As an emancipated Turkish woman, Janissary fights against Muslim extremist forces who want to revive the Ottoman[38] past.

During the Izmit earthquake[39] rescue efforts, we see her in her shorts, ponytail, and cap. She is with the Red Crescent working on equal terms with men. She appears as an ideal female soldier of the Republic, an agent in the country's effort to reach Western civilization. She is an unveiled, educated professional in the public sphere.[40] She comforts a Canadian earthquake victim, saying, "My name is Dr. Tolon, I got my degree at Stanford. Now just relax." When another earthquake victim she is trying to rescue from under the rubble asks where the men are, she confidently turns to her and says, "We don't need *men* for this, ma'am. Just a little leverage."[41]

These conversations are a foreshadowing of her origin story. When she finds herself thrown into a ditch during an aftershock,[42] she discovers Ottoman sultan Suleiman's scimitar which Merlin has blessed with power. The scimitar and Merlin's book were left there in 1566 to be removed by a champion as brave and wise as Suleiman himself, with the hope that, one day, this *man* will have the strength to wield both weapons in battle. Janissary turns out to be that *man* who will help protect and rebuild modern Turkey.

She takes on the duty to protect the Ataturk Dam in Southeastern Turkey,[43] which when being completed in 1992 cut off the international water flow of the river Euphrates for over a month, and was portrayed as a hostile act by the Arab media, triggering an Iraqi threat of military action and escalating the Turkish-Arab divide over the river.[44] The dam, which bears Ataturk's name, acts as a symbol of Turkey's modernity project and victory over the Arab world, and Janissary, as a soldier of the republic, swears to fight for it.[45]

The dichotomy between the vast Ottoman Empire, represented as a backward, oppressive, despotic, theocratic monarchy, with close ties to the Muslim/Arab world, and the modern, secular, progressive Turkish Republic, an ally of Israel,[46] is evident throughout Janissary's adventures. When Iblis asks her to join forces with him in reviving the Ottoman Empire—"Join me, we'll make this country a paradise"—she responds, "I love my country as it is."[47] Similarly, Iblis promises to make Kazim the sultan of an empire, not the president of this "pathetic little country," aka Turkey.[48] Incidentally, Merlin's Eternity Book which aids her in her heroine work is not in Arabic; it is "Ancient Turkish."[49]

However, since use of the *hijab* was also discouraged by the state[50] as discussed previously, the modern Janissary's veil and red *hijab* seem puzzling, a contradiction in itself. Andrivet attempts to explain this puzzle by referring to her secret identity and argues that "Janissary's veil and hood are chiefly intended to protect her secret identity—as a modern Turkish Muslim, she does not wear any special headgear in her civilian identity."[51] What is significant in this interpretation is how "modern" and "unveiled" are equated, and how the Western dress code adopted by Selma Tolon represents modern Turkey. In the following section, the Islamic Turkey that Janissary also represents and how it becomes subject to Orientalism will be discussed.

Janissary as the Muslim Other

According to Said, "the Orient is not only adjacent to Europe; it is also the place of Europe's greatest and richest and oldest colonies, the source of its civilizations and languages, its cultural contestant, and one of its deepest and most recurring images of the Other."[52] The images associated with this popular Other are presented as colorful, veiled, and exotic, but also barbarian, backward, and uncivilized. As such, the West always has the "relative upper hand" in this relationship to the Orient, "describing it, teaching it, settling it, ruling over it . . . dominating, restructuring, and having authority over" it.[53]

Muslims, particularly, are often represented as people whose values are culturally incompatible with those of the West.[54] Since representations construct socially shared knowledge, attitudes, ideologies, norms, and values,[55] Muslims are oftentimes perceived not only as religiously different but also as threats to freedom, equality, and secularism. And the veiled Muslim woman, practicing a habit which is not expected or acceptable in many Western nations, becomes a symbol for this different and threatening culture. It symbolizes "the non-European 'Other' which must be excluded, and the danger this 'Other' poses to liberal democratic notions of society, and to 'our' civilization, where freedom and gender equality is valued."[56]

As Mohanty argues, similar to the Orientalist perception of the West toward the religious covered Muslim women, there is a tendency to create a homogeneous notion of the oppression of women as a group. This in turn, Mohanty argues, "produces the image of an 'average third world woman.'"[57] She further argues that

> this average third world woman leads an essentially truncated life based on her feminine gender (read: sexually constrained) and being "third world" (read: ignorant, poor, uneducated, tradition-bound, domestic, family-oriented, victimized, etc.). This, I suggest, is in contrast to the (implicit) self-representation of Western women as educated, modern, as having control over their own bodies and sexualities, and the freedom to make their own decisions.[58]

In what follows, it will be argued that this Orientalist ideology of the West is also supported in the story of Janissary and her representation as a veiled Muslim woman, which in turn brings her closer to Islamic Turkey.

We meet a "modern" daughter of the republic, Selma Tolon, as a medical doctor, working at one of Turkey's oldest hospitals, Ankara Numune Hospital, after a long shift. The next thing we find out about her, however, is the fact that she is a practicing Muslim who is fasting during the month of Ramadan—a notion which does not have a place in the secular, feminist discourse.

"They've probably got me on hold through Ramadan." In the next panel, the very second of the story, she approaches a veiled woman and says, "Periham Hanım [the name should have been "Perihan," literally an archfairy], your husband is recovering nicely." The name "Perihan" sounds different and exotic. She is called in for another emergency when she decides to pass the job on to a colleague, Olhan (the name should have been "Orhan," literally great ruler), as she has a more pressing appointment. As she goes into her hideout we get a first glance at her secret identity: she has a costume with a Turkish flag, which incorporates a crescent and a star; a veil; and a scimitar.

A few pages later, Wonder Woman greets her with the traditional Arabic greeting phrase among Muslims, "*Sallamalaykum* [Peace be unto you] *efendim.*"[59] *Efendi*[60] is a Turkish title of respect, meaning lord or master, equivalent to English "Sir." *Efendim* is the possessive form. Wonder Woman mistakenly refers to Janissary, a woman, as "*efendi*," but the phrase serves the purpose of "Othering" the non-Western character and reinforcing the us/them dichotomy.

Cultural differences between the East and the West, between Christianity and Islam, which are the basis of Orientalism, are stressed on several other occasions. For instance, the misunderstanding between Janissary and Green Lantern on what caused the trouble and what the Jinn are contributes to the exoticization and mystification of Islam: "The Jinn happened. You may know them by their Westernized name. Genies. They are sprits made of fire, created by Allah. They are not the innocuous lamp dwellers."[61]

Similarly, Iblis is explained to be a non-Western Satan: "Iblis is Koran's Satan. He is also one of the Jinn."[62] Accordingly, a "Muslim version of the exorcist" takes place when Janissary's body becomes a host for Iblis.

The iconic images of flying carpets, dark-skinned Turks, crocodiles in the river, the glass mosque Kazim hides in, Batman—which is not "just the name of a hero, but also a city in Southeastern Turkey"[63]—the rope Wonder Woman puts on when she enters this "sacred ground," and Janissary's veil and *hijab* all contribute to the mystique of the East.

The East is not only mystified but also emasculated through the castration of Janissary, historically a member of the Ottoman *male* infantry unit. As such, a person of the Orient is both conceptually[64] and literally emasculated. The castration of Janissary fits perfectly with the Orientalist representation of the West as "masculine" and the East as "feminine." Symbolically, the East is rendered powerless and patronized by the West. In this Orientalist picture, Janissary, a veiled Muslim woman warrior, becomes a symbolic representation that marks this fundamentally alien, powerless culture both in the eyes of Western readers and the Turkish secularist elite.

THE REJECTION OF JANISSARY AND GENERAL DISCUSSION

As we argued in the beginning of this chapter, the presence of Janissary is a symbol that represents the separate ideologies not only in their answer to the "woman question" but also to the general divide that exists within Turkey today: the secular versus Islamist dichotomy. For this very reason this chapter, via the analysis of Janissary, demonstrated that it is not easy to position women into one single pillar. This was, we argue, evident in our inability to prove which group—the Islamic or republican women's groups—Janissary belonged to. This positionlessness of Janissary seemed to create a tension among the critiques and the readers of Turkish DC Comics.

When the comic book was translated into Turkish in 2005, Janissary made her way into the mainstream Turkish media, and the reactions she got were mainly negative. The secularist political elite were not happy because the only Turkish superheroine was wearing a veil and fasting. The military elite were not pleased with her either. In an interview, retired general Hursit Tolon, who later became the leading suspect in the Ergenekon[65] trials, was asked whether the name resemblance was a coincidence. He replied, "I have no relative called Selma Tolon. The choice is completely coincidental. Furthermore, not only the armed forces but everyone in Turkey sees *irtica* [Islamic reactionism] as a threat."[66]

Dogu Pelincek, the chairman of the Workers' Party, claimed that the comic book's release was part of a greater plan: "As part of the Great Middle East Project, Turkey is depicted as a power fighting against the forces of the East and Southeast. Turkey is serving as the West's gendarme."[67]

Umut Kirecci, a writer for the popular comic book website Cizgi Roman (Comic Book), on the other hand, claimed that Janissary's story bore likeness to U.S.-Turkish politics, and "the bridge between the East and West, fundamentalist Muslims who want to destroy Atatürk's legacy, pro-Sharia soldiers, the South East presented as a problem zone" were all very familiar.[68]

These reactions point to the polarization of religion and politics in Turkey, where Janissary is embraced neither by the Islamists nor the secularists. She is either shunned as part of the bigger plan to destroy modern Turkey or because she is neither secular nor Muslim enough. Her worst crime, however, is subjecting "modern" Turkey to an Orientalist discourse, something that the Kemalists were fighting against since the establishment of the Republic.

NOTES

1. Valentine Moghadam, "Women, Revolution, and Identity in the Middle East," in *The Women and International Development Annual*, ed. Rita Gallin et al. (Boulder, CO: Westview Press, 1995), 119.

2. With the foundation of the republic in 1923, Turkey's official ideology became Kemalism, which has its roots in Mustafa Kemal Ataturk's ultrasecular views and the top-down modernization project.

3. Hande Eslen-Ziya and Umut Korkut, "Political Religion and Politicized Women in Turkey: Hegemonic Republicanism Re-visited," *Totalitarian Movements and Political Religions* 11, no. 3 (2011): 312.

4. Ibid.

5. The Turkish Republic abolished monarchy in 1922 and the Caliphate in 1924 in an attempt to sever ties with the Ottoman and Islamic past. K. Karpat, *Ottoman Past and Today's Turkey* (Leiden: Brill, 2000).

6. Elizabeth Klaus and Susanne Kassel, "The Veil as a Means of Legitimization," *Journalism* 6, no. 3 (2005).

7. Yvonne Y. Haddad, "Islam and Gender Dilemmas in a Changing World," in *Islam, Gender and Social Change*, ed. Y. Y. Haddad et al. (New York: Oxford University Press, 1998).

8. Literally, the member of the infantry unit Janissaries who were recruited almost exclusively from ex-Christian converts. They reached the height of their power in the mid-seventeenth century when only candidates approved by the janissary corps could be appointed grand vizier. M. Kunt, "Suftan, Dynasty and State in the Ottoman Empire: Political Institutions in the Sixteenth Century," *Medieval History Journal* 6 (2003).

9. Janissary, *Comic Vine*, last modified December 2, 2012, http://www.comicvine.com/planet-dc/39-56262.

10. Graham Huggan, *The Postcolonial Exotic: Marketing the Margins* (London: Routledge, 2001).

11. Eslen-Ziya and Korkut, "Political Religion."

12. Aysan Sever and Yurdakul Gökçeçiek, "Culture of Honor, Culture of Change: A Feminist Analysis of Honor," *Violence against Women* 7, no. 9 (2001).

13. Eslen-Ziya and Korkut, "Political Religion," 316.

14. Ibid., 317.

15. Afet Inan, *Atatürk ve Türk Kadın Haklarının Kazanılması Tarih Boyunca Türk Kadınının Hak ve Görevleri* (Istanbul: M. E. B. Yayinevi, 1968), 157.

16. Berna Turam, "Turkish Women Divided by Politics: Secularist Activism versus Pious Non-Resistance," *International Feminist Journal of Politics* 10, no. 4 (2008): 478.

17. Zehra Arat, "Turkish Women and the Republican Reconstruction of Tradition," in *Reconstructing Gender in the Middle East: Tradition, Identity and Power*, ed. Fatma Müge Gökçeçiçek et al. (New York: Columbia University Press, 1994).

18. Gül Aldıkaçtı Marshall, "A Question of Compatibility: Feminism and Islam in Turkey," *Middle East Critique* 17, no. 3 (2008): 229.

19. Deniz Kandiyoti, "Islam and Feminism: A Misplaced Polarity," *Women against Fundamentalism* 8 (1996): 11.

20. Marshall, "A Question of Compatibility," 227.

21. Brian K. Vaughan (s), Steve Scott (p), and Hector Collazo (i), *Unveiling: The Janissary!*, JLA Annual, no. 4 (National Comics Publications, 2000).

22. Geoff Johns (s), Phil Jimene (p), and Andy Lanning (i), *Infinite Crisis: Day of Vengeance*, vol. 1, no. 6 (National Comics Publications, 2006).

23. Simone Bedard (s), Scott Sequiera (p), and Hazlewood Riggs (i), *Birds of Prey* (National Comics Publications, 2007).

24. Bill Willingham (s), Steve Scott (p), and Wayne Faucher (i), *Shadowpact #5: "One Year Later"* (National Comics Publications, 2006).

25. Vaughan, *"Unveiling: The Janissary!,"* 5.

26. Ibid., 6.

27. Ibid., 15.

28. Sébastien Andrivet, "Janissary—Turkish Super-Hero," Writeups, last modified July 16, 2013, http://www.writeups.org/fiche.php?id=355.

29. Vaughan, *"Unveiling: The Janissary!,"* 20.

30. Ibid., 15.

31. Andrivet, "Janissary—Turkish Super-Hero."

32. Bedard, *"Birds of Prey."*

33. Johns, *"Infinite Crisis, Day of Vengeance,"* 20.

34. Vaughan, *"Unveiling: The Janissary!,"* 3.

35. Ibid., 24.

36. The struggle of Mustafa Kemal Ataturk and his followers between 1919 and 1923 to form a new republic and the war between the Greek and Turkish armies in the years 1919 to 1922 are referred to as the Turkish Independence War.

37. Itir Erhart, "Ladies of Besiktas: A Dismantling of Male Hegemony at Inönü Stadium," *International Review for the Sociology of Sport* 48 (2013).

38. Vaughan, *"Unveiling: The Janissary!,"* 13.

39. The Izmit earthquake was a 7.4 magnitude earthquake that struck northwestern Turkey on August 17, 1999, and killed around seventeen thousand people.

40. Nilufer Gole, "Islamism, Feminism and Post-modernism: Women's Movements in Islamic Countries," *New Perspectives in Turkey* 19 (1998).

41. Vaughan, *"Unveiling: The Janissary!,"* 35.

42. Ibid., 30–33.

43. Numerous structures are named after Ataturk: Ataturk Dam, Ataturk Cultural Center, Ataturk Airport, and so forth. This dam on the Euphrates River in Southeastern Turkey, the largest structure built in Turkey, and one of the largest dams in the world is the main unit in the Southeastern Anatolia Project (GAP).

44. Brahma Chellaney, *Water, Peace, and War: Confronting the Global Water Crisis* (Lanham, MD: Rowman & Littlefield, 2013), 199.

45. Vaughan, *"Unveiling: The Janissary!,"* 12.

46. Ibid., 13.

47. Ibid., 23.

48. Ibid., 5.

Itir Erhart and Hande Eslen-Ziya

49. After the foundation of the Republic, under the influence of the sociologist Ziya Gokalp's writings, the Turkish language came to be perceived as the heart of Turkish identity. Purifying Turkish of its Arab and Persian borrowings and rediscovering Turkish folktales, heroes, and culture became parts of the nation-building project, in Barbara Celarent, "Book review: *The Remembered Village*, by M. N. Srinivas," *American Journal of Sociology* 117, no. 6 (2012).

50. Eslen-Ziya and Korkut, "Political Religion."

51. Andrivet, "Janissary—Turkish Super-Hero."

52. Edward W. Said, *Orientalism* (New York: Vintage, 1979), 1–2.

53. Said, *Orientalism*, 3.

54. Edward W. Said, *Covering Islam: How the Media and the Experts Determine How We See the Rest of the World* (London: Vintage, 1997); and Yvonne Y. Haddas, "Islam and Gender Dilemmas in a Changing World," in *Islam, Gender and Social Change*, ed. Y. Y. Haddad et al. (New York: Oxford University Press, 1998).

55. Teun A. Van Dijk, "Principles of Critical Discourse Analysis," *Discourse & Society* 4, no. 2 (1993).

56. Maryam Khalid, "Gender, Orientalism and Representations of the 'Other' in the War on Terror, Global Change, Peace & Security," *Peace, Security & Global Change* 23, no. 1 (2011): 21.

57. Chandra T. Mohanty, "Under Western Eyes," in *Feminism without Borders: Decolonizing Theory, Practicing Solidarity* (Durham, NC: Duke University Press, 2003), 333.

58. Ibid., 337.

59. Vaughan, "*Unveiling: The Janissary!*," 11.

60. From Greek *avthéntis* (αυθέντης), lord, master. Sevan Nisanyan, *Sözlerin Soyağacı: Çağdaş Türkçenin Etimolojik Sözlüğü* (Ankara: Adam Yayinlari, 2007).

61. Vaughan, "*Unveiling: The Janissary!*," 10.

62. Ibid., 14.

63. Ibid., 20.

64. Said, *Orientalism*, 291.

65. An alleged secularist, clandestine organization. The alleged members of Ergenekon, which includes army officials, politicians, as well as academics and journalists, are being tried for attempting to stage a coup to overthrow the government.

66. "Yeniceri ile alakam yok," *Haber 7*, last modified March 11, 2005, http://www.haber7.com/kultur/haber/80508-org-tolon-yeniceri-ile-alakam-yok.

67. "Yeniçeri," *Aksam*, last modified March 11, 2005, http://arsiv.aksam.com.tr/arsiv/aksam/2005/03/11/gundem/gundemprn1.html.

68. Umut Kirecci, "Yeniceri," *Cizgi Roman*, last modified January 16, 2008, http://www.cizgiroman.gen.tr.

Chapter Nine

Representations of Motherhood in *X-Men*

Christopher Paul Wagenheim

Since its advent in 1963, Marvel's *Uncanny X-Men* (originally published simply as *X-Men*) has become a pillar of American popular culture. In the six decades since its debut, the *Uncanny X-Men* has crossed over into successful television, film, and video game franchises and remains wildly popular in print, both the original and the multitude of spinoffs. Marvel's line of comic books—both classic and contemporary—continue to be ground zero for creative ventures outside of nonprint media. Credited with ushering in an era of comic books that were critical of the society and culture they were inked in, Marvel has used the *Uncanny X-Men* and the ever-expanding Marvel Universe as a vehicle for social commentary—especially commentary concerning racism, sexism, and xenophobia. And while Marvel's oblique commentary on racism, sexism, and xenophobia has been thoroughly explored by the academic community, a thorough investigation of the roles of mother figures, motherhood, and maternal influence within the Marvel Universe (and the X-Men in particular) has been absent. Using the first three publication years (1963–1966) of the *Uncanny X-Men*[1] and the first two volumes (2006–2007) of *X-Men: First Class*,[2] this chapter will establish that the representation of mothers and mother figures within the foundational/origin story of the X-Men has remained static and problematic despite almost five decades in between the publications at hand. In both volumes mothers are largely absent, and when they do appear they are superfluous at best and adversarial at worst. This chapter will link the absence of mothers and their problematic representation to the psychoanalytic and sociological theories of mother-disidentification in regard to hegemonic male development and suggest that the *Uncanny X-Men* and the modern expansion in *X-Men: First Class* is teaching the "mostly male comics consumer"[3] that separating themselves from their mother is an integral part of moving from boyhood to manhood. Additionally this chapter will argue that Jean Grey, as the only female member of the team, partakes in this mother-separation process as a way of earning her status as an X-Man and that normative cultural markers of womanhood (specifically acts of domesticity and mothering) have all but disappeared from 1963 to 2006. While the stripping of normative feminine markers can be seen as transgressive, further examination points to masculinization, not gender progressivism as the major reason for Jean Grey's transformation. This masculinization allows Jean Grey to further participate in mother-disidentification—Jean Grey is driven toward a masculine identity in order to teach young readers to disidentify with their own female influences. Focusing primarily on the adolescent years of the X-Men as they attend Professor X's School for Gifted Youngsters will reveal much on the view of masculine development in the United States and the role of mother (or lack thereof) within that development.

I have chosen these two data sets because of the age of the characters and the nature of the narratives. The first three years of the *Uncanny X-Men* and the recently released *X-Men: First Class* are in essence the same origin story—they depict the same adolescent mutants coming to grips with the same uncanny abilities that relegate them to the same fringes of the same society. The origin story is an often-deployed narrative arc within Marvel franchises that focuses on the complex past of individual characters. Origin stories often ask how and why a particular character turned out the way they eventually did. This is not dissimilar to the transitional period between adolescence and adulthood. What is adolescence if not the origin story of the adult a person has become? In addition to depicting the original members present in the *Uncanny X-Men*—Cyclops, Beast, Angel, Jean Grey, Iceman, and Professor Charles Xavier—*First Class* often references or revisits story arcs from the initial run in the 1960s. The editor of *First Class* says of the limited series, "With *X-Men: First Class* we have a chance to look at [creators] Stan Lee and Jack Kirby's creations with a fresh set of eyes, all within the continuity structure of Marvel's established universe."[4] This retrospective is not a direct remake of the original comic book series, nor is it a reboot like *The Amazing Spiderman*; it is an expansion of the origin story and an homage to its founding. In combination with the original series, *First Class* offers an exciting chance at comparative analysis.

Within academic circles, comic books have historically ranked below literature and film in terms of serious attention, but they have nonetheless found themselves a niche within cultural studies and literature programs alike. Starting in the 1970s, comic books found traction in college curriculums and publications due in part to a surging popularity among American readers and in part to a palpable relevance within the narratives.[5] With the emergence of the Silver Age of comic books in the 1960s came a "shift in comic-book content from oblique narrative metaphors for social problems toward direct representations of racism and sexism, urban blight, and political corruption."[6] With this new ideological identity came great ideological responsibility. The comic book industry in general, and those produced by Marvel in particular, "committed to the antiracist and antifascist ideals of democratic politics" and "used visual culture as a space for modeling new modes of radical critique that offered alternatives to direct-action politics and the discourse of civil liberties."[7] Thanks to Marvel's mass appeal, unparalleled financial success, and their long history of creative output, a large body of academic work now exists pertaining to its universe alone. And while much has been written on gender, race, body image, and xenophobia within that universe, too few articles tackle representations of motherhood within the genre—and there has been a complete absence of work that specifically explores the role of comic book mother figures and their influence on a child's transition from adolescence to adulthood. I am not arguing that comic books and their consumption change adolescent behavior—a topic too complex, too broad, and too debatable for this analysis—but central to this chapter is the idea that Marvel is cognizant of both popular opinion and scholarly conjecture that espouses that "comic-book constructs are part of childhood socialization."[8] I am arguing that Marvel is aware that their product may be influential in the lives of young boys and girls transitioning out of adolescence.

Marvel themselves directly alludes to this socialization process in the eleventh issue of *First Class*[9] when a group of adolescent teenagers (two boys, Marin and Doyle, and one girl, Kell) working together in a comic book store discover a shipment of comic book issues that foretell the future. In retelling their story to the X-Men, the teens explain that they "were now privy to the greatest secrets of the world and with that knowledge came great responsibility. We secretly intervened whenever threats to our own reality—our very continuity—would arise."[10] The trio tells the X-Men that they had retired because they had grown too comfortable with their powers and began negatively affecting events: "We were just unthinking teenagers, and the years were changing us. It became time to put away our special comics . . . and become men."[11] An echo of what mothers have undoubtedly told their sons in the non-diegetic world, this excerpt draws not only a connection between youths and comic books, but between child development and comic books. It is also important to note that Kell—like Jean Grey—is recognized as one of the boys. At first it appears that the teens had acquiesced to the idea that comic books are a barrier to manhood; that is, until they use their unique comic book knowledge to save the very fabric of space and time. Sacrificing themselves to oblivion in order to save their universe, Marin reveals that he never stopped reading comic books, despite his declarations of doing so.

Kell, in turn, expresses her love for Marin. In this final scene, comic books—and specifically the adolescent consumption of them—not only saves the universe but sparks a heteronormative union. It should be noted that Doyle also begins, but does not finish for the readers—because the tear in space and time closes—professing his love to Marin. With a palpable feeling of humor, this unfinished proclamation simultaneously reinforces heteronormativity and endows comic consumption with cross-orientation powers of attraction. In this issue Marvel directly supports the notion that comic books are not an impediment to manhood, but instead serve an integral function in the development process.

It is clear that Marvel and the *X-Men* are interested in the socialization of children, specifically the process of moving from boyhood to manhood, but how do mothers fit into the transitional narratives? Looking at the formative years of the X-Men reveals much about mothers and their role, or lack of one, in the development of the young mutants enrolled at Professor X's School for Gifted Youngsters. In a word, mothers are absent. In the first fifteen issues of *Uncanny X-Men*, mothers only make brief appearances four times[12] —two of which are flashbacks. The two appearances of a mother set in the diegetic present are fleeting, and their respective children are almost immediately called away by their patriarch Professor X.

In each of their four appearances mothers are framed as problematic, unreliable in terms of decision making, or ineffectual in the lives of their children because "in a genre obsessed with perpetuating a fantasy of hegemonic masculinity the options for maternal roles are clearly limited."[13] In the fifth issue of the *Uncanny X-Men*,[14] Jean Grey's parents visit her briefly at the school. In her six-panel appearance, Jean Grey's mother almost removes Cyclops' glasses—which restrain the volatile and dangerous energy beams that emanate from his eyes—in addition to accidentally trapping him inside the Danger Room, a room that creates very real, very dangerous combat scenarios. This almost kills him. In the twelfth issue of the *Uncanny X-Men*,[15] Professor X flashes back to the memory of his father's funeral where his mother Sharon, who appears in seven panels, seeks comfort from her husband's former colleague, Kurt Marko, a man the young Professor X does not trust. The longest of all appearances of a mother in the first fifteen issues, the three-page narrative describes Sharon's decision to marry Marko, their abusive marriage, the tenuous and often violent relationship between Professor X and his new stepbrother Cain Marko, Sharon's death, and finally Kurt's death. Sharon's decision to marry Kurt inextricably links Professor X to Cain, who becomes the Juggernaut, a powerful and lifelong adversary to the X-Men as a whole. In the fourteenth issue of the *Uncanny X-Men*, Angel visits his parents for two panels before being called away. Despite the extremely short appearance, Angel's mother is cast as unimportant and unaware. When Angel directs his gaze at his father—a very deliberate act in the pictorial form—and says he must leave, his mother stutters, "But, Warren—I—I don't understand . . . !"[16] She is then interrupted by her husband who offers his understanding to his son and assures him that he is now (seemingly after his time at Professor X's school) a man that can make his own decisions. Finally, in the fifteenth issue of the *Uncanny X-Men*,[17] Beast is forced to reveal his "innermost secrets,"[18] which consist of, in part, a two-panel appearance of his mother. This appearance is a flashback to when he was recruited by Professor X—his mother merely says that she is proud and supportive of her son. No subsequent appearance or mention of her is made.

These appearances of mothers in the *Uncanny X-Men* can hardly be called appearances. Together four mothers constitute seventeen panels in fifteen issues, making them nearly an invisible part of the series. And when mothers do appear they cause problems for their children, or in the case of Beast's mother and Angel's mother, they are predominantly ineffectual in the lives of their children. Not quite vilified, mothers in the *Uncanny X-Men* represent either impediments to the team's role as crime fighters or they represent nothing at all. It can be argued that one of the X-Men's longest-running nemeses within the franchise, Cain Marko/Juggernaut, is a product of Sharon's decision to marry Kurt. Jean Grey's mother is represented as a bumbling idiot who nearly gets herself and the X-Men team leader, Cyclops, killed. Alternatively, Angel's mother and Beast's mother are unimportant to the point of narrative superfluity, or in Angel's case easily dismissed by the men in her life.

While the appearance of mothers in the *Uncanny X-Men* is lacking, it would be a fair contestation that the time period of the first fifteen issues (1963–1965) is partly at fault. Although a valid point, it is not the sole reason for such representation. In the first two volumes of *First Class*,[19] there is actually a decrease in the presence of mothers. Three mothers appear in only eight panels over twenty-four issues, but their framing as either problem makers or seemingly invisible entities remains problematically intact. Two out of the three nearly invisible mothers are those of Jean Grey and Angel in the fourth and twelfth issues of *First Class*,[20] respectively. While Angel's parents make the longest appearance in the research set, Jean Grey's mother only appears in one panel with her back turned—an example of a mother who is literally faceless. Angel's parents arrive at the school to tell him that his favorite aunt has gone missing, at which point he vanishes from the grounds in order to find her—that is the last readers see of Angel's mother. The issue instead focuses on Angel's aunt. The last appearance of a mother is found in two panels of the tenth issue of *First Class*[21] with the introduction of a mentally unstable mutant adversary named Frederick. While Frederick is unconscious, Professor X probes his mind and discovers that his father was exposed to extreme amounts of radiation during his employment at a mine which led to his early death and that his mother was committed to a mental institution as a result of the loss. The unnamed mother's institutionalization and Frederick's subsequent plunge into his own mental instability are narratively linked in a single panel. The artwork itself is visually inseparable and alludes to continuity. The panel begins with the revelation that his mother has been committed, then moves to a doctor saying that he won't go anywhere near Frederick due to his mutation, and finally to Frederick squatting in the abandoned mine his father had once worked at. Frederick's fall from grace is inextricably tied, narratively and visually, to his mother and her failure to mentally cope with the passing of Frederick's father.

References to mothers, as opposed to appearances, although limited, are more frequent in *First Class*. In the issue in which Jean Grey's mother appears,[22] Iceman laments that he misses his parents but has no desire to go home: "You know where I'm from sir. I miss my folks but I don't miss the rednecks who hate anyone different."[23] Beast also mentions his parents in the same issue, but only in passing. After these brief mentions, Beast and Iceman go on a vacation/adventure by themselves without another mention of their mothers.

So why are mothers framed in such a way within the pages of the X-Men franchise? I think the answer lies, in part, with Iceman, Bobby Drake. Drake, in both *Uncanny X-Men* and *First Class*, is often referred to as the youngest member of the team, and his story arcs often have to do with him growing up and becoming more mature in order to meet the expectations of his teammates and his mentor/patriarch, Professor X. Part of this maturation process—a process the entire team is going through—is a figurative and literal separation from the mother. Alan Klein in "Comic Book Masculinity" writes that in the United States, "the movement through puberty often involves the following elements: social isolation, generational-same sex contact, pain, [and an] emphasis on conformity." Klein goes on to explain that "in male-dominant societies this often results in some sort of men's house or male-only place in which the initiates are traumatized, sequestered and instructed."[24] This description falls perfectly in line with Professor X's School for Gifted Youngsters, where primarily male students are isolated from society due to their mutant abilities, are traumatized and exposed to pain through combat, are forced to conform aesthetically through uniforms and mentally through discipline, and are instructed by the ultimate paternal figure in Professor X.

The team's isolation, however, is not just from the rest of society, but from their mothers, in what one scholar says is "the (lesser known) negative Oedipus complex," a Freudian theory that "involve[s] the little boy's desire to be like Mother, his primary love object—to nurture and bear children and then become Father's love object," but one that states that "if the boy was to become man, those desires must be renounced."[25] This theory was expanded on by Robert Stoller and Ralph Greenson in the 1960s in Greenson's article "Disidentifying from Mother":

> The disidentification hypothesis can be simply summarized as follows: "the male child, in order to attain a healthy sense of maleness, must replace the primary object of his identification, the mother, and must identify instead with the father." To become "man," the boy must make a complete break from mother and the "feminine"; only then is the stage set for the true transition to "maleness" to begin. [26]

Nowhere is this break more prominent within the research set than in the first issue of *First Class*. [27] The entire issue is narrated by Drake in a letter to his mother: "Dear Mrs. Drake, please wire your son Bobby more money so he can attend a field trip to Europe—Chuck Xavier. Ha! jk mom. I'm sorry I haven't written in a while—we stay pretty busy here at Xavier's School for Gifted Youngsters—so I'll make this a long one." [28] The letter continues as narration throughout the issue, concluding on the last page with Drake writing,

> Wow this turned out to be a long one for me! I guess I kind of lapsed into those "therapy journals" you used to make me write when I first realized I was a mutant. It still works—I got across some stuff I didn't know I was thinking. But just like Professor X is afraid of if we had e-mail, I'm letting too much information out. [29]

It is at this point that Drake uses his ability to freeze the letter to his mother and throw it out the window where it shatters and is gone. What at first appears to be an embrace of the mother turns out to be an extensive exercise in the youngest X-Man (with both figuratively and literally the furthest to go in his journey into manhood) separating from his mother. Although he identifies with her through fondly remembered past experiences, he verbally assents to psychological separation by acknowledging that he has let out too much information—information that can be read as identification with his mother. Drake also physically sets himself apart from the temptation to identify with his mother by literally smashing the physical manifestation of his connection to the maternal on the ground. By partaking in "the genre's overall dismissive attitude regarding the maternal," [30] Drake is clearly taking what are considered "necessary steps toward emotional autonomy, psychological separation, and most important here, securing the masculine self." [31] Drake does not make contact with his mother for the remainder of the two volumes. [32]

A subsequent example, which encompasses the entire team, links the mother-rejection and mother-as-problematic paradigms together. In the third issue of *First Class*, [33] the adolescent X-Men find themselves trapped in

Professor X's subconscious, and while his mother, Sharon, does not make an appearance, another female mother figure does: his childhood maid Ms. Lafitte. The very absence of Professor X's mother from his own subconscious is a rejection at the deepest level in its own right. And while it could be argued that Professor X does embrace a mother figure in Ms. Lafitte, she seems to serve a more important role for the young team that is trapped in his subconscious. She serves as a monstrous mother figure that the young X-Men are able to reject as "out of place."[34] The X-Men are initially unaware that what they are experiencing is a fabrication and so accept Ms. Lafitte as a part of their reality—she is cooking them breakfast. However, as the narrative progresses, the X-Men begin to understand that things are not as they seem and confront Ms. Lafitte (dialect and bold as intended by original publication):

Jean Grey: Why are you here?

Ms. Lafitte: Where else would I be? My job ees to feed Charles Xavier.

Hank McCoy (Beast): Yes . . . but you cooked for him when he was a boy. I remember now. He would tell us about the delicious meals you would make.

Ms. Lafitte: Merci m'sieur McCoy.

Hank McCoy (Beast): But that came up **last year**. He had been thinking about you . . . because . . . he . . . he attend . . . your . . . **funeral.**

Ms. Lafitte: Young man! Are you saying that I am **Dead?**

It is at this point that Ms. Lafitte turns into a living corpse and attacks the X-Men. This scene not only allows the X-Men another opportunity to reject a mother figure; it highlights "female bodies as unstable and uncontrollable agents of abjection."[35] Ms. Lafitte is quite literally an "example of femininity as both literally and figuratively monstrous."[36] She is, yet again, another example of the mother or mother figure posing a threat to normal psychological development and function. This only supports the notion that the female body, in the form of mother, is something that the X-Men must reject, be on guard against, and battle physically if necessary.

So then where does Jean Grey, as the only female member of the X-Men, fit into this boyhood-to-manhood paradigm? Based on the evidence, Jean Grey is just as invested/involved in the negative Oedipus complex as the rest of her team and potentially more. Jean Grey not only sees less of her mother in *First Class*, but she also rejects hegemonically feminine roles, traditionally maternal assignments, and an opportunity to establish more permanent ties with a new mother figure. Jean Grey participates in these rejections in order to participate in mother disidentification which in turn is intended to help her achieve manhood. Despite her biological assignment and aesthetic sexualization, she is "striving . . . for masculinity." She, like her male counterparts, partakes in a highly psychological and complex process of defeminization:

> For a boy attempting to achieve manhood, the need to separate from mother is crucial; working within his patriarchal society, he often resorts to sexist tactics to facilitate the separation: "A boy represses those qualities he takes to be feminine inside himself, and rejects and devalues women and whatever he considers to be feminine in the social world."[37]

And while there was a repression of feminine qualities by Jean Grey in the first fifteen issues of the *Uncanny X-Men*, there is a more forceful and vociferous rejection in the two volumes of *X-Men: First Class*.

While Jean Grey's character, in the first twenty-one issues of the *Uncanny X-Men*,[38] rejects some aspects of hegemonic femininity—emotional and physical fragility, passivity—she does participate in others, albeit infrequently. In the fourth, fifth, and thirteenth issues of the *Uncanny X-Men*,[39] Jean Grey is seen as a subordinate assistant/caregiver, either helping Professor X with medical procedures or nursing injured teammates back to health. However, in the thirteenth issue,[40] Jean simultaneously rejects and embraces the role of both mother and sex object as she, in a single panel, tends to her injured teammates:

Cyclops: We've never all been injured at the same time before!

Angel: Who cares? With a nurse like Jean, it's a pleasure!

Hank McCoy (Beast): My mother used to kiss me to expedite my recovery!

Iceman: That's for sure.

Jean Grey: I do not happen to be your mother, Mr. McCoy.

Despite Jean Grey's ambiguity in terms of rejection or acceptance, this panel frames her as having only two choices—Madonna or Whore. The remaining examples of Jean Grey's feminization—the sixth and seventh issues of the *Uncanny X-Men*[41]—fall into the Madonna category. Jean Grey, for the first and only time, is seen emerging from the kitchen to serve a meal[42] and subsequently chastises her teammates for their table manners. She also schools Beast in proper cultural etiquette when interacting with a woman.[43]

Jean Grey makes an almost complete break from hegemonically feminine roles and motherhood roles in *X-Men: First Class*. Only once does she seemingly embrace motherhood when she comforts a young Professor X in his own subconscious in the third issue of *First Class*.[44] And only once does she appear to partake in domesticity when she is chopping vegetables with Cyclops in the thirteenth issue of *First Class*[45]—it should be noted here that an angry Jean Grey seems to be wearing a gender-neutral apron while Cyclops' appears more feminine. Both the anger and the gender-neutral apron can be read as a rejection of the seemingly domestic act of preparing a meal. This kitchen scene also happens to be the site of Jean Grey's most direct rejection of motherhood when the X-Men have been asked to mentor a sentient android (Aaron) developed by a friend of Professor X. Jean Grey rejects Aaron's presence and her role in the mentoring process: "He's not an X-Man! He's a science project, and I don't feel like showing Pinocchio how to be a real boy!"[46] While the Jean Grey in the 1960s may have been more likely to take Aaron under her wing, the Jean Grey of the 2000s rejects his presence and her culturally constructed, and expected, role as mother entirely.

The connection between rejecting the mother and masculine development continues when Sue Storm of the Fantastic Four appears at Professor X's behest in the eleventh issue of *First Class*.[47] She is asked to mentor Jean Grey who had recently encountered a roadblock in the development of her abilities. And while she and Sue Storm fight crime, the rest of the X-Men begin to worry that she will choose to leave them for the Fantastic Four—this can be read as trepidation over whether she will embrace or reject this new mother figure. At the end of the issue, however, Jean Grey informs the X-Men that she never had any intention of joining the Fantastic Four and returns home with her team. This issue is especially enlightening because it directly explores Jean Grey's development as an X-Man, connects it to a mother figure, and ultimately rejects said mother figure.

It appears that Jean Grey's rejection of the hegemonic trappings of femininity serves to increase her association with the negative Oedipus complex. Her participation is twofold: on the one hand, she is accepted more readily by her teammates who are also participating in the complex, and on the other hand, her masculinization—her voyage from boyhood to manhood—repudiates any "threats of emasculation that would undermine the masculine fantasy on offer" within the pages of the X-Men.[48] So then, by having Jean Grey trek the same path as her male counterparts, readers are offered a single choice when it comes to adolescent development: reject mom and the feminine and you too will be a man, an X-Man.

The almost complete absence of mother figures, and their negative framing when they do appear, is ultimately linked to the masculine journey from boyhood to manhood and is directly and indirectly referenced in the *Uncanny X-Men* and *First Class*. This link, and its subsequent references, are illustrations of the negative Oedipus complex, which theorizes that a boy must reject his mother and all things feminine in order to reach masculine adulthood. It appears that Marvel and the X-Men franchise is reinforcing this process of mother disidentification, despite the theory's checkered past.[49] Even if the theory is scientifically disputed, there is no question that these comic books are espousing that childhood separation from the mother is at the very least beneficial to his or her adjustment into adulthood. This process as a male-only socialization is called into question with the addition of Jean Grey. Jean Grey's participation in mother disidentification is evidence of the universality and social/cultural construction of masculinity and its attainment. Masculinity is not a biological inevitability but a socialization process that can equally apply to boys and girls. *Uncanny X-Men* and *First Class*, then, is not a reflection of masculinity but a roadmap to obtaining it in its dominant hegemonic form.

NOTES

1. Stan Lee and Jack Kirby, *Marvel Masterworks Presents the X-Men: Reprinting the X-Men, Nos. 1–10* (New York: Marvel Comics, 1994); Stan Lee et al., *Marvel Masterworks Presents the X-Men, Reprinting the X-Men, Nos. 11–21* (New York: Marvel Comics, 1988).

2. Jeff Parker et al., *X-Men: First Class—Tomorrow's Brightest* (New York: Marvel, 2007); Jeff Parker and Nick Dragotta, *X-Men: First Class—The Wonder Years* (New York: Marvel Enterprises, 2009).

3. Jeffrey A. Brown, "Supermoms? Maternity and the Monstrous-Feminine in Superhero Comics," *Journal of Graphic Novels and Comics* 2, no. 1 (2011): 77.

4. Parker et al., *Tomorrow's Brightest*, no. 1.

5. Ramzi Fawaz, "'Where No X-Man Has Gone Before!' Mutant Superheroes and the Cultural Politics of Popular Fantasy in Postwar America," *American Literature* 83, no. 2 (2011): 356.

6. Ibid.

7. Ibid., 356–57.

8. Alan Klein, "Comic Book Masculinity," *Sport in Society* 10, no. 6 (2007): 1101.

9. Parker and Dragotta, *The Wonder Years*.

10. Ibid., no. 11.

11. Ibid.

12. Lee and Kirby, *Marvel Masterworks Presents the X-Men: Reprinting the X-Men, Nos. 1–10*, no. 1; Lee et al., *Marvel Masterworks Presents the X-Men: Reprinting the X-Men, Nos. 11–21*, nos. 12, 14, 15.

13. Brown, "Supermoms?," 81.

14. Lee and Kirby, *Marvel Masterworks Presents the X-Men: Reprinting the X-Men, Nos. 1–10*, no. 5.

15. Ibid., no. 12.

16. Lee et al., *Marvel Masterworks Presents the X-Men: Reprinting the X-Men, Nos. 11–21*, no. 14.

17. Lee and Kirby, *Marvel Masterworks Presents the X-men: Reprinting the X-Men, Nos. 1–10*, no. 15.

18. Lee et al., *Marvel Masterworks Presents the X-Men, Reprinting the X-Men, Nos. 11–21*, no. 15.

19. Parker et al., *Tomorrow's Brightest*, no. 4; Parker and Dragotta, *The Wonder Years*, no. 11.

20. Ibid., no. 12.

21. Parker and Dragotta, *The Wonder Years*, no. 10.

22. Parker et al., *Tomorrow's Brightest*, no. 4.
23. Ibid.
24. Klein, "Comic Book Masculinity," 1078.
25. Clifton Edward Watkins, "The Evolving Psychoanalytic Vision of Boyhood(s) and Masculinity(ies)," *Thymos: Journal of Boyhood Studies* 5, no. 2 (2011): 176.
26. Ibid., 178.
27. Parker et al., *Tomorrow's Brightest*, no. 1.
28. Ibid.
29. Ibid.
30. Brown, "Supermoms?," 77.
31. C. Blazina, "Gender Role Conflict and the Disidentification Process: Two Case Studies on Fragile Masculine Self," *Journal of Men's Studies* 12, no. 2 (2004): 151.
32. Parker et al., *Tomorrow's Brightest*, no. 4; Parker and Dragotta, *The Wonder Years*, no. 11.
33. Parker et al., *Tomorrow's Brightest*, no. 3.
34. Ibid.
35. Brown, "Supermoms?," 77.
36. Ibid., 78.
37. Klein, "Comic Book Masculinity," 1076.
38. Lee and Kirby, *Marvel Masterworks Presents the X-Men: Reprinting the X-Men, nos. 1–10*, no. 1; Lee et al., *Marvel Masterworks Presents the X-Men, Reprinting the X-Men, nos. 11–21*, nos. 12, 14, 15.
39. Lee and Kirby, *Marvel Masterworks Presents the X-Men: Reprinting the X-Men, Nos. 1–10*, nos. 4, 5; Lee et al., *Marvel Masterworks Presents the X-Men, Reprinting the X-Men, Nos. 11–21*, no. 13.
40. Lee et al., *Marvel Masterworks Presents the X-Men, Reprinting the X-Men, Nos. 11–21*, no. 13.
41. Lee and Kirby, *Marvel Masterworks Presents the X-Men: Reprinting the X-Men, Nos. 1–10*, nos. 6, 7.
42. Ibid., no. 6.
43. Ibid., nos. 6, 7.
44. Parker et al., *Tomorrow's Brightest*, no. 3.
45. Parker and Dragotta, *The Wonder Years*, no. 13.
46. Ibid.
47. Ibid., no. 11.
48. Brown, "Supermoms?," 78.
49. Watkins, "The Evolving Psychoanalytic Vision of Boyhood(s)," 181.

Chapter Ten

Negotiating Life Spaces

How Marriage Marginalized Storm

Anita McDaniel

Refuse, then—crawl back into your cave. Flee from duty and responsibility. It is easily done. A path you have already walked. But if I truly craved that oblivion . . . I would have let Wolverine kill me in the cave. Or will myself to death as MjNari did on this hilltop. I have found my home—it is the whole of the world—and with it, the reason for my being! —Storm[1]

"It's the wedding of the year for comic book fans," claimed the *Houston Chronicle*.[2] Storm (mutant weather goddess and co-leader of the X-Men) and the Black Panther (former Avenger and current king of Wakanda, the wealthiest and most technologically advanced African nation in the world) tied the knot in *Black Panther* #18. Two high-profile writers, Eric Jerome Dickey (popular black romance novelist) and Reginald Hudlin (program director for Black Entertainment Television and screenplay writer), were brought on board to pen the background story of the love affair in *Storm* #1–6 and the nuptials in *Black Panther* #14–18, respectively. During a Marvel teleconference, Dickey and Hudlin regarded writing the early courtship and marriage of the couple as an opportunity to reveal another side of these characters—a side that would attract new readers.[3] Paul O'Brien, Ninth Art columnist, regarded the whole affair as a dubiously conceived publicity stunt to attract black readers.[4]

Six years later, the union of Marvel Comics' only black god couple ends. Absent the tradition and grandeur of their wedding, T'Challa informs Ororo that their marriage has been annulled.[5] The strangeness of the breakup was matched only by the coldness of the announcement. Close followers of the narrative speculated that the king had to divorce his wife due to her ties to the person who destroyed Wakanda.[6] Followers of the industry's buzz said the divorce was necessary to resolve casting issues for a Black Panther movie.[7] When asked about the divorce in an interview, Marvel editor Tom Brevoort simply stated, "To be honest, I don't know that we handled Storm and the Panther as a married couple as well as we could have consistently."[8]

Prior to the wedding and after the divorce, fans had mixed feelings about this union in particular and the idea of a "black comic book" in general.[9] Some fans agreed with O'Brien. They felt that the wedding was a publicity stunt—a convenient way to increase the sales of *Black Panther* by pandering to black readers. Others agreed with Hudlin and Dickey. These readers viewed the union as an opportunity to showcase "blackness" in this popular medium. Online conversations following the divorce speculated about the impact that this event would have on Storm and readers' perceptions of the industry. Many readers felt that Storm was better off without Black Panther "weighing her down," while other fans interpreted Brevoort's excuse as subtle racism that set this union up for failure.[10] A common thread in fan reactions to the marriage and divorce was the importance of race to the average reader's appreciation and acceptance of a superhero.

Marvel Comics' use of "blackness" to attract readers deserves some praise as well as some criticism. The decision to feature black characters like Storm and Panther in multiple one-shot story arcs and their own titles where their "blackness" had been incorporated into the narratives is noteworthy. However, yoking their high-profile black characters with traits like Eurocentric blue eyes and long, flowing hair and a Tarzan-like leadership style leads one to question Marvel's motives. According to van Dyk,

> Words and images never operate within a vacuum; they have an impact and effect on those exposed to them. . . . Marvel's representations of [blackness] are commodifications exactly because they have either perpetuated black stereotypes or ignored black culture completely.[11]

I would argue that all black characters are not created equally in the Marvel Universe. From the perspective of black comic book readers, it may or may not be a matter of responding to or identifying with an authentic versus stereotypic presentation of a black character. But, from the perspective of comic readers in general, I would assert that it is a matter of experiencing the adventures of a black *superhero* rather than the exploits of a black *character* that attracts and maintains the interest of a comic book audience.

SUPERHERO TEXTS AND SPATIATION

Storm and Black Panther are a combination of written and visual texts that establish their importance/relevance as superheroes in the Marvel Universe.

According to Fingeroth, a superhero is fundamentally someone who represents the values of the society that produces him/her and someone who possesses skills and abilities that normal humans do not.[12] Rhetorically, the visual representation of a superhero is associated with his/her identity—what he/she represents in the comic book reality in which he/she exists. This identity is a construction of the character's social demographics (i.e., race, gender, and economic status), physical attributes (i.e., attractiveness and body type), and private/secret and public personas such that when readers see any rendering of the character, the idea of "superhero" registers.

Central to a reader's visual understanding of a superhero is the costume/tights—the superhero "uniform." The costume is designed to define the character's purpose and affiliation. Panther's costume is primarily ceremonial—it establishes his link to the panther god and legitimizes his claim to the throne of Wakanda. Storm's costume, however, identifies her as a member of the X-Men, a mutant superhero team. The costumes are important because they highlight the superhero identity elements that are valued by the reader. For example, a costume that exposes a lot of skin draws the reader's attention toward less-valued, human elements such as race, gender, and physical attractiveness, whereas a costume that covers the body and hides the identity draws the reader's attention toward the more valued, superhero elements such as strength and the ability to perform heroic acts.

The superhero's narratives describe the character's special abilities and skills beyond those of normal human beings in tales of his/her origins and subsequent heroic acts. These narratives contextualize the superhero's visual representations by establishing and justifying the character's motivations behind his/her appearance and actions. The Black Panther uses Batman-like agility, intelligence, and gadgetry to rule and protect those within and connected to the Wakandan realm. Storm uses her weather-controlling abilities to protect mutant and humankind from the prejudices and other evil forces that would harm both groups. Although a character's narratives should make room for growth and development, they are not supposed to change the character into something he/she was not intended to be.[13] That is, a writer could make a character lose his/her powers or commit immoral acts in order to help the reader understand some of the more human qualities of that superhero or gain an appreciation for that superhero's inner strength, but a writer cannot make those changes permanent. A superhero is perceived as a superhero because he/she deals with morality and conflict on a grander scale. Routine hardships and crises of faith are part of the human experience; they are issues to be overcome, not endured, by a superhero. A comic book reader is not interested in soap opera drama; he/she wants to read about superpowers used to address drama on an epic scale.

Storm is an important black female character in the Marvel Universe because she has been drawn and written to be important. Few black or female characters (not to mention black *and* female characters) have achieved her status as a superhero. Traditionally, female and other minority characters have been marginalized in comic books. Female characters have been hindered visually due to too much emphasis on their physical beauty and form (i.e., skimpy costumes, exaggerated features, and suggestive poses) such that their heroic narratives become irrelevant or nonexistent. Black characters (and other racial minorities) sometimes suffer from the incongruence between origin narratives that place too much emphasis on their cultural uniqueness and heroic texts that do not justify the need for cultural variation. That is, black characters become distanced from the average comic book reader because he/she can neither connect with the "otherness" of a racially specific origin story nor understand why writers continue to include race (i.e., use of language or references to cultural belief systems and traditions) in story lines that do not necessitate diversity.

Storm is a successful, black, female character because her narratives and visual representations work together to meet her readers' expectations about what and who a superhero is. Unlike other black and female characters, her cultural heritage and gender have been incorporated seamlessly into her narratives. She is not a marginalized character; she has not been written or drawn in a way that assigns her to a supporting cast member role. Storm has been drawn and written to claim a center-stage space among other important superheroes in the Marvel Universe.

When I talk about "claimed space," I am referring to uninterrogated space—a situation in which one does not have to give, take, and/or exchange some aspect of his/her identity in order to gain or maintain his/her status in his/her social environment.[14] "Assigned space," on the other hand, is a situation in which one must accept a designated status because only certain aspects of his/her identity have value in his/her social environment. According to Jackson,

> Spatialization is a metaphorical construct that reminds us that social beings occupy certain life spaces. . . . At times we may choose to abandon or disengage ourselves from those ontological and geopolitical locations, but these terrains are still observed as socially constructed residences. Although the space may have been temporarily vacated, the social expectation presupposes these spaces are where we live. Naturally, this social and political assignment of spatialization has slippage in that it fails to account for both those who do not intend to return to their "assigned homes" once they have left, and those who never lived in these spaces.[15]

Never has Storm lived in an "assigned home." Over time, she has been visually and narratively represented in countless ways that have showcased her physical beauty, her African roots, her human frailties and strengths, and her mastery of her mutant powers. Yet these qualities *combined* have led to her assuming a leadership role among the X-Men and her acceptance as a superhero among her readers. I believe that has occurred because she has been single. As a single woman, Storm has been allowed to focus on her superhero "career" and demonstrate how her connection to her African roots enhances her ability to lead and use her mutant powers. As a married woman, particularly as queen of Wakanda, Storm had to give up her superhero status in the X-Universe that was recognizable to her readers for a second-in-command position in Wakanda—an environment that may have been unfamiliar culturally to many readers. Now, the natural assumption to make is that her black readers did not mind this cultural shift. As indicated by some of the earlier-mentioned wedding bloggers, black readers implied that they might embrace it as a move toward more authentic representations of black characters. I do not think so. Storm is important to black readers because she is a strong, black, female *superhero*, not just because she is a strong, *black woman*. Married, Storm lost significance on the Marvel landscape because her status as a superhero had to take a backseat to her strength as a black woman.

The purpose of this chapter is to discuss my view of the narratives and visual representations of Storm in *Uncanny X-Men* and various *Black Panther* titles. Specifically, I want to examine the rhetorical space that Marvel's writers have allowed her to "claim" as a single, black woman and compare it to the rhetorical space that Hudlin "assigned" her to as Panther's wife. The ideas presented in this chapter are not meant to suggest that women have to focus on their careers to be relevant or that being a wife and/or mother is unimportant. This is not about determining whether Storm is happier or feels more fulfilled as a single or married woman. I am suggesting that a black woman who no longer functions as a superhero in a superhero comic book drastically loses status in the eyes of her readers—black and white. I feel that the marriage between Storm and Black Panther rhetorically negated her critical superhero identity qualities and thereby devalued the important space that she claimed in the Marvel Universe.

STORM AS A SINGLE BLACK SUPERHERO

As a single woman, Storm claims space in the foreground because she is recognized primarily as someone who has mutant powers and someone who is a superhero. Even though Storm began as the physically alluring, female member of the new International X-Men,[16] she has developed considerably as a visual and written text. Over the years, she has moved away from a character who was defined primarily by her beauty (and gender, by extension) and cultural "otherness" toward a character who is respected primarily for her mastery of her powers and her desire to use them to preserve life. According to Housel,

> [Storm] has a perfect face and body. Of course, there is a rich tradition in superhero comics of women apparently introduced just because of their exaggerated physical beauty, but Storm isn't on the scene for her physique or face. And she is not the center of a traditional, patriarchal heterosexual matrix—the classic male-female relationship. She is her own person, and brings considerable substance to the X-Men. [17]

Part of the substance that Storm brings to the X-Men is reflected in her costume choices. As noted earlier, a superhero's costume defines his/her purpose and affiliation. Storm has undergone numerous costume changes, alternately signifying her individual personality and group membership. [18] Of these different "looks," the costume that consisted of Storm shaving off her hair into a Mohawk and donning a 1980s punk rock outfit may be most salient rhetorically when discussing her ascendency in superhero status. Storm adopted this look to symbolize her need to reclaim her spiritual self as a woman—to reconnect with her emotions and how they influence her ability to control her powers. [19] Thus the Mohawk and black leather clad Storm was a manifestation of her need to be "wild." "'Wild' is the metaphoric expression of that inner will to rebel, to move against the grain, to be out of one's place." [20] "Wild" Storm was allowed to claim space beyond the place of most women and minorities in comic books. The fact that *Uncanny X-Force* writer Sam Humphries lobbied hard for the return of the "wild"/Mohawk look immediately after the divorce speaks to its rhetorical significance in Storm's single life. [21]

Originally, Storm adopted the "wild"/Mohawk look when she made the shift from follower to leader. It was during this time that her character was allowed to assume leadership of the X-Men from Cyclops in spite of the fact that she had lost her powers. Cyclops' claim to leadership was in jeopardy because his loyalties were divided between his responsibilities as a husband and new father and his responsibilities to the X-Men. Storm may have felt a need to prove herself as an X-Man after accepting the fact that her mutant powers possibly were gone forever. During a pivotal narrative in *Uncanny X-Men* #201, Storm challenged Cyclops to a duel in the Danger Room. [22] There, she bested him using "human" cunning and physical strength. No longer would readers see Storm as merely a beautiful black woman whose behaviors were directed by others. Comic fans would see her as someone who pushed herself beyond the physical limitations and psychological crises of faith of the average human being to become the leader of a mutant superhero team.

Later narratives further explicated Storm's unique contributions as a superhero. With her powers restored, readers got to experience Storm's decision making as the X-Men faced new challenges and their roster changed.

Due to unmanageable numbers, the X-Men broke into teams such as X-Factor, X-Force, and the Blue and Gold teams. As Storm became leader of the Gold team and Cyclops led the Blue team, readers began to see differences in their leadership styles as well as how team members functioned under their direction. Although equally committed to Xavier's dream of peaceful coexistence between humans and mutants, Cyclops led in a way that adhered strictly to the letter of that dream, whereas Storm was more inclined to apply a more personalized (i.e., cultural and gender-based) sense of right and wrong to achieving the same goal. That is, Cyclops seemed to follow a masculine ethic (a rules-based approach to decision making), whereas Storm seemed to follow a feminine ethic (a care-based approach that is based on a strong belief in individual rights, equality, and the common good). [23]

> [Storm] is not bound to one conception of ethics over another. She seems clearly to understand that different situations require different ways of thinking. Ethical action may be based on an abstract sense of justice and corresponding duty, or it can arise out of proper emotion. In her understanding of this, she functions outside of typical gender expectations, both in terms of mythology and moral psychology. Storm is perhaps the perfect hero. She has mental and physical toughness, beauty, and a nurturing feminine side, as well as a focused rational side. [24]

In short, Storm's gender and cultural connection to the natural world were integral to her heroic narratives because they made her a more complex decision maker and a more complete leader/superhero to her readers.

Her first encounter with the Phalanx is an appropriate illustration of this seamless integration of culture, gender, and epic heroism. In *Uncanny X-Men* #312, Storm led Gambit (a member of the Blue team) and Yukio (a member of Xavier's Underground) in a battle against the Phalanx (a techno-organic entity designed to eliminate genetic anomalies). [25] Throughout this encounter, Storm creatively used force (and encouraged her teammates to do the same) equal to the threat of the Phalanx and expected by her readers. She used lightning bolts to drag the construct through an electrified billboard and to destroy the ground where it stood, produced gale force winds to keep the construct from reforming, and dropped the temperature of the construct in a concentrated area to separate the techno from the organic. However, the narrative also explicitly and repeatedly referenced her nurturing concern for the safety of her teammates and the civilians in the area (a feminine quality) and her belief in a higher power that connects all life—the Bright Lady (a cultural element)—and would come to her aid.

There was a lot of conversation between Storm and the Phalanx that established a context for the excessive force used during the battle. The reader learned that the Phalanx was a collection of individuals fighting specific threats to humanity's claim to a life space much like the X-Men who fight threats to mutantkind's claim to a life space. Readers could tell that Storm recognized the similarity as well. At the close of the altercation, it was not surprising that Storm said, "How long will it be until we are forced to accept that this lifeform might lay claim to their own place in this world? . . . Will it cost us our souls to ultimately defeat them?"[26] Storm's concern about the X-Men's response to the Phalanx made sense because her gender and racial elements led her to think beyond some "abstract sense of justice and corresponding duty." As one who can control the weather and related elemental forces of the Bright Lady, Storm is connected to her superhero activities on a more natural, primal, and/or instinctual level. Thus, in her narratives, she draws on her maternal concern for her allies and enemies and the way that she embraces the natural world to guide her decision making.

Additionally, Storm's comment metaphorically erased the "otherness" that can be created by gender and race. That is, it may not be necessary to separate individuals into "us" and "them" categories based on some arbitrary determination of who has a greater claim to a center-stage life space. She is black, but that does not diminish the role she plays as a superhero. She is a woman, but that does not necessitate that her heroic acts take a backseat to the heroic deeds of male superheroes. Her race and gender identify her as an "Other," but they do not hinder her readers' understanding of her as a superhero. Her race and gender *enhance* her readers' acceptance of her as a superhero. Rhetorically, Storm is more than just another single, black, female comic book character. Single, she is a superhero icon in the Marvel Universe because her narratives and visual representations allow her to claim superhero icon status.

STORM AS A MARRIED BLACK WOMAN

As a married woman, Storm was assigned background space because she functioned primarily as a complement to her new husband, King T'Challa. Instead of being known for her mutant powers and superhero exploits, she was known as the black female lead character in *Black Panther*. For Storm, marriage meant giving up her superhero career—the specific element that allowed her to claim space in the Marvel Universe. Sure, she got to become Queen Ororo of Wakanda, but that is not a superhero position; thus she had no claim to important space in a superhero comic book. Being king of Wakanda is central to a reader's understanding of who T'Challa is as a superhero. Such is not the case for Storm. She is a superhero and a weather goddess without the title of "queen." As a result, it was necessary to marginalize Storm's superhero status (or eliminate it completely) while married because she could not "out superhero" Panther in his book.

Rhetorically, it was important that Storm from *Uncanny X-Men* became known as Queen Ororo in *Black Panther* because it signified a shift from "claimed" space to "assigned" space—a shift from being known as someone who maintained a *lead* character position in *her* book toward being known as a *supporting* character in *her husband's* book. According to bell hooks,

> more than ever before in our history, black women who enter the work force are encouraged to feel that they are taking jobs from black men or de-masculinizing them. For fear of undermining the self-confidence of black men, many young college-educated black women repress their own career aspirations. While black women are often forced by circumstances to act in assertive ways, most black women . . . believed men were superior to women and that a degree of submission to male authority was a necessary part of woman's role. [27]

Single, Storm's narratives cast her as a leader of a superhero team that represents what is best in mutantkind. Married, she was written to be not much more than *Panther's* wife in *Panther's* country. Single, readers were allowed to explore her persona as "a weather goddess" in self-titled projects and solo story arcs. Married, readers were limited to "Ororo Munroe coping with her new life and her new husband in a new country" stories in *Panther's* book. If *Black Panther* had been renamed *Panther and Storm* after the wedding, readers would have been assured that her high-profile status as a mutant and a superhero would have been maintained in *their* title. However, in *Black Panther*, her role was reduced to Ororo following T'Challa around helping *him* do *his* work on behalf of *his* people in order to maintain *his* superhero status.

There is ample evidence illustrating how Storm was marginalized in *Black Panther*. Engagement and postmarriage representations of her as a visual and written text placed more emphasis on feminine qualities that marked her as inferior rather than her superhero abilities that maintained her importance. Throughout the first Hudlin relaunch of the title, Storm was dressed in her X-Men uniform—the tiara and caped, full-body unitard uniform that is reminiscent of the classically styled superhero outfits of her teammates. [28] Rhetorically, this should have reminded the reader of her superhero status and position among the X-Men. However, the narratives in *Black Panther* #16 repeatedly subjected her to the male gaze. [29] In the beginning of the issue, there was a lengthy discussion about her suitability as queen of Wakanda among the country's citizens. Objections that were raised because she was an outsider or because the courtship was too brief were quickly dismissed with comments like, "But she is beautiful," as if her physical appearance was the only important criterion to rule beside King T'Challa. When her teammates learned of the nuptials, Cyclops was the only male to lament the loss of "one of our best team leaders." The other males simply referred to her decision to marry as another lost dating opportunity. In the end, the reader may have wanted to continue "seeing" Storm as a superhero, but the narratives contradicted that view.

Additionally, in Panther's title, all of Storm's acts of heroism were minimized. She had the potential to be an excellent superhero partner to Panther. The weather goddess and the panther god, a black couple protecting everyone in their sphere of influence—what a concept! Yet it was a disappointment to see no development in Storm's use of her powers as a married woman. After the wedding, the title's narratives regularly featured T'Challa using new forms of Wakandan technology (i.e., full-body light armor) and *Matrix*-like fighting skills.[30] But Storm was featured doing nothing more than summoning lightning bolts and gusts of wind. The few narratives in which she used her powers creatively (i.e., creating a weather vortex that could slingshot an aircraft from one side of the world to another)[31] were in various X-titles.

While it is obvious that Ororo played a more submissive role relative to T'Challa to make him more superhero-like to readers, Marvel occasionally erased her from the superhero landscape entirely to promote the Black Panther as the hero in his book. There have been three relaunches of *Black Panther* since the wedding—*Black Panther: Dark Reign*, *Black Panther: The Man without Fear*, and *Black Panther: The Most Dangerous Man Alive*. Storm's costume was changed in *Dark Reign* and thereafter. Artists abandoned her "claimed space" superhero unitard and adopted the typical uniform of the marginalized female character—a one-piece bathing suit and thigh-high boots. In *Black Panther: Dark Reign* #6, when she made the supreme sacrifice for her new husband and country—literally giving up her life in exchange for his life[32] —Storm was not in any uniform: finally, a *Black Panther* narrative where Storm was written to be the hero, and the artist dressed her in a string bikini and gossamer robes. Ultimately, the couple was saved from Death as a result of a plan devised by T'Challa's sister, Shuri—the newest incarnation of the Black Panther. Because she was not in uniform, Storm could not claim superhero space in the narrative. Because she did not look like a superhero, Storm's actions could not be interpreted as anything more than a loving wife trying to help her husband and his family. In the end, Storm and her act of heroism were rendered meaningless because the superhero symbol of the panther god remained the star.

Hudlin wrote T'Challa to be a proud black man—someone who exudes a "coolness" that is heavily laced with arrogance. While some readers may view Panther's "coolness" as a quality that makes it difficult for them to relate to him in general, black readers are more likely to see his "coolness" as something that validates his claim to the throne of Wakanda and enhances his appeal as a superhero.

As an ancient and indigenous part of black culture, the idea of cool bears a spiritual meaning: sense of control, symmetry, correct presentation of self, and sophistication. Coolness is a part of character—"ashe." To exhibit grace under pressure is akin to exuding a royal demeanor. A noble confidence and mystic coolness of character, "ashe" reveals an inner spirituality and peace that marks the strongest of men. [33]

T'Challa's "ashe" keeps him cool in a crisis, always in charge of all of the pieces on the chessboard. But, as the master strategist, Panther closely guards his thoughts and controls his emotions such that he keeps most people at arm's length. Unfortunately, the king's "ashe" was used to distance T'Challa from his wife and, consequently, her fans from his book.

Even though Wakanda was created to be a technologically advanced society, the royal husband-and-wife dynamic was medieval. Marvel writers saddled T'Challa with language that bespoke confidence and superiority when communicating with equals and subordinates. This behavior was somewhat charming when he spoke about his wife ("You hurt my wife and I'll hunt your entire race to extinction"), [34] but off-putting when he spoke to her ("This is a conflict between Von Doom and myself. Do not interfere."). [35] In response, Storm was deferential more often than defiant. The late Dwane Duffie felt that Ororo's presence grounded T'Challa, kept him in touch with his humanity, and made him more accessible to readers. [36] That is, she helped him transcend his "cool pose." However, in doing so, Storm ceased to be the progressive superhero leader fans knew her to be. She became the damsel in distress in *Doomwar*. [37] She became the wife ordered to stay out of her husband's business in *Black Panther: The Man without Fear*. [38] She became the mutant outsider summarily dismissed from her role as wife and queen. T'Challa's "ashe" is central to his superhero narratives, specifically when those narratives involve the king being in control of something or someone. Rewriting Storm as someone the king controls rhetorically changed her superhero footprint. Storm never may have lived in the assigned place of supportive female character, but in the pages of *Black Panther*, it is obvious that space was her new home.

CONCLUSION

In *X-Men: Worlds Apart* #1, Cyclops asked Storm, "Are you an X-Man or a queen? I know how Storm would have answered. I'm not sure how the Black Panther's wife will." [39] As a single superhero, Storm claimed space. That is, her gender and race were not considered hindrances to her superhero status. "Being wild," spiritually Afrocentric, and nurturing allowed Storm to deal with morality and conflict on an epic scale in ways that were relatable to her audiences. As a woman married to King T'Challa, Ororo was assigned the role of helper/obedient follower. She was limited to routine hardships and soap opera dramas that were part of the human experience. The narratives that emphasized her physical beauty and willingness to defer to her husband forced her into a cultural box that readers neither appreciated nor could understand. Just prior to the wedding, Charles Xavier told Storm that being T'Challa's wife trumped *everything* that she had done in her single life.[40] For Storm, married life should have been a respite from her superhero duties, not a substitute for them.

I have mixed emotions about the portrayals of Storm in *Black Panther*. I liked the tender moments shared between the couple—her kindness and deference brought out similar human qualities in him. But I was not satisfied reading narratives of Storm doling out the occasional lightning bolt or windstorm at the behest of her husband. Storm claimed space as a powerful, decisive, and moral leader; it was hard accepting her as a submissive follower who knew her "assigned" place. The writers, artists, and editors of the *Black Panther* series are responsible for the poor handling of these characters and their lack of readers. And Hudlin, in particular, squandered the opportunity to feature Storm as part of a strong, black *husband-and-wife* superhero team by displacing her in order to claim space for Panther. The continued success of Storm as a black, female character depends on her readers' perceptions of her as an iconic superhero. Being married challenged those perceptions, and being married to T'Challa almost erased her from the Marvel landscape completely.

NOTES

1. Chris Claremont, Barry Windsor-Smith, and Tom Orzechowski, "Lifedeath II," *Uncanny X-Men*, no. 198 (October 1985): 32.

2. Lara Berkowitz, "For Storm and Black Panther, It's My Big Fat Superhero Wedding," *Houston Chronicle Online*, February 22, 2006, http://www.chron.com/disp/story.mpl/life/3675702.html.

3. Jennifer Contino, "Black Panther/Storm Wedding Conference," *PULSE News* Forum at Comicon.com, May 26, 2006, http://www.comicon.com/cgi-bin/ultimatebb.cgi?ubb=get_topic;f=36;t=004700.

4. Paul O'Brien, "Article 10: Nice Day for a Black Wedding," *Ninth Art*, January 30, 2006, http://ninthart.com.

5. Jason Aaron, Brian Michael Bendis, Ed Brubaker, Matt Fraction, Jonathan Hickman, and Adam Kubert, *A vs. X*, no. 9 (October 2012).

6. Jim Smith, "Panther/Storm/Foresight Is My OT3," *Mightygodking Dot Com*, August 3, 2012, http://mightygodking.com/2012/08/03/black-pantherstormforesight-is-my-ot3.

7. Steve Morris, "Spoiler: Black Panther's Decision in Avengers vs. X-men 9," *The Beat: The News Blog of Comics Culture*, August 1, 2012, http://comicsbeat.com/spoiler-black-panthers-decision-in-avengers-vs-x-men-9.

8. Albert Ching, "Avengers vs. X-Men Post Game, Week 19: 'TilAvX Do Us Part,'" Newsarama.com, August 3, 2012, http://www.newsarama.com/9964-avengers-vs-x-men-post-game-week-19-til-avx-do-us-part.html.

9. Rich Watson, "What's a Nubian? Special Edition: Coming to Wakanda," *Pop Culture Shock*, January 26, 2006, http://www.popcultureshock.com/features.php?id=1277.

10. Steve Morris, "Spoiler."

11. Michael van Dyk, "What's Going On? Black Identity in the Marvel Age," *International Journal of Comic Art* 8, no. 1 (2006): 468.

12. Danny Fingeroth, *Superman on the Couch: What Superheroes Really Tell Us about Ourselves and Our Society* (New York: Continuum, 2004), 17.

13. Ibid., 468.

14. Ronald L. Jackson, "White Space, White Privilege: Mapping Discursive Inquiry into the Self," *Quarterly Journal of Speech* 85 (1999): 47–48.

15. Ibid., 38.

16. Jennifer Novick, "Let There Be X-Men," *X-Men Anniversary Magazine* 1, no. 1 (1993): 21.

17. Rebecca Housel, "Myth, Morality, and the Women of the X-Men," in *Superheroes and Philosophy: Truth, Justice, and the Socratic Way*, ed. Tom Morris and Matt Morris (Chicago: Open Court, 2005), 78.

18. Ruth Luzifer and Peter Luzifer, "Storm: Costume Gallery," UncannyXmen.net, 2004, http://www.uncannyxmen.net/db/spotlight/showquestion.asp?faq=10&fldAuto=76&page=11.

19. Chris Claremont, Barry Windsor-Smith, and Tom Orzechowski, "Lifedeath," *Uncanny X-Men*, no. 186 (October 1984).

20. bell hooks, *Black Looks: Race and Representation* (Boston: South End Press, 1992), 49.

21. Joseph Hughes, "Artist Kris Anka & Sam Humphries on Uncanny X-Force Fashion (Interview + Exclusive Art)," ING Comics, October 10, 2007, http://www.comicsalliance.com/2012/10/10/uncanny-x-force-costume-design-kris-anka-sam-humphries-marvel-now-interview/#ixzz28vXdyn3w.

22. Chris Claremont, Rick Leonardi, and Whilce Portacio, "Duel," *Uncanny X-Men*, no. 201 (January 1986).

23. Housel, "Myth, Morality, and the Women of the X-Men," 80.

24. Ibid., 81.

25. Scott Lobdell, Joe Madureir, and Dan Green, "Romp," *Uncanny X-Men*, no. 312 (May 1994).

26. Scott Lobdell, Joe Madureir, and Dan Green, "Hands across the Water," *Uncanny X-Men*, no. 313 (June 1994).

27. bell hooks, *Ain't I a Woman: Black Women and Feminism* (Boston: South End Press, 1981), 83.

28. Ruth Luzifer and Peter Luzifer, "Storm: Costume Gallery."

29. Reginald Hudlin, Scot Eaton, and Klaus Janson, "Bride of the Panther Part Three," *Black Panther*, no. 16 (July 2006).

30. Reginald Hudlin, Turnbull Koi, and Don Ho, "War Crimes Part One," *Black Panther Dark*, no. 23 (February 2007).

31. Christopher Yost, Diogenes Neves, and Ed Tadeo, "Conclusion," *X-Men: Worlds Apart*, no. 4 (March 2009).

32. Reginald Hudlin, Ken Lashley, and Paul Neary, "The Deadliest of Species, Part 6," *Black Panther Dark Reign*, no. 6 (September 2009).

33. Richard Majors and Janet M. Billson, *Cool Pose: The Dilemma of Black Manhood in America* (New York: Lexington Books, 1992), 57–58.

34. Jason Aaron, Jefte Palo, and Jefte Palo, "See Wakanda and Die, Part 3," *Black Panther*, no 41 (November 2008).

35. Reginald Hudlin, Scot Eaton, and Andrew Hennessy, "World Tour Part One: Holiday in Latveria," *Black Panther*, no. 19 (October 2006).

36. Richard George. "Fantastic Four Interview: Dwane Duffie Chats about Marvel's First Family," ING Comics, June 13, 2012, http://www.ign.com/articles/2007/06/14/fantastic-four-interview?page=2.

37. Jonathan Maberry, Scot Eaton, Andy Lanning, and Robert Campenella, "Part 1," *Doom-war*, no. 1 (April 2010).

38. David Liss, Jefte Palo, and Jean-François Beaulieu, "Storm Hunter Part Two!," *Black Panther: The Man without Fear*, no. 520 (August 2011).

39. Christopher Yost, Diogenes Neves, and Ed Tadeo, *X-Men: Worlds Apart*, no. 1 (December 2008).

40. Reginald Hudlin, Scot Eaton, and Klaus Janson, "Bride of the Panther Part Five," *Black Panther*, no. 18 (September 2006).

Chapter Eleven

The Mother of All Superheroes

Idealizations of Femininity in Wonder Woman

Sharon Zechowski and Caryn E. Neumann

Wonder Woman is the oldest feminist icon in popular culture and one of the very few superheroes to survive for over seventy years. First appearing in a comic book in 1941, she also had a mid-1970s television show that prompted a generation of little girls to spin around "just like Wonder Woman" and that inspired other female-heroine shows such as *The Bionic Woman* and *Buffy the Vampire Slayer*. Central to her power is the idea that any woman (or girl) could be a Wonder Woman. She is a long-standing symbol of female independence and gender equality in a popular culture dominated by male characters and patriarchal narratives.

Yet Wonder Woman is often dismissed or ignored. A major textbook on comic books identifies Wonder Woman as one of DC Comics' "most iconic characters," along with Superman and Batman, but then forgets about her.[1] Other works dismiss her as an object for male sexual fantasies or take away her feminist power by emphasizing her skimpy costume and large breasts.[2] Her presence in contemporary media culture is rare. Unlike her male equivalents, Wonder Woman has not been revived and appropriately franchised through various media synergies. Her character, when represented today, is relegated mostly to the world of print (e.g., graphic novels) or kitsch (e.g., Halloween costumes and assorted nostalgia).[3] Her general absence from the popular culture, in spite of the public's recent obsession with the superhero genre, raises several questions about Wonder Woman's cultural relevance as a progressive female character today. Is Wonder Woman a feminist? Was she ever?

The progressive elements of the Wonder Woman comics are clear and reflect some of the concerns of the era in which she was introduced. She was the earliest female superhero and the most prominent, born of a matriarchal society called Paradise Island.[4] An Amazon, she possessed powers that enabled her to fight evil and bring peace to "man's world." More accessible than other superheroes, however, Wonder Woman gained her powers through hard work and determination rather than a radioactive spider or status as a refugee from an alien planet. She did have the aid of gadgets, such as a magic lasso, that forced people to tell the truth.[5] At the time of World War II, when women were being encouraged to join the war effort, there is a clear message that any woman could be a Wonder Woman. The comic reinforces this as women inspired by Wonder Woman burst their bonds, with characters in one book declaring, "We **are** strong—we **can** fight! Follow **Wonder Woman**."[6]

Like Rosie the Riveter, Wonder Woman symbolically disrupted the gender norms that had prevented real women from achieving full equality with men in the public sphere. From this perspective, one might say she was a prototype for feminism's Second Wave of the 1960s and 1970s. (Feminist leader Gloria Steinem recalled reading Wonder Woman as a child in the 1940s and famously put her on the cover of the first edition of *Ms.* magazine in 1972.[7]) However, as Rosie also discovered, there were limits to equality.

Wonder Woman possessed characteristics that were regressive and stereotypical. For example, she falls in love with the first man she ever sees, Steve Trevor, and leaves her home to be with him. Once in America, she easily slides into subordinate positions. As her alter ego Diana Prince, Wonder Woman serves as a nurse during World War II, not a physician. She took orders from men, as she would do throughout the rest of her career, although her job changes. In the 1950s, she even served as the romance editor at the *Daily Globe* newspaper, a position that presumably never was offered to Clark Kent.

As the 1954 code for comics required romantic stories to emphasize the value of the home and the sanctity of marriage, Wonder Woman became just another female character, albeit one with a strong right hook.[8] Few women recall being inspired by the rather bland Wonder Woman of the 1950s and 1960s. In 1968, as the feminist movement was gaining strength, Wonder Woman even surrendered all of the gadgets that had made her powerful, as well as her iconic costume, and accepted control by a man. It took several years and a protest by feminists for Wonder Woman to appear as she once had been.

The contradictions within Wonder Woman are evident. Although her mission is to combat the evils of patriarchy, Wonder Woman is also its ultimate projection of female perfection. As such, it is this idealization of her femininity that weakens her status as a progressive female character. Wonder Woman—strong, beautiful, nurturing, and wise—is a mother figure above all.[9] Moreover, the narratives that span the Golden, Silver, and Bronze ages of Wonder Woman comics (roughly 1941 to 1986) reinforce a central essentialist ideology. Across all periods, despite various changes to her character, Wonder Woman is represented as being morally superior to men.

Feminist and queer readings of Wonder Woman emphasize that much of her appeal has been grounded in two competing feminist ideals—equality and difference. While many feminists, Gloria Steinem among them, cite being inspired by Wonder Woman's superhero qualities and equality with men, there is another reading offered by those who have felt marginalized in a patriarchal, heteronormative culture. For these readers, it is how Wonder Woman differed from established gender norms that made her significant. [10] These interpretations address issues of polysemy, whereby the meaning of cultural texts is not always monolithic and culturally determined, but, more importantly for this analysis, provide a way in which to see how Wonder Woman's feminist message is subsumed into a larger patriarchal framework, one that is much less culturally progressive than has been previously suggested. This message, in stressing the moral superiority of women and feminine values, serves to validate women *and* undermine them.

Historically, arguments made about the moral superiority of women have been used by men and feminists (e.g., radical, eco, care-based). For example, social movements such as suffrage and temperance owe some of their success not to the wide-scale embrace of women's equality and liberation, but rather to the socially constructed ideology of femininity. Second Wave feminists fought against this constructivist platform, emphasizing that women were equal to men and deserving of the same opportunities in the arenas of work and civil rights. However, women who would later be referred to as radical feminists rejected the idea that women should strive to be like men. Patriarchal society was the problem, as well as the attributes ascribed to masculinity. Reclaiming and reappropriating the feminine, this type of feminist and feminist theory celebrated feminine values instead of dismissing them as unimportant. This idealization of femininity (by feminists) was radical in its orientation because it was still grounded in the processes of women's social liberation *and* female self-actualization. The idealization of femininity that occurs in the Wonder Woman narratives is much different, however, informed by a specific patriarchal sensibility.

Cultural texts may be interpreted in a number of ways, many of which are informed by subject positions related to social class, race, gender, and sexual orientation. This perspective, emphasizing that audiences are active rather than passive consumers of media, is evident in the scholarship and popular writings about Wonder Woman. Immortalized in Stuart Hall's classic encoding/decoding model, this perspective allows for Wonder Woman to be read as a character with multiple significant roles. However, in spite of the polysemic nature of cultural texts, all interpretations are framed by a central dominant ideology (capitalism, patriarchy, etc.) that is either resisted or reinforced. For example, understanding Wonder Woman as a woman who is morally superior to men supports both feminist and patriarchal ideologies.

The idealization of femininity that occurs in Wonder Woman is both progressive and regressive. Through a close reading of the comic books, especially those of the Golden Age, it is difficult to argue that Wonder Woman was merely a stereotypical projection of heterosexual male desire. Dr. William Moulton Marston created her as a female superhero, and in doing so challenged stereotypes related to sex and gender.[11] Wonder Woman was a woman who could do all the same things as a male superhero like Superman, shattering myths related to women being "the weaker sex." The cover of *Sensation Comics'* first edition depicts the patriotically clad Wonder Woman triumphantly deflecting gangsters' bullets with her bracelets. Considering the political climate in which she was created, Wonder Woman (like Rosie the Riveter) was radical—up to a point. She was a superhero first and a woman second, safely contained within the familiar conventions of the male-dominated comic book genre.

Determining the meaning of a cultural text requires examining it at the levels of production, distribution, and consumption. This allows for a comprehensive analysis that locates Wonder Woman within specific historical, economic, and cultural contexts. Existing scholarship supports that Wonder Woman provides a useful lens through which to understand shifting social attitudes about women over several decades. The Golden Age establishes Wonder Woman as a strong female character who introduces many progressive ideas about women to a mass audience. The backlash against such attitudes is apparent during the Silver Age, when new writers—all of whom were male—cast Wonder Woman as more concerned with traditionally feminine issues, such as relationships. This period concludes with Wonder Woman losing her powers. The Bronze Age encompasses attitudes reflected in these two eras. Wonder Woman's powers are restored when she is reclaimed by the feminist movement as an icon of liberal feminist values. However, by the middle of the 1980s she is finally disempowered through her marriage to Steve Trevor and restored to her appropriate role within "man's world."

These interpretations illustrate with certainty the process of "ideological normalization" that occurs within popular-culture texts, such as comic books.[12] In Wonder Woman, the dominant ideology of patriarchy is challenged and reinforced. This is elicited through a textual analysis of the comic books (semiotics) as well as a genre analysis (ideological critique). To avoid accusations of "reading too much into" these texts, historical contextualization is key. For example, Wonder Woman is considered progressive within the context of the 1940s because she is the first female superhero. After the women's liberation movement, it might be easier to dismiss her progressive qualities. Women have more rights in the real world, so what need for Wonder Woman? In identifying the characteristics that made Wonder Woman radical for her time, it may also be revealed that what she represents is still radical, given both her absence and the overall misrepresentation of women in the media today.

Those who control the production of a text imbue it with their individual and cultural values, determining to a large extent what it will mean to consumers. Genres are the larger thematic structures through which stories are told and made familiar. They create certain expectations for audiences and, in doing so, normalize cultural values and ideologies. In the case of Wonder Woman, dominant ideologies about gender are reinforced (standardization) and disrupted (differentiation). The audience's familiarity with the superhero genre allowed Wonder Woman's story to be told, but the transgressive elements of her story were safely contained within a dominant masculine narrative, thus preserving the gender status quo.

Nevertheless, the process of differentiation that occurs in the Wonder Woman narrative is still unique and worthy of critical inquiry because the inversion of gender norms rarely occurs within popular-culture genres. When it does, the reversal of roles almost always serves a comedic function, undermining the possibility of real gender equality altogether and further trivializing the feminine. In possessing traditionally male attributes such as physical strength and speed, along with her ability to save the world, Wonder Woman allows for a temporary reimagining of gender norms that is believable. This theme, while consistent throughout the series, is the most transgressive in the issues which comprise the Golden Age, written by Marston.

It is difficult to deny the progressive gender messages in the original Wonder Woman series. Themes such as gender equality, peace, female camaraderie, and the overall celebration of feminine values were, and still are, anomalies within popular culture. Finding the expression of such ideas in a devalued genre such as comics, written by men for young boys in the 1940s, is even more unique. This is perhaps why much inquiry into Wonder Woman has acknowledged, and to some extent revered, the feminist sensibilities of her creator, psychologist Marston.

Marston's interest in gender is reflected in his scholarship as well as his popular writings directed at women, which appeared regularly in publications such as *Ladies' Home Journal* and *Reader's Digest*. Wonder Woman, however, is perhaps the most famous manifestation of his professional and personal beliefs about the moral superiority of women. Through her, he celebrated the "natural" propensities of women, such as being loving and nonviolent. Characteristics that had deemed women the "kinder, gentler sex" were represented in Wonder Woman as signs of strength rather than weakness.

Marston openly criticized the violent, war-laden world created by men. For him, the problems related to "the hatreds and wars of men in a man-made world" could be eradicated if women possessed more self-confidence and could rule the world according to their value system. In "The Five Tasks of Thomas Tighe," Marston has female characters doing feats that men refuse to do. At the end, Tighe says, "You win Wonder Woman! And I must confess, that you and the girls have made me change my mind about women! I'm no longer a woman-hater!" Wonder Woman replies, "Then *you're* the real winner, Mr. Tighe! Because when one ceases to hate, he becomes stronger!"[13] Wonder Woman was the cultural projection of this very unconventional idea.

The most radical aspect of Wonder Woman is that she existed, period. Although the visual culture of the 1940s produced its share of strong female role models—Katharine Hepburn, Rosalind Russell, Barbara Stanwyck, and Joan Crawford to name a few—the types of films these women appeared in were intended for adults. Any alternative readings of these actors (feminist or queer) were the product of adult imaginations. Children's popular culture (books, movies, toys), by contrast, has consistently perpetuated the least imaginative and most rigid of gender roles. Wonder Woman challenged the normalization of these stereotypes—she was no Snow White.

Comic books and the films of Walt Disney were intended for a general audience of children. A closer examination of the narrative structure of each genre implies a more targeted, gender-specific audience, however. Some of the most beloved and enduring Disney stories are based upon classic fairy tales (with the addition of a happy ending for many). These fairy tales confirm basic stereotypes about victimized, passive women and heroic, active men. Superman, the first DC superhero, reiterated this theme within the comic book genre. Wonder Woman did not. She was, in many ways, a male version of Superman whose actions implied that women were no different than men. This may have been the intended message of Marston, but did children get it?

Children are socialized into specific gender roles as soon as they are born. These roles and expectations are so pervasive that they go unquestioned (unless they are violated in some way). For this reason, it is likely that boys reading Wonder Woman perceived her differently than girls. Interpreting her as "a woman who acted like a man," and therefore progressive, may not hold true for both sexes. Boys were the target audience for all comic books, and advertisements in Wonder Woman overwhelmingly confirm this. Toy soldiers, tanks, ant farms, stamp collections, and muscle-enhancement products appear regularly throughout the decades examined here. Gender-neutral ads, such as those for Blammo bubble gum, depict boys and the occasional girl enjoying the product. The only indication that girls may have also been reading is indicated by a few isolated segments from the 1960s ("Marriage a la Mode" and the "Wonder Women of History"), and a lone ad for the Dusty/Skye doll which appeared in 1976.

Marston's own account of his "pro-woman" message suggests that he was intentionally trying to enlighten boys and empower girls. (This distinguished him from his successors.) Wonder Woman also served as a popular vehicle through which Marston could advance his professional opinions about gender, some of which would resonate within liberal feminist circles more than twenty years after his death.

The strongest liberal feminist themes are found within the Golden Age series written by Marston. Readers of the first issue are immediately exposed to an alternative gender narrative, one whose appeal to girls is obvious. Wonder Woman is strong, smart, and beautiful, a female who will fight the evils of "man's world" for all "womankind." In spite of its abundantly clear message that men were the problem and women the solution, boys continued to read Wonder Woman. Why?

Encountering Wonder Woman for the first time would provoke numerous reactions. Boys and girls could accept or reject her, for infinite reasons. However, the popularity of her character confirms a shared interpretation. Wonder Woman is represented as an idealized woman who functioned as a fantasy figure for girls and boys, supporting feminist and patriarchal ideologies about sex and gender. As such, the character is empowering and nonthreatening.

A quick glance at the covers of forty-plus years of Wonder Woman comics shows the classic superhero motif: superhero violently battling foes or facing some kind of impending doom. It is Wonder Woman's clothing which signifies her status as a biological woman (becoming more sexually provocative as the series continues), but above all, her clothing is a patriotic uniform suggesting that her duties are about nation first. She is almost always shown having to physically defend herself against mostly male villains (or later on, male superheroes). During the Golden Age series, her status as a "good American woman" (rather than a "good feminist") takes priority, especially in the issues where she battles Hitler and Hirohito. The imagery supports that Wonder Woman is an otherworldly visitor helping to support the war effort, in a way very similar to Superman. Like Rosie the Riveter, her status is always coded as temporary. However, unlike Rosie, Wonder Woman will continue to be a symbol of shifting gender roles after the war.

The dominant, patriotic themes definitive of the Golden Age series allow for the existence of a progressive gender subtext that will inform how Wonder Woman was and would be interpreted. This minor discourse comprised numerous elements. The feminist imagery associated with Wonder Woman emphasizes how she is equal to men. Physical attributes such as strength and speed are represented as her natural abilities. Even though these skills are connected to her Amazonian identity, Wonder Woman often encourages the regular women she encounters that they, too, are strong (against the Seal Men, for example). Gender roles are again reversed when Wonder Woman creates a winning all-girls baseball team and a college, attended by her female friends, the Holliday Girls. Like all superheroes, Wonder Woman's physical strength also allows her to rescue people in trouble, including men. Her love interest throughout the series, Steve Trevor, is consistently in need of rescue by Wonder Woman. She is often shown physically carrying him out of danger, a truly unique motif if one considers the time period and genre. It is rare to see women rescue men in popular narratives; rarer still is when a woman demonstrates possessing greater strength than a man (who is coded as masculine) to do so. One only has to think of this type of role reversal in any classic fairy tale to appreciate its feminist overtones.

Wonder Woman's physical strength is culturally acceptable because it is balanced by her physical beauty. Without it, her physical strength alone would make her unfeminine and more symbolically threatening. (Even so, the character could not escape charges of promoting lesbianism).[14] It is permissible for Wonder Woman to save Steve Trevor because she is doing it out of love (rather than competition or a sense of superiority). Although she defies the stereotype of the passive woman in need of rescue, her actions toward Trevor still support a heteronormative ideology. Wonder Woman is often motivated by her love of a man (and by extension, his country).

Like soap opera, the comics are a genre which relies heavily upon open-ended narratives. This device helps to sustain a loyal fan base by perpetually deferring their need for narrative closure. Romantic relationships are especially well suited for this type of storytelling. The first issue of Wonder Woman establishes that she is in love with Steve Trevor, and this remains a central subplot throughout the series. Their relationship during the Golden Age is less stereotypical than Silver or Bronze because of the public stance Wonder Woman takes against marriage as something that will render her powerless. To some degree she views marriage (not love) as a trap, a theme that foreshadows *The Feminine Mystique* in 1963. In addition, Wonder Woman makes clear that her career comes before marriage. For example, in "The Talking Tiara," Steve Trevor proposes to Wonder Woman, asking her to wear his wedding ring. She replies, "I will Steve! As soon as there is no need to battle evil and injustice."[15] In other words, no. Her advice to other women is to be self-reliant, reminding them that they possess the power to determine their own lives.

After Marston, Wonder Woman remains single, but themes related to marriage become more prominent, evidence perhaps of an increasing number of female readers and a postwar backlash against women as well as the influence of the Comics Code. Wonder Woman continues to fight crime, but many issues emphasize plots related to relationships with men (e.g., will she choose Steve Trevor or Mer-Man as her husband?). When Steve Trevor and Wonder Woman get married, he is quickly dismayed to find that he must share her with the world. After the wedding, a bystander asks her if she will be able to "combine marriage while taking distress calls." While she is able to continue as a superhero, her husband resents being second to her career. A married Wonder Woman is unable to cook, but she can still rid the world of a nuclear missile. Her lack of domestic skills, combined with having a career, make her an undesirable wife. A pouting Wonder Woman is shown alongside a much relieved Steve when he tells her their marriage was just a dream. He has the last word, and she is clearly disappointed.

In addition to plotlines such as these, the Silver Age also features sections that address marital traditions and relationships, such as "Marriage a la Mode," "Curious Courtships," and "No Kissing Allowed." Fan mail during this period also confirms that girls are reading Wonder Woman, too. This type of subject matter normalizes heterosexuality and privileges it. Moreover, many of these plotlines serve as a cautionary tale. Wonder Woman thought she could have it all until her husband decided otherwise, in spite of what liberal feminists were beginning to tell real women in the 1960s.

Scholars and fans point to the creation of *The New Wonder Woman* as being most representative of the backlash against the women's movement. During this period, Wonder Woman voluntarily relinquishes her superpowers and exists solely as her alter ego, Diana Prince. Her "mod" look emphasizes fashion, accessorizing, and sex appeal, issues that were now being openly critiqued by feminists as superficial distractions women were socialized to care about. Although Diana Prince still fights crime, she does so with karate, taught to her by a male mentor, I Ching. Critics of this period see this story line as regressive. A letter to the editor from a girl named Jade states that Wonder Woman should have her superpowers back because she is "sort of dull without them." It would be equal to producing a "New Superman" series built around the adventures of Clark Kent.

Creators of *The New Wonder Woman* imply that the character is changed to represent a more realistic woman, one who will experience the difficulties faced by ordinary people. A letter that follows Jade's is from a boy named Keven who agrees, stating, "I like the New Wonder Woman . . . because now she's with it. She's in! She's part of the new scene! Now I can identify with her because she is human with the same problems that face all of us, especially the young people like myself."[16] While it is true that Diana Prince is confronted with real issues such as how to earn a living and find an affordable, safe place to live, they are not represented as *women's* issues. If truly realistic, in the late 1960s Diana Prince would find that she probably could not secure a business loan or an apartment on her own. Moreover, there are no references to the women's liberation movement in *The New Wonder Woman* (odd if one considers how often current events served as a backdrop within story lines), which would provide a feminist context in which to interpret her character. At a time when women were becoming empowered, Wonder Woman disappeared. The pressure upon writers to revive the original character came from adult women who could appreciate the symbolic significance of Wonder Woman's disempowerment. Their acknowledgment of it is suggestive of Wonder Woman's feminist appeal prior to the "New" series.

When the feminist movement became more radicalized, the tendency of the mainstream media (controlled exclusively by men) was to distort issues (e.g., bra burning) or omit coverage. When the women's liberation movement disappeared from the media's agenda, the Wonder Woman who symbolized it did, too. Backlash and postfeminist culture is officially mainstreamed with the rise of the Moral Majority and the popularization of conservative talk radio in the 1980s. A misogynistic popular culture regularly extolled images of the classic madonna/whore dichotomy. Career women or those who challenged traditional gender roles were regularly demonized in the media—women like Wonder Woman.

The ideological influence of a socially conservative, antifeminist status quo is symbolized in the final issue of Wonder Woman in 1986. Her image on the cover belies her final fate. A defiant, muscular Wonder Woman stands ready to do battle with numerous foes. By her stance, one can assume she will be triumphant. For those who had admired Wonder Woman in the past, this might prove a comforting image, one reminiscent of her original feminist message.

After a final battle to save Paradise Island, Wonder Woman marries Steve Trevor. She is the one who finally "comes to her senses" and, realizing that "life is short," tells him, "I want us to seal our love as man and woman." As a final issue, her marriage is significant because it effectively kills the character. The marriage is not a temporary plot device used to send (as in the past) an antimarriage, procareer message. It is not as though Wonder Woman decided to get married after thinking it over. Instead she chooses to be a powerless, married woman, one who is anxious to fulfill the contract of the nuclear family and have a child (saying so dressed in a revealing, white nightgown). This plotline is the most regressive because it is final. It is regressive because it reinforces the dominant backlash culture of the time, requiring "good" women to resume their rightful place as wives and mothers.

When compared to *The New Wonder Woman* series, this final issue provides much less room for alternative readings. In TNWW, she is clearly upset that she relinquished her powers. It was her choice, not mandated by another or issued as a punishment. More significantly, she does so not for love, but in order to continue her mission. Although many expressed disappointment with TNWW, Diana Prince remained independent. As such, she (unlike Mrs. Steve Trevor) could not be assumed to "live happily ever after," leaving readers to forever wonder what she would, or more importantly *could*, do next.

NOTES

1. Randy Duncan and Matthew J. Smith, *The Power of Comics: History, Form, and Culture* (New York: Continuum, 2009), 43. The book contains three references to Wonder Woman, with the longest coverage—a paragraph—at the end of the book.

2. Bradford W. Wright sees Wonder Woman as entertainment for men in *Comic Book Nation: The Transformation of Youth Culture in America* (Baltimore, MD: Johns Hopkins University Press, 2001). Scott Beatty's guide to the character provides a history but emphasizes Wonder Woman's body rather than story lines. A good history of the character in comic books, television, and kitsch can be found in Les Daniels, *Wonder Woman: The Life and Times of Wonder Woman, the Complete History* (San Francisco: Chronicle Books, 2000). The best history of the comic book character, though one that manages to completely miss the feminist aspects of Wonder Woman, is in Robert Greenberger, *Wonder Woman: Amazon, Hero, Icon* (New York: Universe, 2010).

3. The recent documentary on Wonder Woman attempts to restore her prominence but has had fairly limited impact. It divides focus between the comic book character and the television character. See *Wonder Woman: The Untold Story of American Superheroines*, dir. Kristy Guevara-Flanagan, prod. Kelcey Edwards (Vaquera Productions, 2012).

4. Miss Fury, a socialite who acquires superpowers when she dons a leopard skin, appeared in newspaper comic strips about six months before Wonder Woman made her comic book debut. Drawn by June Tarpé Mills, Miss Fury had an erratic existence that ended in 1951. She never had the impact of Wonder Woman. See Trina Robbins, ed., *Tarpé Mills and Miss Fury: The First Female Superhero Created and Drawn by a Woman Cartoonist* (San Diego: IDW, 2011).

5. Perhaps not coincidentally, Wonder Woman creator William Moulton Marston, a psychologist, invented an early lie detector machine. Marston wrote under the pen name of Charles Moulton.

6. Emphasis in original. Charles Moulton, "Wonder Woman: The Icebound Maidens," 1945, in Gloria Steinem, ed., *Wonder Woman* (New York: Holt, Rinehart and Winston and Warner Books, 1972), n.p.

7. Steinem, *Wonder Woman*, 1–2.

8. The Comics Magazine Association of America published its code in October 1954, and a comic could not be published without receiving the seal of the Comics Code Authority. See Wright, *Comic Book Nation*, 172–73.

9. Lillian Robinson, *Wonder Woman: Feminisms and Superheroes* (New York: Routledge, 2004), 11–25.

10. Trina Robins, "Wonder Woman: Queer Appeal," *International Journal of Comic Art* 10 (2008): 89–94.

11. William Moulton Marston, "Why 100,000,000 Americans Read Comics," *American Scholar* 13 (1943): 42–43.

12. Peter Coogan, "Reconstructing the Superhero in All-Star Superman," in *Critical Approaches to Comics: Theories and Methods*, eds. Matthew J. Smith and Randy Duncan (New York: Routledge, 2012), 207.

13. Emphasis in original. Steinem, *Wonder Woman*, n.p.

14. Fredric Wertham, *Seduction of the Innocent* (New York: Rinehart, 1953), 192.

15. Charles Moulton, "The Talking Tiara," in *Wonder Woman* (New York: Tempo Books, 1978), n.p.

16. Mike Sekowsky, *The New Wonder Woman*, no. 188 (New York: DC Comics, May–June, 1970), n.p.

Chapter Twelve

Wonder Woman: Lesbian or Dyke?

Paradise Island as a Woman's Community

Trina Robbins

In his now-infamous 1954 indictment of comic books, *Seduction of the Innocent*, Dr. Fredric Wertham called the Wonder Woman comic book of the 1940s and 1950s[1] "the Lesbian counterpart of Batman," whom, along with his young sidekick, Robin, he had already accused of membership in NAMBLA. Using acrobatic leaps of logic, Wertham went on to make the following connection about Wonder Woman's sidekicks, students at the all-woman Holliday College: "Her followers are the 'Holliday girls,' i.e. the holiday girls, the gay party girls, the gay girls."[2]

Later critics would echo Wertham's theory. In the 1970 classic, *All in Color for a Dime*, Jim Harmon describes how Wonder Woman would "exchange hugs and kisses of delight with the readily available Holliday Girls." He adds, "It was a very sick scene."[3]

In a 1996 private phone interview, Robert Kanigher, who took over writing the comic in 1948 after the death of creator William Moulton Marston—who wrote the comics under the pseudonym "Charles Moulton"—let me in on what he called the truth about Wonder Woman: the Amazons from her home, Paradise Island, where no men are permitted, were all lesbians.

Not everyone agrees. Jules Feiffer, clearly wishing for something closer to *Hothead Paisan*, draws a different conclusion in his 1965 memoir, *The Great Comic Book Heroes*. "Wonder Woman," he writes, "wasn't dykey enough. Her violence was too immaculate, never once boiling over into a little fantasmal sadism."[4] In her introduction to the Bonanza Books 1972 collection, *Wonder Woman*, and again in her introduction to Abbeville Press's 1995 collection of Wonder Woman covers, also titled *Wonder Woman*, Gloria Steinem avoids the issue entirely, preferring to write about "sisterhood." And in the 2000 Chronicle Books production, *also* titled *Wonder Woman*, writer Les Daniels, hired by DC Comics, writes off the accusation in one short sidebar of the 206-page book: "(Wertham) saw innuendo every-where, and . . . managed to work himself into a lather because he thought Wonder Woman contained 'Lesbian overtones.' . . . As Robert Kanigher later pointed out, surely some inhabitants of Paradise Island must have had Sapphic tendencies. Not in the comics, however!"[5]

So, are the Amazon princess Diana, her hometown Amazons, and her Holliday girl sidekicks lesbians? And is this a *bad* thing? William Moulton Marston was a successful pop psychologist, and also happened to be the inventor of the lie detector. The man knew what he was doing, and if there is lesbianism in the Golden Age Wonder Woman,[6] he put it there. What hints does he give the reader?

Well, there's the hugging, but, as previously mentioned, women *do* hug.[7] What about lovers? Marston occasionally hints that Wonder Woman might be in a Xena and Gabrielle relationship with another woman. In *Sensation Comics* #19, 1942, Wonder Woman's Amazon best friend, Paula, is called in to help when the princess runs amok because her bracelets have been removed.[8] Stopping Wonder Woman in the act of strangling a suspected fifth columnist, Paula says, "Easy, darling—it's your Paula!"

Another story[9] deals with Marya, a beautiful eight-foot-tall "Mexican mountain girl," who definitely has a crush on Wonder Woman. She calls Wonder Woman "brave princess" and "beautiful princess." When the two women are captured in nets, Wonder Woman, ungraciously considering only her dumb blond "boyfriend," Steve Trevor, tells her, "I'm sorry for you, Marya, but at least we've saved Steve." Marya, with the selflessness of true love, replies, "I care not what happen to me if I help save your friend, Preencess!" Finally, Marya is encased in cement up to her chest. But when the Amazon princess is about to be killed, "driven desperate by her great love for Wonder Woman, Marya wrenches savagely at the solid cement which encases her legs." Leaping from the cement, she shouts, "My preencess—I *come!*" Finally, Wonder Woman freed and the villains vanquished, Wonder Woman declares, "The credit goes to the biggest girl and the bravest—my little friend *Marya!*" Marya kneels at the Amazon's feet, clutching her hand rapturously, saying, "Oh Preencess!"

Getting in the way of Wonder Woman's relationships with other women is always Steve Trevor, the Token Boyfriend.[10] The Lois Lane to Wonder Woman's Superman, he seems to exist only to be rescued. She always puts him off when he asks her when they will marry with statements such as, "When justice has finally triumphed over wrong!" or "When evil and injustice vanish from the earth!" In other words, it'll be a cold day in hell, buster. Her reluctance to marry Steve may have had nothing to do with her interest in other women, but rather her reluctance to spend the rest of her life with someone so stupid that he constantly fails to make the connection between the Amazon princess Diana and her alter ego, army nurse Diana Prince.

It is generally accepted that Marston created Wonder Woman for girls, as an alternative to the male-oriented superhero comics of the time; however, I could find no actual statement on his part saying that. In her introduction to the collection of Wonder Woman covers, Gloria Steinem writes, "[Marston] had invented Wonder Woman as a heroine for little girls, and also as a conscious alternative to the violence of comic books for boys."[11] Of course, Steinem was not there, nor did she ever interview the good doctor. The statement I have found by Marston that comes closest to reflecting Steinem's conclusion is from an article written by him in *The American Scholar*:

> It seemed to me, from a psychological angle, that the comics worst offense was their blood-curdling masculinity . . . it's smart to be strong. It's big to be generous, but it's sissified, according to exclusively male rules to be tender, loving, affectionate. . . . "Ah that's girls stuff!" snorts our comic reader. "Who wants to be a girl?" And that's the point; not even girls want to be girls as long as their feminine stereotype lacks force . . . strength.[12]

I have also found no statistics that show just how many girls *did* read Wonder Woman,[13] so my only evidence is anecdotal. Obviously, as she tells us in her writings, Gloria Steinem read, and was strongly influenced by, the amazing Amazon. In her introduction to the collection of Wonder Woman covers, she describes the origin of *Ms.* magazine: "Since Joanne Edgar and others of its founding editors had also been rescued by Wonder Woman in their childhoods, we decided to rescue Wonder Woman in return [by putting her on their first cover]." On the back cover of my book *The Great Women Superheroes*, author Jane Yolen writes, "I was one of the legion of young girls who adored Wonder Woman back in the 1940s." In her article, "Looking for Wonder Woman,"[14] Lillian Robinson writes of "devouring monthly installments of Wonder Woman." She continues, "I didn't know she was an icon, of course. But she was certainly the apotheosis of the female hero I . . . sought."

And of course there's my own memory. When I was a young girl, my girlfriends and I all read and loved Wonder Woman.

Much information can be gleaned from the letters pages of a comic. The original Golden Age Wonder Woman comics had no letters pages, but as late as the early 1960s, when Robert Kanigher was writing and editing the book, the letters page reveals the demographics of his readers. The April 1962 issue contained letters from two girls and one boy, the May 1963 issue had letters from five girls, and the October 1964 letters page was another all-girl affair, with letters from five girls. Judging from their letters, the writers were all young, and they wrote to Wonder Woman herself, rather than to the writer or editor (in this case, the same person), as later, older male fans would do. In her letter from the 1963 issue, Linda Parson, from White Castle, Louisiana, wishes to actually visit Paradise Island:

> When another reader begged you to take her to Paradise Island with you, you answered that Paradise Island is imaginary. Well, how about taking me on an imaginary trip there?

In asking to go to Paradise Island, Linda Parson is expressing a desire to go to a woman-only world, the world of Golden Age Wonder Woman comics. Steve Trevor is not only the Token Boyfriend in these comics, but often the Token Male in stories that otherwise feature only women. Any other males in these stories are usually villains, like Mars, god of war and sworn enemy of the Amazons.

Many Golden Age Wonder Woman stories, especially the ones that take place on the all-woman Paradise Island, do not include even Steve, because men are not allowed on Paradise Island. Some of the women in these stories are butch to an extreme. In "Wonder Woman and the Coming of the Kangas,"[15] male cat-headed alien invaders turn out to be women in disguise. "We're Amazons like you," says the beautiful red-haired leader, after she has been defeated. "We have no home. Won't you let us join your nation?" In "Villainy, Incorporated!,"[16] the evil "Hypnota, magician of the Blue Flame," is a mustached and bearded woman with breasts. Another of the villains in this story is the cross-dressing "Byrna Brilyant, the Blue Snow Man."

Even off Paradise Island, in what Marston referred to as "Man's World," the Amazon princess mostly interacted with women. In "A Human Bomb,"[17] Suzan Patience, "the famous woman penologist," wants Wonder Woman to help her convince the governor to make her warden of the new woman's prison. Steve Trevor, whose imagination is on par with his IQ, says, "Impossible! Whoever heard of a female prison warden?" Of course Wonder Woman agrees to help, and she starts by giving the prisoners new outfits. As they toss off their gray uniforms and try on the colorful dresses, the prisoners exclaim, "These clothes aren't like prison uniforms at all!" "Cute!" and "We don't look like convicts anymore—all the uniforms are different!"

For at least a few years after Marston's death, Wonder Woman continued, in the spirit of her deceased creator, to interact with women. In the 1950 story "Hollywood Goes to Paradise Island," the Amazon puts together the "first all-girl crew in cinema capital history," including a "directress," "the only woman director in Hollywood!"[18]

Even Wonder Woman's birth, as related in the very first issue of *Wonder Woman*, is an all-woman affair, without even the aid of a turkey baster. In a feminist reversal of mythic hero birth stories, in which a virgin mother is magically impregnated by a male deity,[19] the virginal Amazon Queen Hippolyta, desiring a baby, is instructed by the goddess Athena to mold one from clay. Then Aphrodite bestows the gift of life upon the statue, who becomes the baby princess Diana. Thus, like Heather, Diana has two mommies. [20]

The world of boys and men can be threatening to girls. [21] In *The Reader's Companion to U.S. Women's History*, Marie Wilson has this to say about adolescent girls:

> Sexual comments, jokes, and threats become more intimidating as girls develop an understanding of sexuality and as boys, on average, become physically bigger and stronger than girls. . . . They begin to realize that good looks are necessary for certain kinds of success, and that good looks lead to being looked at, which for young adolescent girls can seem threatening. [22]

In the 1940s, sexual harassment in the workplace and in schools, although never approved of, was accepted as an unavoidable evil, as was domestic violence, which was not then illegal. At home, young girls saw their mothers being hit by their fathers, and accepting it. [23] In school, it has only recently been understood by educators that traditional teaching has focused on boys' interests and behaviors. Teachers have traditionally called on boys more often than girls. They have accepted that boys tend to act out and disrupt the classroom in various of ways, meanwhile encouraging girls to be passive and quiet. [24]

Girls have needed, at least in their fantasy lives, a safe place to be with other girls, where they could express themselves without being threatened by boys. British girls' magazines seem to have recognized this need more than American comics. In my study of four British girls' magazine annuals, from 1956, 1958, and 1963, [25] I found comics in which the protagonists, usually students from all-girl schools, interacted with other girls, and any male in the stories is usually a villain. In a typical story from 1958, three schoolgirls dress up as "the Silent Three," in hooded robes and masks, [26] to help a younger girl whose dog has been stolen by a wicked man who hopes to use the dog to retrieve a hidden paper that will lead to treasure.

In "Staunch Allies of the Swiss Skater," from 1956, two British schoolgirls, vacationing in Switzerland, befriend a young Swiss ice skater, buying her a dress to wear for a skating contest. When the girl's cruel uncle locks her up, forbidding her to enter the contest, they free the girl and find a paper proving he is an impostor, masquerading as her dead uncle "to steal the legacy her mother left her!" One of the contest judges knew the real uncle and would have recognized him. In the end, a British girl hugs the skater and says, "Your troubles are over, Odette dear. You're free—free to skate!"

American girls' comics from that period are very different. Instead of the sisterhood themes of the British comics, the American comic stories usually revolve around the theme of the eternal triangle—two girls, one of which is the protagonist, fighting over the Token Boyfriend. Patsy Walker and Hedy

Wolfe fight over Buzz Baxter, Betty and Veronica fight over Archie Andrews, and so on. Although the comic books were aimed at and read predominantly by girls, the message seems to be of the importance of boys in their lives. Perhaps the publishers, using Wertham's logic, feared that without boys in the stories, they might be interpreted as promoting lesbianism?

In the women's community of Paradise Island, girls did not *have to* have boyfriends; they could be "free—free to skate!" or free to be themselves and to interact with other girls.

Marston's message to girls lasted for at least twenty years after his death, although it was progressively watered down. By 1968, however, as comics grew more and more male oriented, new creators started aiming Wonder Woman at the new larger male audience by disempowering her, thus making her less intimidating to men. Writer Denny O'Neill divested the Amazon heroine of both her powers and her costume, putting her instead into a mod jumpsuit. Worst of all, he sent Paradise Island off to another dimension. Without her community, Wonder Woman was alone and had to turn for help to a man, an old Chinese martial arts instructor with the unlikely name of I Ching.

This unhappy state of affairs lasted three years, during which time the book continued to lose what female readers were left. Although Wonder Woman regained Paradise Island and her old costume in 1971, the costume slowly shrank over the years as her bust size increased. After disempowerment came hypersexualization. By 1994, when the Amazon was drawn by Brazilian artist Mike Deodato in her most sexually provocative style, her starry shorts shortened to thong size, sales of the book skyrocketed, but the new readers buying it were men. As for Paradise Island, it had become a place of conflict, where a vicious, minimally clad Amazon named Artemis battled with Diana for the title of Wonder Woman. Sisterhood was a thing of the past, and the safe place for girls was long gone.

It will never be known if Wonder Woman's creator really intended any hidden lesbian agenda in his comics, or if suspicions of Sapphism were simply products of Wertham's McCarthyist mentality, but for over ten golden years, William Moulton Marston provided a haven for girls in the pages of his comics, away from Man's World.

NOTES

1. Comics from these years are referred to by collectors as "Golden Age."
2. Using this same kind of logic, one might question the gender preferences of actor/comedienne Judy or singer Billie, not to mention the subversive hidden agenda that must be concealed in the classic film *Holiday Inn.*
3. Page 186. Actually, although Wonder Woman is indeed seen hugging her friends and her mother in the pages of these comics (women *do* hug!), she doesn't kiss them. She's never even depicted kissing her "boyfriend," Steve Trevor!

4. Page 45. Feiffer also refutes Wertham's argument that Batman comics were producing gay youth. He writes, "If homosexual fads were certain proof of that which will turn our young queer, then we should long ago have burned not just Batman books, but all Bette Davis, Joan Crawford, and Judy Garland movies."

5. Page 103. Daniels also writes of Wonder Woman, "No overt eroticism of any type was present in these comics." Yet he devotes eight pages in the first chapter to bondage and domination scenes in Wonder Woman. DC Comics, for whom Daniels wrote this book, has courted a male audience to the exclusion of females since at least the late 1960s. Possibly the DC theory is that descriptions of kinky sex will interest the boys in reading Wonder Woman, but God forbid they should mention lesbianism!

6. For purposes of this chapter, I have defined Golden Age as the 1940s and early 1950s. Even though Marston died in 1948, he left some scripts behind, and as late as the early 1950s, certain Wonder Woman stories seem to bear the Mark of Marston.

7. With the exception of the French, Russians, and Italians, white heterosexual men, fearful of being considered gay, do *not* hug.

8. Removal of Wonder Woman's bracelets causes her to become "*Too Strong.* The bracelets bound my strength for good purposes—now I'm completely uncontrolled! I'm free to *destroy* like a *man!*"

9. This comic book is coverless and bears no dates, but is probably postwar, because a character says to the villains, "You—you are Nazis! But Germany . . . is licked—"

10. Possibly so that readers will not suspect them of lesbianism, fictional American heroines for young girls always seem to be given Token Boyfriends. Nancy Drew had Ned Nickerson, and Barbie, of course, has Ken. In the early 1990s when I was one of the writers on Marvel's *Barbie Comics,* I did some research with two young girls who were playing with their Barbies at my local photocopy center. They told me that they each had five Barbies and one Ken, but that they did not play with their Ken doll much. I asked them what they used their Ken doll for, and the answer was that when they dressed Barbie up and played bride with her, they needed Ken so that she would have someone to marry.

11. Page 11.

12. "Why 100,000,000 Americans Read Comics," *American Scholar,* Winter 1943–1944.

13. Obviously, neither does DC Comics, or Les Daniels would have quoted them in the 2000 Wonder Woman book when he makes the dubious statement, "It's an open secret, however frequently acknowledged, that Wonder Woman's readers have always been predominantly male" (Daniels, *Wonder Woman,* p. 33). Gloria Steinem refutes this in her introduction to the collection of Wonder Woman covers: "Wonder Woman did attract some boys as readers, but the integrated world of comic book trading revealed her true status: at least three Wonder Woman comic books were necessary to trade for one of Superman." On the other hand, in recent times, as Wonder Woman's bust size has grown and her pants have shrunk, and girls no longer read comics because there are no comics for them to read, her readership has become predominantly male. In the mid-nineties, when Brazilian artist Mike Deodato took over drawing Wonder Woman in what Daniels describes as "the most overly eroticized version of Wonder Woman to see print," sales hit the ceiling.

14. Unfortunately, I do not know the source of this article, which was mailed to me in photocopy form some years back.

15. *Wonder Woman* #23, 1947.

16. *Wonder Woman* #28, 1948.

17. *Wonder Woman* #30, 1948.

18. The writer of this story, probably Robert Kanigher, was wrong. In 1949, screen star Ida Lupino made her uncredited directorial debut with the film *Not Wanted,* co-written and co-produced by her along with Anson Bond and Collier Young. Director Elmer Clifton fell ill shortly after shooting began, and Lupino took over but insisted that he retain screen credit. She went on to direct five more features, the first two (*Never Fear* and *Outrage*) of which were made in 1950. But Kanigher was unlikely to know this when in his script, Wonder Woman pep talks her all-girl film crew, "We are the first all-girl company to produce a movie in Hollywood history! Many men think we'll be unsuccessful! But I have faith and confidence in you! I know

that all you need is a chance and you will show that you can *at least* equal anything men have ever done!"

19. Some of these more familiar myths are Leda, impregnated by Zeus as a swan; Danae, also impregnated by Zeus (he got around) as a shower of gold; and of course the Christian Virgin Mary.

20. It is also significant that, in the Golden Age Wonder Woman stories, the Amazons only relate to two deities: Athena and Aphrodite. The only male deity in the stories, Ares, who is called by his Roman name, Mars, is the Amazons' enemy. Later, more contemporary Wonder Woman comics (from the 1980s on) changed this, so that Mercury figures strongly in more recent comics, and Diana and her sisters acknowledge the supremacy of Zeus—an unlikely act for a matriarchal culture.

21. And the world of girls can scare the pants off boys. In *The Great Comic Book Heroes*, Jules Feiffer writes, "I can't comment on the image girls had of Wonder Woman. I never knew they read her—or any comic book. That *girls* had a preference for my brand of literature would have been more of a frightening image to me than any number of men being beaten up by Wonder Woman."

22. Page 244.

23. More recent statistics are not encouraging. An article by Kate Raphael from the *San Francisco Sentinel*, October 11, 1990, reports that almost half of married women are beaten at least once by their husbands.

24. This information comes from the Women's College Coalition website, http://www. academic.org/surprise.html.

25. *Girls' Crystal Annual* from 1956, 1958, and 1963; *School Friend Annual* from 1958.

26. Coincidentally, the first superheroine in American comics, the Woman in Red (1940), costumed herself in a hooded robe and mask.

Chapter Thirteen

Homicidal Lesbian Terrorists to Crimson Caped Crusaders

How Folk and Mainstream Lesbian Heroes Queer Cultural Space

AprilJo Murphy

Comics are art, and they are literature, and, yes, they are entertainment. None of these things must exclude the others. For any story to be successful, it must reflect the truths of our own world. —Greg Rucka [1]

Communities are to be distinguished, not by their falsity/genuineness, but by the style in which they are imagined. —Benedict Anderson [2]

While the over seven billion people who share space on planet Earth exhibit significant diversity, American cultural representations have tended to fore-close that variation in ways that privilege members of some historic majority populations. People produce and inhabit cultural space as well as literal space in the world. Some people create narratives (books, movies, musical theatre), others do it in imagined spaces (video game worlds, tabletop gaming, Disneyworld), and sometimes these different cultural space creators are lesbians. Sometimes the people creating cultural space are not lesbians, but they are creating lesbian characters and lesbian narratives to inhabit their spaces.

In keeping with a history that physically and culturally centers on heterosexuality, lesbians are likely to be mistreated or misunderstood in many spaces. Sometimes, but not always, nonlesbian lesbian space creators know what they are doing, and treat the minority character well. Sometimes they do not. Sometimes these space creators do not even create minority characters at all. This absence is unfortunate, because as Greg Rucka says in this chapter's epigraph, the absence of minority characters is a lie. It is a lie about the real world that is being reproduced in a lying cultural space.

The critical connection between lesbian identity and how it inhabits space is not a new idea.[3] In her seminal book on the subject, *Heroic Desire: Lesbian Identity and Cultural Space*, Sally R. Munt describes several lesbian narrative archetypes and explores how each of these identities inhabits or explores literal space and incorporates it into lesbian culture. Lesbian culture, as I define it, is a cultural space that is created by and for other lesbians and women-oriented persons who identify as female. I will return to Munt's work later, as it will lay the basic foundation for the arguments in this chapter.

So why, then, if all of these spatial and lesbian theories abound, is it necessary to now turn our gaze to the world of comics? Comics, as serialized and sequential narratives, offer a wide cultural space for lesbian characters to inhabit and thrive. Jeffrey Brown, a scholar of (heterosexual action) heroines, has said that "whether on television, in novels, or in comic books, serialized heroines benefit from the ability of longer formats to fully develop and explore characters."[4] By giving individual characters the temporal space to expand to their widest breadth of potential, Brown is essentially agreeing with lesbian scholars that space is necessary to the process of transcending the heteronormative bind of "passive female character" and that purposefully inhabiting space allows one to become a hero, regardless of orientation or gender identity. Just as Batman is the hero suited to Gotham and Superman has Metropolis, so too are lesbian heroines connected to and reflected in the spaces they inhabit.

Yet I would hazard a caveat to those who would believe that simply existing makes a lesbian comic character heroic. Marilyn Falwell has posited "that the struggle for control over the definition of heroism is between the lesbian image in [a] text and the narrative system which presents it,"[5] which brings the creator and publisher of lesbian comics into an interesting sociological-narrator position. Whoever produces lesbian comic characters must undergo a thorough "processing" wherein the intentions of all involved are vocalized and considered to determine whether or not these characters can be accepted into the "real world" lesbian culture (you thought we could talk about lesbians without a good deal of processing? Ha!). Beyond that minority culture, how do they inhabit mainstream cultural space? How do they claim it for the actual lesbian and queer nations?

So, then, the purpose of this chapter is to propose an intersection between queer identity and theories about lesbian identity by identifying some early alternative lesbian comix creators/comics characters as what I term "folk heroes." Claiming them as heroes allows the comparing of these characters to their relatively new mainstream lesbian superheroic counterparts, in addition to recognizing their important cultural status within lesbian history. Then I will look at how both folk and mainstream heroes embody these lesbian identities and alter them to work together to queer existing cultural spaces.

Specifically, I'll be discussing how lesbian heroic narratives, as defined by Sally Munt, describe lesbian heroic archetypes that are attached to how one creates or lives in cultural space. To search for these spaces, I look at the protagonists of several alternative publishers (Diane DiMassa's *Hothead Paisan* and the cast of Alison Bechdel's *Dykes to Watch Out For*) and see how alternative comics/comix representations embody and inhabit their worlds (and ours), as lesbian folk heroes. Then I will apply the same lens to mainstream lesbian superheroes (Renee Montoya, aka the Question; Kate Kane, aka Batwoman), and reinterpret Sally Munt's heroic archetypes within a superheroic context and a queer context.

I suggest that while these mainstream incarnations of the lesbian heroic may be flawed to a lesbian-oriented cultural perspective, they are still significant. I reinterpret these new cultural worlds as a "queer" nation created by mainstream comic book publishers, and respectfully suggest they work in tandem with their independent predecessors.

Finally, I maintain that mainstream lesbian superheroic comics narratives are creating queer cultural spaces for a spectrum of comics readers to actually inhabit, and inspire new queer revolutions against gender, digital, and other binaries. *Queer*, as I define it, is an extension of the lesbian identity (this is also where I respectfully disagree with Munt). I will expand on this redefinition of *lesbian* to include *queer* throughout the chapter, where it is relevant.

PART ONE: THE QUESTION OF TRAILBLAZING FOLK AND HEROIC OUTLAWS, AVENGERS

It's perhaps no surprise that prior to entering mainstream comic books, lesbian heroes existed mostly as a part of alternative comix, independent press culture (starting in the 1970s) and later evolved inside of DIY zine culture (1990s).[6] Queer theorists have traditionally claimed that "[l]esbian perspective originates through denial and resistance, through a sense of difference," which can lead to "furious self-creation."[7] If we, lesbians, do not see a space for ourselves within a dominant culture structure (often represented by patriarchy, but "external reality" would also suffice), then we must choose to deny that culture (coming out to ourselves, recreating a notion of personal identity). If we make this choice, then lesbians must reform our external reality by openly being ourselves (coming out to others, evolving our public identity), despite the dangers such actions pose to our existence. We become an "other," an outsider, by challenging the oppressive structure. To some extent, then, to have a lesbian identity and accept it is to be a hero; it is a personal revolution. To be that heroic person regardless of the concerns existing in external reality is not to only (re)claim that space for lesbian heroics, but to (re)claim it for queer heroism, too.

Revolutionaries are wont for comrades. Yet, a paradox of queerness, of lesbianism, is that the revolution is internal (and eternal). Thus, in order to create culture, the internal reality must be made visible. Queer and lesbian culture are inherently visual,[8] and often what is most visible in a minority culture is stereotypes. Early lesbian visual and folk culture has two major stereotypes, and these stereotypes are the first lesbian comic heroes: the Lesbian Avenger and the Lesbian Nation.[9] After these groundbreaking alternatives are offered by the independent presses, the mainstream will take them, abuse them, and ultimately transform them.

HOTHEAD PAISAN, HOMICIDAL LESBIAN TERRORIST, THE LESBIAN AVENGER FOLK HERO

Scholars (and consumers) of queer culture never quite know what do with *Hothead Paisan*. As an angry, leather-jacket-sporting dyke, Hothead's adventures typically include smashing the patriarchy in the most radical ways: she cuts off penises; she kills men who displease her. But she is an equal-opportunity heterosexist menace; she hates women who are subjugated by patriarchy and perpetuate it with the same venom. She certainly thinks that superheroes are a part of the problem (evidenced in one particular panel where she stuffs a superman-like caped crusader down a manhole titled "outdated patriarchal propaganda" after kicking him in the super-manhood). So she probably would be appalled that I am grouping her in with them. Oh, well. Hothead, you're a hero; get over it.

Hothead's creator, Diane DiMassa, seems to consider the comic a way of creating her own cultural space. In an interview with Elana Bouvier, DiMassa speaks about dealing with addiction and alcoholism, and how creating the cartoon character was a way of healing herself. She says that from an early age, "I was always very aware of who I was and never bought any of the media stereotypes of what women were supposed to be . . . there was no place for me to express myself, so everything got internalized."[10] By taking her internal anguish and using it to create a cultural space for herself in a visual medium, DiMassa's creation of *Hothead* is an incredible and undeniable act of heroism, regardless of how controversial her character may be.

Hothead was originally published as a quarterly "zine" (an independently made magazine-type publication) and sold in mostly lesbian and gay bookstores. The character proved popular enough in the early 1990s that her adventures were collected into two anthologies that are still published by Cleis Press and easily found now, via one aptly named website.[11] Cleis Press, founded in 1980 by Felice Newman and Frederique Delacoste, is a purpose-fully queer and feminist press that focused on publishing work that was "activist-based and concrete."[12] These ladies talk the talk and walk the walk about purposefully inhabiting and creating cultural space.

Hothead's later commercial success has caused some comics scholars like Liana Scalettar to say that Hothead is neither "alternative" nor "mainstream" because the character "both partakes of mass culture and rejects it."[13] While I see the value in this argument (and agree with Scalettar that *Hothead* is essentially a comic about "political resistance"), I must insist that *Hothead* is alternative, not only in its publishing history, but because its ultraviolent narrative was produced by and for a lesbian-oriented readership. Indeed, one can imagine how off-putting *Hothead* could be for an uninitiated audience.

Yet one of the most heroic things that *Hothead* did was carve out a space for the lesbian avenger/outlaw archetype within the mainstream world. That she now can be found quite easily by a presumably uninitiated heterosexual or mainstream audience is a testament to how trailblazing her narrative has been for queer readers.

Renee Montoya: A Questionable Mainstream Answer to the Alternative Lesbian Outlaw

The first lesbian comic character to become a superhero in the DC Universe was Renee Montoya.[14] Montoya joins the cast of Gotham City in the early 1990s, first appearing as a character on *Batman: The Animated Series*. She shortly thereafter was a recurring cast member of the Gotham Police Force, appearing across DC Comics' Gotham City universe. In 1999, nearly a decade later, Greg Rucka will out her as a lesbian in *Gotham City Central: Half a Life*. Seven years later after that remarkable development, Renee Montoya will make another transition: to superhero. She assumes the mantle of "the Question" after Vic Sage dies of cancer, during a story line written by Greg Rucka for the *52* yearlong series.

The choice was an apt one, given the bifurcated character identity Renee already had. During *Half a Life*, Montoya was rather violently forced out of the closet by the villainous Two-Face. Her external reality, unfortunately, did not evolve alongside her identity. Montoya was disowned by her family and by the end of the series had left the Gotham Police Force. If she was to go forward with her heroic nature, Montoya needed to start operating outside of the boundaries of the law. She needed to become a lesbian outlaw/avenger. Renee Montoya's ascension to superheroic status later during the *52* series quite literally gives her the ability to shed her former identities and transcend the cultural spaces within Gotham that have limited her.

Yet becoming her superheroic identity also places Renee Montoya be-yond the gender binary to which the readers of the comic book are accustomed. When she becomes the Question, Renee has no face; her body is androgynously attired, wearing a simple masculine-style suit and fedora. Such clothing would be a familiar signal to lesbian readers, as it plays with notions of butch-ness and androgyny. This fluid identity gives her the ability to work outside the law without the fear of discovery; it is an interesting evolution to see that this fluidity extends to her gender expression. Specifically, part of Montoya's superpower is her queerness, her ability to transcend gender binaries, to paradoxically leave behind all of her previous affiliations—like her lesbian identity—by extending them, by becoming a faceless entity defined only by difference.

Scholars of superheroic identity have long been vocal about how the splits of super identity parallel the divides within queer identity—one where the superhero's civilian persona lives in "the closet" because they must keep their heroic or "true" identity a secret.[15] Feminist scholars of comics are also incredibly perceptive, noting that there is an inherent problematic bifurcation in how female superheroism is actualized: generally, a woman may be powerful, but only if her body is incredibly sexualized.[16] I bring up these distinctions because while Renee Montoya's lesbian narrative makes her strong and lays the foundation for her superheroism, it will ultimately become a problem for the way she is visually produced for a mainstream audience in a way that her queerness does not.

Rucka, who identifies as a straight heterosexual man, wrote a brilliant and poignant story line for Montoya. He describes his decision to change Montoya's canon sexuality as a nondecision. Acknowledging that "ordinary people have secret identities too," Rucka said, "As far as I am concerned . . . [Renee Montoya] was always gay. We were simply the first story to actually say so, and to say it in no uncertain terms."[17] Rucka's commitment to creating a space for her story within the world of Gotham certainly is heroic.

Renee Montoya's ascension to superheroic status is not without severe flaws, however. As remarked upon earlier in this chapter, a lesbian (or queer) character is defined both narratively and through the style/presentation of the images of that character. While Greg Rucka wrote Renee as an undeniably heroic queer and lesbian character, unfortunately the artists in charge of translating these narratives into images often were distracted by the lesbian sexual identity of the character. Entire story lines suffered from the increasingly sexualized way Renee Montoya was drawn. Most offensive in this litany would probably be "Lust" in The Five Books of Blood[18] series, wherein the entire story focuses on whether or not Renee will sleep with a woman—and this seduction is secretly broadcast over television screens and watched by men (a move that quite literally places the entire lesbian seduction narrative in the male gaze).[19] Sadly, because of poor visual images like this one, the Question's treatment by mainstream comic publishers is problematic. This is especially true given that as of the writing of this book chapter (July 2013), the character has been removed from the DC Universe entirely. Yet Renee Montoya's heroic outlaw trailblazing would lead to the creation of DC's highest-profile lesbian character ever, and the treatment of lesbian and queer characters would evolve again. But the Batwoman would be a reimaging of a different folk heroic: the Lesbian Nation.

PART TWO: WATCHING THE DYKE NATION BEGET THE SUPERHEROIC RED BAT, A QUEER NATION BUILDER

Dykes to Watch Out For, the Lesbian Nation

In 1983, feminist monthly magazine *Womanews* published the first of a new comic strip called "Dykes to Watch Out For," by a young graduate art school reject named Alison Bechdel. The strip was the beginning of the creation of a cartoon countercultural revolution led by a ragtag collection of lesbian friends, academics, and feminists. A core cast of characters—Mo, Lois, Harriet Sydney—eventually grew into a queer city (that may or may not have been Minneapolis) and cartoon universe.

In *The Indelible Alison Bechdel*, a sort of companion piece to the *Dykes to Watch Out For* (*DTWOF*) universe and a prequel to *Fun Home* and *Are You My Mother?*, the unerasable cartoonist speaks about how the widespread cultural misogyny of the 1950s and 1960s was embodied in the women cartoon characters of the time.[20] This lack of cultural space was not only understandably traumatic but led to Bechdel's furious graphic self-creation.

Alison Bechdel said, "As a kid, I was outraged by the gap in the system . . . and the way I dealt with it was to disassociate myself from being a girl."[21] Later, Bechdel created the *DTWOF* comic strip out of a desire to create "a catalog of lesbians" from which she could "derive a universal lesbian essence"; this project, Bechdel hoped, would be an "antidote to the prevailing images of lesbians as warped, sick, humorless, and undesirable." The comic characters would create an immense cartoon universe created for lesbians, but function as a sort of gateway into lesbian culture for the uninitiated.[22] The resulting twenty years or so of *Dykes to Watch Out For* is a testament to this heroic achievement.

Yet for all of its trailblazing heroism, *DTWOF* remained relatively unknown by the cultural mainstream until after Alison Bechdel's memoir *Fun Home* became a phenomenal commercial success in 2007.[23] The comics series ran quietly, circulated across the nation in regional lesbian and gay newspapers and magazines, sold in mostly lesbian and gay bookstores, if sold in public spaces at all. Publication in this manner placed *DTWOF* "even farther outside the traditional comics industry . . . tied [it] strongly to the LGBTQ community and the queer media ghetto."[24] Thus, the lovably diverse cast of *DTWOF* lived on for many years as only lesbian folk heroes, inhabiting a mostly lesbian-oriented cultural space.

In this way, *Dykes to Watch Out For* is a comics folk hero embodiment of an early lesbian stereotype that Sally Munt terms "the Lesbian Nation." She defines it as a "utopic community and a fantasy of autonomy, which offered a kind of heroic alternative for the lesbian feminists of the 1970s."[25] Indeed, the cast and universe of Bechdel's comic is so varied and positive that *Publisher's Weekly* called it "politically correct and diverse to a fault."[26] This is a criticism that doesn't bother the cartoonist. In fact, it seems to reflect her own reasons in creating such a cultural space. Alison Bechdel says,

> I feel like ever since I came out, I've been in search of this elusive lesbian community. . . . I've never found it. . . . Not only is the [comic] strip utopian, it's also utopian in that it's a much more cohesive [lesbian] community than I've ever found.[27]

Again, Bechdel's heroic intentions and ambitions with her *Dykes to Watch Out For* comic strip are laudable. In many ways, the comic strip and its creator are a good example of how a lesbian who is involved with "furious self-creation" can create not one self, but many. She may be able to transcend a single identity and contain multitudes. She may even become a nation unto herself.

Expanding Existing Lesbian Identity: The Lesbian as Queer Nation

Early in *Heroic Desire*, Munt speaks about how lesbian identity is actually a collection of identities. She says, "I think the concept of the heroic, multivalent self has the potential to offer the most resistance to homophobic discourse."[28] It is drawing upon this idea of the lesbian as someone who internally is many selves that I posit a slight reiteration of Munt's "Lesbian Nation" archetype. Because she is capable of identification with many people who are externally different from her (straight men, straight women, people who are transgender, homosexual men, etc.), because the lesbian's root of identity is deeply connected to recognizing and living a cultural difference, the lesbian's multivalent self is not simply a lesbian identity and thus only capable of being a member of a "lesbian nation." Instead, a lesbian identity has the potential to *be* a vast internal nation, an overarching identity that is capable of presiding over different selves. The single lesbian person has the possibility to be an autonomous internal nation. Thus, I would like to introduce the idea of a new archetype: "lesbian as queer nation."

Here is where I finally disagree with the great Sally Munt. Within *Heroic Desire*, published in 1998, when speaking about "the Queer Nation," Munt defines the term as "exhibitionist propaganda" designed to "self-consciously shove the homosexual into America's face."[29] She goes on to say that "queers [do not] share an identity, only an opposition to the discipline of normalization. . . . Queer Nation reversed the parameters and focused on the inclusion of anybody who felt 'different,' although, crucially *sexually* different" (emphasis mine). Ultimately, Munt believes that "a queer identity was fixed in a romantic undifferentiation, but the present reality of inequality and regret kept breaking through."[30]

It would seem that, to Munt, the prospect of opening the lesbian identity to include queerness would be both reductive (seeing lesbians as simply people who have sex with other women) and assimilationist, an attempt to erase the uniqueness of lesbian culture (offensive because it says that a lesbian is different in the same way as somebody else who identifies as queer but may not identify as a lesbian, like a gay man or a person who is transgender). These concerns are understandable, but they echo the sort of divisions that have, for example, radically split feminists and lesbians in the past.

To explain this difference, let us look quickly at another heroic woman: Wonder Woman. There is a reason Wonder Woman is traditionally presented as a heterosexual hero, despite the inherent Sapphic possibilities for the identity of the character.[31] Just as Amazons in the historical past need not be lesbians to be warriors, so too does Wonder Woman with her message of hope for all (wo)mankind not need to be so. She holds all women (and humanity) in her lasso of truth.

Just as all feminists need not be lesbians, or even women for that matter, to benefit from the work that feminists have done, so too does a lesbian identity benefit from the work done in the interest of queerness.

Yet I would contend that reading lesbian identity as a queer identity first and foremost is not only possible; it may be preferable because of the expansion it provides to traditional lesbian identity. Rather than being a member of an existing but self-contained lesbian community, a lesbian has the potential to belong to a queer community internally.

"Queer,"[32] as I define it, is slightly different from the parameters that Munt provided. While I agree with Munt that queerness can be "a romantic undifferentiation" between people who oppose the "difference of normalization," I do not agree with Munt that the queer identity is crucially founded upon nontraditional sex acts. Rather, I believe that like the lesbian, queer identity is about recognizing inherent difference and accepting it, despite the dangers such a revolution poses. I feel that those who oppose the linking of the two identities are reiterating some of the very qualms they seem to have with existing structures: focusing too much on traditional notions of sexual identity or gender identity.

The lesbian identity can be extended. The lesbian has the ability to be an internal queer nation and a member of a larger queer nation that is defined by a shared identity of embodying the inherent differences within humanity.

Every nation needs a hero. Enter the Batwoman.

Batwoman: Kate Kane, Queer Nation Builder

With the introduction of Batwoman in 2006, DC Comics attempted something that they had never done before: giving extreme publicity to a lesbian character, and making her a high-profile superhero. Prior to her actual appearance in comics, Kate Kane was profiled in national newspapers like the *New York Times* and garnered mixed reviews from critics.[33] This mercurial attitude was largely due to the fact that Kate Kane was initially designed, written, and drawn as a closeted lipstick lesbian. Critics were unsure whether her sexuality was merely an attribute of her heroic character, or if her character's sexual identity would overtake the other facets of the superhero. Given the previous treatment of Renee Montoya, expectations were understandably low.

To be honest, when Kate Kane was initially introduced during the *52* series alongside her ex-lover Renee Montoya, these concerns were justified. Kate Kane's sexuality did little, other than provide sexual tension with her ex-girlfriend. It wasn't until Batwoman began appearing in an ongoing narrative written by Greg Rucka within DC's highly popular *Detective Comics* title that the character began to change how lesbian superheroes were being portrayed and treated by mainstream publishers.

During the *Detective Comics* run, Greg Rucka and artist J. H. Williams III completely and literally revamped Kate Kane's coming-out narrative. Where before Kate Kane had been an ashamed, closeted lipstick lesbian, the new Kate Kane was an out and proud lesbian who had been discharged from a West Point–like U.S. military academy for refusing to comply with the military's "Don't Ask, Don't Tell" policy. This narrative was an ideological comics revolution.

With the publication of *Detective Comics* #857, Rucka and Williams took the mainstream comics universe and made it an ally of mainstream LGBT minority culture.[34] To help them do this, the cartoonists consulted with real-life mainstream LGBT activists like Lt. Daniel Choi, who is quite literally drawn into the issue, as he appears within the military school Kate Kane attends. The story line was so exceptional that prominent lesbian cultural icon and mainstream news pundit Rachel Maddow agreed to write the introduction to the hardcover publication of the story line *Elegy* in 2010.

It is obvious that Kate Kane is a lesbian superhero; she inhabits a cultural lesbian nation created by Maggie Sawyer, Renee Montoya (and the patrons of Molly's Bar), and others in Gotham. It would not be difficult to accept that she is a lesbian superhero that is marketed toward a lesbian-oriented culture, as the intersections between the two of them would indicate. But I would like to also claim her as a purposefully *queer*, in addition to "lesbian," superhero.

Kate Kane (and any heroic lesbians who dare to live their personal truth and by doing so challenge their external realities) creates and inspires a queer nation in addition to the lesbian nation. Because queerness is inherently opposed to essentialist arguments, it is a natural ally of feminism, female masculinism,[35] and lesbianism.[36]

This inclusive nature is echoed by J. H. Williams' approach to the character. He says,

> The reality of comics is to entertain those that read it, so it's hard to really define that role until the audience has had a chance to absorb it. Once it's in print and analyzed in greater detail, that's when such a thing can really be defined. I know there are parts of her story that are socially important to American society and I want to explore those, but I really want outsiders to be able to come in and really test the validity of those stories.[37]

Such an attitude is a respectful recognition of the minority cultures that Batwoman is identified with, but also claims her as a sort of ambassador, a recruiter, that queers existing heteronormative space. Such an inclusive attitude parallels the queering of the patriarchal family culture that occurs inside the story line of the character.

Batwoman's supporting cast of characters, or "allies," reveals her queerness to be paramount. Inside the DC Universe, and certainly inside of Gotham City, these sorts of strategic cross-character allegiances are generally considered "families." For example, the patriarchal familial reading of Batman (father) and his sidekick Robin (son), plus an extended network of allies like Red Robin, Night Wing, and others, is considered canon. Postcolonial theorists have long seen the connection between familial metaphors and the relationship of governments to their subjects.[38] If Gotham is Batman's world, it is a patriarchal one. How does Batwoman fit into this bat family?

To be honest, at the time this chapter is being written, Batwoman is not a member of the traditional bat family. Depending on which Batwoman origin you're reading,[39] the interpretation varies. Kate Kane comes to possess her bat powers through her biological father, who co-opts military weapons and tools for her. She borrows the Bat symbol merely to show what side she is on. The Batwoman family is the Kane family; it is a parallel operation to the Batman/Wayne family.

Notice that Batwoman, unlike the Question, was able to become a superhero and keep the support of her biological family. Also, where the Question was purposefully single or sleeping with women, Batwoman has a multifaceted lesbian identity and partner. As of this writing, Kate Kane has proposed to Maggie Sawyer (in costume), and the two are poised to be wed and start their lesbian-oriented family within Kate's biological family.[40] Lesbian love, moving forward.

What about non–Kate Kane identity allies? What about Batwoman, the iconic identity? Who follows her?

"Family" is a word that is multivalent within real queer communities. The term *family* is also often used to refer to the members of a queer nation—the families, the allies, that queer individuals choose for themselves after the potential loss of their biological families and friends when they came out. At the time of writing this chapter, Batwoman's allies include a government agency dedicated to unmasking superheroes (Cameron Chase, Agent Bones, and the DEO) and a nation of religious zealots who happen to be shape-shifting were-beings, half animal and half human, or various combinations of both (the Religion of Crime).

It is not a leap to say that the creation of the Batwoman family illustrates the embodiment of a queer-led universe inside of the DC Comics publishing universe.

After the successful run in *Detective Comics* and during the establishment of Batwoman's own title, the Crimson Caped Crusader has not merely been building a name for herself; she has built a queer family and a queer nation of allies. Kate Kane's, the Batwoman's, support network includes biological family, a lesbian partner, an army of monsters defined by their hybridity—a queer nation. So too does the *Batwoman* title also hold the potential to queer comic popular book shops, malls, bookstores—places that have sadly not incorporated facets of the "GLTBQ ghetto" before.

This queering, I believe, is a necessary and welcome evolution of the Sapphic heroine. The lesbian superhero has goals similar to the ones that Alison Bechdel, Lesbian Nation folk hero creator, articulated earlier in this chapter. She must choose an identity that allows her to purposefully inhabit her life, thus challenging the spaces around her to either accept or reject her new identity. If the focus is on the lesbian identity, then that seems a bit reductive, though it does help. If the focus is on the queer identity, then she can help more. The lesbian superheroine opens up what used to be an exclusively identified community to a wider queer identification and ultimately mainstream audience. There's a lot of potential for greater queer cultural understanding in that power.

A LOOK BACK BY LOOKING FORWARD: A SPECTRUM OF QUEERS CONQUERING BINARY WORLDS

If we accept that the mainstream lesbian comic book superhero is a potent force, a highly visible articulation of the inherent need for changing external reality that comes with a lesbian identity, then the queer nation and queer culture that evolve alongside lesbian culture can be seen as an extension of what used to be considered the lesbian nation.

This queering of cultural space is already continuing the cycle of revolution: queer artists are once again involved in a process of furious self-creation. These comic book writers and artists are quite literally subverting binaries to create their own spaces: web comics have become the new alternative, independent community. These comics creators inhabit various places of the LGBTQIA spectrum, and the characters they create reflect this diversity. For example, Erika Moen's *DAR: A Super Girly Top Secret Comic Diary*[41] chronicles the cartoonists' journey from lesbian-identified and women-oriented person to a queer identity that encompasses woman-oriented passion and others. Such a narrative was rejected by the traditional lesbian-identified cartoonists' culture, and vilified (most vocally by lesbian-identified web cartoonist Ariel Schrag,[42] who draws *Ariel and Kevin Invade Everything*[43]) and accepted by others that see queerness as an extension of, rather than a threat to, lesbian culture (I would posit that the anonymous cartoonist behind *The Life and Times of a Lesbian Chick*[44] would be among Moen's supporters).

Yet despite the potential of radical division that queer identities pose for traditionally identified LGBT nations and their cultures, there is no doubt that they abound on the Internet. Straight-identified creators like Danielle Corsetto of *Girls with Slingshots*,[45] Randy Milholland, the cartoonist behind *Something Positive*,[46] and Jeph Jacques of *Questionable Content*[47] not only have lesbian narratives in their comic cultural worlds, but a slew of queer characters: persons who are transgender, disabled, asexual, bisexual, into drag, or simply just fluid and different. How wonderful. How revolutionary. How heroic.

If you ever want to test a story to find out whether it's a lie—look for the minorities, the oddballs. Is there a person with a disability? Is there an ethnic minority? Is there a transgender person? A gay man? Is there a lesbian? Is there simply somebody who is different? Hopefully all of these things are there, but often they are not. These absences are a tragedy and a lie. But even if there aren't people there that should be—because she is queer like the rest of the lot, if there's a lesbian,[48] there's hope.

NOTES

1. Greg Rucka, "Introduction," *Gotham City Central: Half a Life* (DC Comics, 2005).

2. Benedict Anderson, *Imagined Communities: Reflections on the Origin and Spread of Nationalisms* (London: Verso, 1991).

3. There is also a tradition of exploring how popular-culture lesbian film narratives inhabit space, which also lays a sort of literal foundation for this avenue of comics scholarship. A good example of this would be Lee Wallace's *Lesbianism, Cinema, Space: The Sexual Life of Apartments* (New York: Routledge, 2009). Also the entire *If These Walls Could Talk* HBO series.

4. Jeffrey Brown, *Dangerous Curves: Action Heroines, Gender, Fetishism, and Popular Culture* (Jackson: University Press of Mississippi, 2011), 9.

5. Marilyn Falwell, *Heterosexual Plots and Lesbian Narrative* (New York: New York University Press, 1996), 62.

6. There's an excellent description of this evolution in *No Straight Lines: Four Decades of Queer Comics*, ed. John Hall (Seattle: Fantagraphics, 2012). For those interested in DIY zine

culture and feminism, see Trina Robbins' *From Girls to Grrrlz: A History of Female Comics from Teens to Zines* (San Francisco: Chronicle Books, 1999).

7. Sarah Hoagland, introduction to *Call Me Lesbian: Lesbian Lives, Lesbian Theory*, ed. Julia Penelope (Freedom: The Crossing Press, 1992), xi–xii.

8. Queer culture, in general, I would posit is acutely a culture defined by images. Again, this is familiar theoretical ground as evidenced by the cornucopia of visual queer art/culture/ criticism.

9. I borrow most of (and agree with) the description of the Lesbian Avenger from Sally R. Munt's "The Lesbian Outlaw," in *Heroic Desire: Lesbian Identity and Cultural Space* (London: Cassell, 1998), 95–131. The later discussion of what I call "The Lesbian Nation/Queer Nation Builder" is a disagreement with and reinterpretation of Munt's "The Lesbian Nation" chapter of *Heroic Desire*, 132–61.

10. Elana Bouvier, "An Interview with Diane DiMassa," in *Dyke Strippers: Lesbian Cartoonists A to Z*, ed. Roz Warren (San Francisco: Cleis Press, 1995), 61.

11. Amazon.com.

12. Regina Marler, "About Cleis: An Interview with Cleis Publishers," CleisPress.com.

13. Liana Scalettar, "Resistance, Representation, and the Subject of Violence," in *Queer Frontiers: Millennial Geographies, Genders, and Generations*, ed. Boone, Dupuis, Meeker, Quimby, Sarver, Silverman, and Weatherson (Madison: University of Wisconsin Press, 2000), 261.

14. Maggie Sawyer (1980s) and Holly Robinson (1990s) are the two lesbian characters who preceded Renee Montoya, but they never achieved superheroic status. Robinson, interestingly, assumed the mantle of antihero femme feline Catwoman. Scandal Savage (1990s) isn't included because she's technically a villain. I have stuff to say about all this, but other chapters, other days.

15. Catherine Williamson involves the metaphors of the closet and drag and connects them to superheroic identity in "Draped Crusaders: Disrobing Gender in *The Mark of Zorro*," *Cinema Journal* 36, no. 2 (1997): 3–4.

16. Most of this anthology probably touches on this subject, but good primers are Chuck Tate's "The Stereotypical (Wonder) Woman," in *The Psychology of Superheroes: An Unauthorized Exploration*, ed. Robin S. Rosenberg (Dallas: BenBella Books, 2008), 147–62; or Larry Niven's "Man of Steel, Woman of Kleenex," in *All the Myriad Ways* (New York: Ballantine Del Ray, 1971).

17. Greg Rucka, "Introduction."

18. The art is drawn by Jesus Siaz. *The Question: The Five Books of Blood* (DC Comics, 2008).

19. Again, the idea of "the male gaze" is not new, but if you need further explanation, it can be traced to Laura Mulvey's essay "Visual Pleasure and Narrative Cinema," *Screen* 16, no. 3 (1975): 6–18.

20. Bechdel separates these archetypes into four visual categories. *The Indelible Alison Bechdel* (Ithaca, NY: Firebrand Books, 1998), 16–17.

21. As quoted in Katie Brown, "An Interview with Alison Bechdel," *Dyke Strippers*, 20–21.

22. Alison Bechdel, "The Cartoonists' Introduction," in *The Complete Dykes to Watch Out For* (New York: Houghton Mifflin, 2008), xiv–xv.

23. See "Oppressed Minority Cartoonist" in *No Straight Lines*, p. 130, for Bechdel's own take on this.

24. Justin Hall, "File under Queer: Comix to Comics, Punk Zines, and Art during the Plague," *No Straight Lines* (2012).

25. Munt, *Heroic Desire*, 113.

26. As quoted in Katie Brown's interview, 21.

27. Ibid., 21.

28. Munt, *Heroic Desire*, 25.

29. Ibid., 152–53.

30. Ibid., 153.

31. Oh, I would love to talk about Wonder Woman and Batwoman more, but alas this is not the place. A good primer for this eventual discussion is Mitra C. Emad's "Reading Wonder

Woman's Body: Mythologies of Gender and Nation," *Journal of Popular Culture* 39, no. 6 (2006): 954–84.

32. Perhaps the theorist I most closely identify with on this would be Lee Edelmen, in *No Future: Queer Theory and the Death Drive* (Durham, NC: Duke University Press, 2004).

33. George Gene Gustines, "Straight (and Not) out of the Comics," *New York Times*, May 26, 2006.

34. I recognize that many contemporary LGBTQIA activists dislike the mainstream LGBT activist agenda and would consider such moves by DC Comics as "safe." I agree, but even if I disagree with the priorities and the order, I cannot discount that some things are getting done. I may not like what DC does with their lesbian superheroes, but I cannot deny that they exist. That's new.

35. Specifically the sort defined by Judith/Jack Halberstam in *Female Masculinity* (Durham, NC: Duke University Press, 1998). While I disagree with Halberstam's attitudes toward femininity, s/he knows a great deal about female masculinity. Duh, s/he wrote the book on it.

36. Mimi Marinucci provides an excellent explanation of this connection using Foucault and D'Emilio in *Feminism Is Queer: The Intimate Connection between Queer and Feminist Theory* (London: Zed Books, 2010).

37. J. Skyler, "Interview: Batwoman and LGBT Visibility with J. H. Williams III," *Comicosity*, March 26, 2013.

38. A nice overview of this is provided in Maureen Molloy's "Imagining (the) Difference: Gender, Ethnicity, and Metaphors of Nation," *Feminist Review*, no. 51 (Autumn 1995): 94–112.

39. There are three different origin stories: *52* (2006), wherein Kate is defined by her romantic past with Renee Montoya; *Elegy* (2009–2010), wherein Batman inspires Kate to work with her biological father and become the night; and finally *Batwoman* #0 (2011) keeps Kate's biological family, but has Batman discovering her secret/family identity and giving her his blessing. Troubling.

40. Allying DC Comics with the mainstream LGBT goal of marriage equality roughly six months before the Supreme Court overturned DOMA.

41. Erika Moen's web comic has since been collected into two volumes and self-published through Periscope Studios in Portland, 2010.

42. The blistering article (which I disagree with) is Ariel Schrag's "Comics 'n Things: Queer Identities in Comics," *After Ellen*, November 18, 2010.

43. The web comic is located at http://invadeeverything.com.

44. A delightful web comic that can be found at http://thelifeandtimesofalesbianchick.smackjeeves.com.

45. Follow the adventures at http://www.girlswithslingshots.com.

46. Check it out at http://www.somethingpositive.net.

47. Enter this universe at http://questionablecontent.net.

48. Human being.

Part III

Contemporary American
Graphic Novels/Comics

Chapter Fourteen

Punching Holes in the Sky

Carol Danvers and the Potential of Superheroinism

Nathan Miczo

The Lord put us here to punch holes in the sky. —Helen Cobb to Carol Danvers

There is a certain lyricism in Helen Cobb's sentiment, expressed in a letter to Carol Danvers. It invokes the idea of soaring up to the heavens, transcending the limitations of an earthbound existence to realize one's potential. When the receiver of that sentiment is a superhero (as Carol Danvers is), the notion of flight is more than just figurative language. However, the term *punching* suggests aggression, violence, and the urge to fight. In the further context of one woman addressing another in Western society, with our "traditional association of men with what is higher (reason) and women with what is lower (emotion),"[1] not to mention the existence of "glass ceilings," Helen's words are susceptible of a more somber reflection on the aspirations of the superheroine.

Can a superheroine ever be a super*hero* first, or will her femaleness (i.e., the fact that she is a hero*ine*) always be her most defining characteristic? Madrid argued that "female superheroes are often not allowed to reach their potential; they are given powers that are weaker than their male compatriots, and positions of lesser importance."[2] Superheroines can also fail to reach their potential when they are placed in situations that make salient negative female stereotypes (e.g., that females are fragile, hysterical, "catty") and/or when they are objectified by repeated emphasis on their physical appearance. Under these conditions, can a female superhero stand on her own, reach her potential, without having her femininity become a liability? The question itself can be addressed at two levels. At one level, superheroes exist in a

171

fictional world, and the plotlines and situations they are placed in have been created by writers and artists. Those creators decide what aspects of a hero's identity are made salient to audiences. The second level concerns the reactions of fans, who, at times, can be very vocal about their preferences regarding any changes to a character, as well as plotlines. These two levels are not mutually exclusive; they influence and interpenetrate each other, together defining the horizon of a character's abilities.

Marvel Comics' Carol Danvers (aka Ms. Marvel, and more recently, Captain Marvel) is a perfect character with which to explore this issue. According to Madrid, she was intended to be "an iconic female superhero that could headline her own title."[3] Her debut issue in 1977 declared, "At last! A bold new superheroine in the senses-stunning tradition of Spider-Man!"[4] Her first volume lasted twenty-three issues, followed by ongoing appearances with both the X-Men and the Avengers.[5] Her second solo outing began in 2006, in the wake of the *House of M* story line, and that volume ran for an impressive fifty issues. In July 2012, volume 3 began with Danvers dropping the title "Ms. Marvel" and adopting the mantle of the fallen Kree warrior Mar-Vell, becoming the new Captain Marvel.[6] Though she may have lacked the ongoing continuity of some of her male counterparts, relative to many female superheroes, Carol has shown a staying power suggesting that she has indeed achieved headline status.

PLOTLINES AS A LIMITATION UPON THE SUPERHEROINE

From her inception, however, Danvers has been plagued with a particular perspective on what it means to be a superheroine. In other words, some of the situations she has been placed in have emphasized the femaleness of her character rather than her "heroic-ness." I will highlight two incidents in particular that associate Danvers with negative female stereotypes.[7] The first concerns Ms. Marvel's origin story. As told in *Ms. Marvel* Vol. 1 #2, Carol Danvers was caught in a fight between the Kree warriors Mar-Vell and Yon-Rogg. An "alien machine" exploded, and though Mar-Vell tried to shield Carol from the blast, radiation from the machine bonded his Kree DNA to her body, resulting in her acquisition of superpowers, including flight, strength, and the ability to absorb energy. There is nothing inherently unique about the acquisition of superpowers via radiation or cosmic rays (e.g., the Hulk, the Fantastic Four). What was different about Carol Danvers' situation was that she remained unaware of her new powers. For the first few issues, Carol literally experienced a "loss of self" when she became Ms. Marvel (and vice versa).[8] Furthermore, when her psychiatrist learned of her dual nature during a session involving hypnosis, he concluded she was the victim of a "massive paranoid delusion." Although Carol shortly thereafter recovered

Punching Holes in the Sky

173

her memories of her alter ego, the message had already been sent: rather than her superpowers being an extension and reflection of Carol's inner self, this "bold new superheroine's" powers were literally alien to her and entailed a loss of self for their manifestation.

The second incident concerned another "loss of self," this time at the hands of the mutant Rogue in *Marvel Super-Heroes Annual* #10. Based on the prediction that Danvers might harm Rogue, the shape-shifting mutant Mystique (who had come to feel very protective of Rogue) made several attempts to destroy Ms. Marvel. Taking matters into her own hands, Rogue confronted the heroine, and as the two battled over the Golden Gate Bridge, Rogue made "flesh to flesh contact" to absorb Carol's powers. However, not only did Rogue absorb Carol's powers, but she also unwittingly stole her memories. Rogue then hurls the unconscious Danvers into San Francisco Bay, where she is rescued by Spider-Woman, who just happens to be flying by. When Professor X is called in to try and uncover the comatose woman's identity, he discovers that "her unconscious mind has been completely erased," her mind "a blank slate." There is nothing unusual about Rogue using her powers to absorb a foe's abilities; in fact, in *Avengers Annual* #10 she absorbs the powers of both Captain America and Thor. In those cases, however, her victims do not experience the total loss of self and consciousness that Carol experiences. The official story line is that Rogue stayed in contact too long with Danvers, and she was careful not to do that with Captain America and Thor. Even if we presume that Danvers' condition was simply a plot device in a larger story line, the message remains: the female sense of self, in this case rooted in memory and consciousness, is more fragile and fluid than the male, which is more inviolate.

Once again, it may be pointed out that there is nothing all that out of the ordinary about a superhero suffering a loss of identity. It happens to Wolverine quite frequently.[9] It may be a general rule that physically invulnerable heroes are more susceptible to mental manipulation. But when Wolverine is taken over by enemies, the end result is often that he is actively used to commit atrocities (see, for example, the following story lines: "Weapon X," "Enemy of the State," "Wolverine Goes to Hell"). In Ms. Marvel's case, however, her loss of self rendered her fully passive. As with her earlier situation, where her (male) psychiatrist was the first to discover her dual identity, it was once again a male (Professor X) who was needed to help her recover her consciousness.

Thus, in some of her early adventures, certain aspects of Ms. Marvel's femaleness seem to have been emphasized. In particular, these were aspects that depicted her as fragile, vulnerable, and weaker than her male counterparts. Recently, however, there have been signs that Carol Danvers may finally be positioned to gain acceptance as a superhero in her own right. In *Ms. Marvel* Vol. 2 #9–10, Carol and Rogue worked together to stop a Carol

Danvers from an alternate dimension who was bent on seeking revenge on Rogue. During the more recent Avengers vs. X-Men event (2012), in *X-Men Legacy* #269–270, Rogue risks her life to break Carol out of Limbo after Danvers is sent there by the mutant Magik.[10] Rogue even refers to Carol as "a friend" when she confronts Magik. In literally overcoming herself and teaming up with Rogue, Carol rose above the stereotype of the vengeful, "catty" female.

The Avengers vs. X-Men event also created the opportunity for Carol to once again get her own ongoing title. Mar-Vell had sacrificed himself during an early attempt to stop the Phoenix from reaching earth. In *Captain Marvel* #1, Captain America persuaded Carol to adopt his mantle as a way of honoring his legacy. The first story arc returned Carol to her early love of flying when she inherited a plane from her mentor Helen Cobb. The plane ended up taking Carol back through time, however, where she met a younger Helen. In the midst of their adventures, the pair was transported to the cave in Florida where Mar-Vell confronted Yon-Rogg. In other words, Carol was taken back to the moment when she first acquired her superpowers. It then unfolds that this was no random occurrence. Helen dangled before Carol the opportunity to undo what had happened to her, to prevent her younger self from being affected by the blast from the Psyche-Magnitron. In the end, Carol not only chose to leave the past intact, but she also had to race a superpowered Helen back to the plane in order to save herself and return to the present. Thus, with the first story arc, Carol was given the opportunity to finally own her own superpowers. Dropping the "Ms." and taking the title "Captain," owning her powers, even making peace with Rogue—all these experiences indicate that, perhaps, Carol was at last being allowed to be a superhero first, and a superheroine second (i.e., being someone weaker and in a position of lesser importance).

FAN REACTIONS AS A LIMITATION UPON THE SUPERHEROINE

Descriptive Analysis of Fan Letters

Except that fans seemed determined to make her femaleness (her physical appearance) once again the most salient aspect of her character. As mentioned earlier, Carol's recent makeover included a new costume and hairstyle; fan reaction to that change is revealing for what is suggests about the struggle of being a superheroine. Ms. Marvel's original costume was red and black with a yellow star on the chest (reminiscent of Mar-Vell's costume at the time); it was basically a one-piece long-sleeve bodysuit with the midsection cut out exposing her navel, complete with gloves, calf-high boots, a diamond-shaped mask revealing just her eyes, and a short cape. Her hairstyle was in the fashion of a "70's female tennis player"[11]: thick blond hair cut shorter, parted in the middle and extravagantly feathered back. That costume lasted for almost twenty issues. In volume 1, issue #20 (1979), she changed her costume to a one-piece, sleeveless, turtleneck black bathing suit that covered her midsection, with a yellow lightning bolt across the chest. Her ensemble was completed with a red sash tied around her hips, black gloves, thigh-length black boots, and a diamond-shaped mask that revealed much more of the expressive area under her eyes. Her "tennis player" hairstyle was replaced with long, flowing blond hair. According to Madrid, the costume change was an attempt to make the character sexier and increase male readership.[12] This is the costume that became iconic for Ms. Marvel. By contrast, the new Captain Marvel costume completely covers Carol's body; it is a full bodysuit, including leggings, predominantly dark blue in color, with a red collar, red gloves, red sash tied around her waist, and red calf-high boots. A yellow border around the red turtleneck collar culminates in a small yellow star on her chest. She lost the mask and also changed her hair from long to short (though hair length somewhat varied as the issues and illustrators changed).

Virtually all superheroes undergo costume changes over the years. Sometimes these costume changes signal a change in affiliation. For example, when Wolverine dons his black and silver X-Force uniform it signifies his undertaking a mission that would never be sanctioned by the Avengers or the X-Men. At other times, the costume change accompanies a reboot to a series or an entire comic line. When Johnny Storm (aka the Human Torch) "died" and the Fantastic Four took on Spider-Man as a replacement, the entire team adopted new uniforms so as not to dishonor Johnny's memory. Fan reaction to these changes can be, understandably, mixed. In the case of Carol Danvers as the new Captain Marvel, fan reaction as gleaned from the "Letters to the Editor" page across the first eight issues of the series reveals a tendency, at least early on, to keep her appearance a salient issue.

With the caveat that only what has been revealed (or in this case, printed) is available for analysis, there were twenty-two letters printed in the "Let's Rap with Cap" page at the back of issues 2 through 8 (in issue 1, there was a letter from the editor, in which he acknowledged that there would likely be strong reaction to the changes). Eleven of those letters were from males, nine from females, and two could not be definitively established (e.g., JayDot). Thirteen of those letters mentioned something about Captain Marvel's appearance (usually the costume change, but some mentioned the hair), and nine were about other aspects of the series. Of those thirteen, four expressed negative attitudes toward the costume change, and nine expressed positive attitudes. Males were more likely to mention the costume than females (eight of eleven versus three of eight); females always expressed approval of the costume change (three of three), while males were split (four approved, four disapproved). Finally, there was some evidence that the focus on Carol's physical appearance diminished somewhat over time. In the first eleven letters, published in issues 2 through 5, there were eight references to her appearance; in the second eleven (issues 6 through 8), there were only five references to her appearance.

The point of this brief content analysis is not to suggest that one gender overwhelmingly approved of the costume while the other gender hated it. What is particularly noteworthy is that 59 percent of the letters contained a reference to Carol's physical appearance, though references grew less frequent over time. It must be borne in mind, however, that Carol's costume change did not alter the manner in which her physical body was depicted. She was still drawn with the characteristics McGrath claims objectify female superheroes: "tight buttocks, ample breasts, long yet muscular legs, narrow torso, muscular arms, and fuller hips."[13] The references to Carol's physical appearance, whether positive or negative, suggest that the heroine was continuing to be viewed as an object first and a hero second.

Thematic Analysis of Fan Letters

A more qualitative reading of the letters suggests several points that further contextualize and reinforce the descriptive analysis:

First, negative comments tended to be advanced without explanation.

"Every time I see that new costume I want to vomit" (Alan, issue 2).

"You've given her a hideous new costume" (Eric, issue 2).

"I don't hate the new costume, but I sure don't love it" (Chuck, issue 4).

"I won't lie, I still prefer her last costume, but we can't agree on everything, right?" (Chip, issue 7).

Second, positive comments, by contrast, were more likely to be made with some sort of explanation:

"How could someone as independent and confident as Carol Danvers not update her outfits? I think she looks fabulous!" (Michael, issue 4).

"Here we have a United States Air Force Colonel, a fighter pilot, a super hero who represents many feminist qualities . . . yet she fights crime with her ass hanging out. So you have no idea how thrilled I was when I saw the ad with Carol in a full body costume" (Lucas, issue 5).

Interestingly, several fans specifically mentioned the practicality of the new costume:

"I like the new look—the hair, the outfit: the sash as useful tool beyond mere adornment" (Matt, issue 3).

"I love seeing Carol as a leader! It is so refreshing to see Carol wearing a practical costume too!" (Claire, issue 5).

"This version of Carol, with a new costume that is practical and still attractive, her strength and choice to adopt the legendary Captain Marvel title, and the importance of her friendships with other women is fantastic, especially for a young woman like myself" (Kelsey, issue 6). "As for the costume change, I like it. Yes, the black bathing suit with the sash looked great, but I strongly like the practical style of having a full body suit" (Rob, issue 7).

Insofar as practicality was often mentioned in conjunction with praise for the costume change, it appears that "being practical" is being viewed as a positive characteristic. By implication, the old costume was therefore impractical, however sexy it might have been. An interesting polarity is thereby established between practicality and sexiness.

Finally, a number of fans mentioned positive traits or characteristics that transcended an exclusive focus on appearance. The letter from Kelsey above is one example. Matt, who mentioned the usefulness of her sash, went on to say, "Captain Marvel vs. the Hulk? No contest: she'd reason with him, create mutual success." Additionally, some fans linked the costume change to the larger issue of women in comics:

"I think the opponents of Carol's new name and new costume don't realize that this is a huge step for female super heroes" (Claire, issue 5).

"Finally, a female comic book hero who has not been fetishized for a male readership that is largely imagined" (Imogen, issue 6).

It is clear, however, whether fans loved or hated the changes that accompanied Carol's transformation to Captain Marvel, that her costume change set the terms of the debate. It echoes the point made earlier that her physical appearance was a central preoccupation surrounding the launch of her new title.

OBJECTIFICATION THEORY

The objectification theory of Barbara L. Fredrickson and Tomi-Ann Roberts can help account for this phenomenon.[14] Objectification theory posits that in the United States, and the West more generally, males scrutinize and evaluate women's physical appearance from the standpoint of their own subjectification. This "male gaze" treats female bodies as objects to be consumed and otherwise used for the purposes of the gazer. To the extent that they desire and/or are forced to be participants in this masculine culture, females internalize the objectified perspective, self-objectifying and subsequently coming to devalue their own subjective experiences in favor of conforming to societal standards of beauty; further, they also turn this adopted male gaze upon one another. One of the mechanisms by which such internalization proceeds is media consumption. Aubrey, Henson, Hopper, and Smith, for example, found that females exposed to models who were barely dressed were less positive about their own appearance and somewhat more self-objectifying than a control group.[15] A study by Zurbriggen, Ramsey, and Jaworski found that consumption of objectifying media was related to partner objectification, which in turn predicted reduced relationship satisfaction.[16] Exposure to, and consumption of, objectifying media thus has effects upon both one's sense of self and one's relationships.

In addition to direct effects of media exposure upon self-conceptions and standards applied to others, there are likely indirect effects of media via the use of media as social capital. That is, viewers do not passively take in media in isolation; rather, they use the content of films, magazines, television shows, and even comic books as fodder for conversation.[17] This is especially likely to be the case to the extent that affect and identity are wrapped up in the contents of one's viewership, as they are for fans of any genre.[18] The implication for Carol Danvers is that as fans, both male and female, make salient her physical appearance and thereby objectify her, they actively construct a discourse in which female heroes are, at least partially, defined by one aspect of their femaleness that reinforces their subordinate status in society.

There is evidence, however, that this does not have to be the case. Johnson and Gurung exposed female undergraduates to photos of one of three provocatively dressed females: in one picture, the female was standing by a swimming pool and holding a trophy plaque; in another she was standing by a white board completing a complex math equation; the third was a control condition, where the female was standing against a white background.[19] The results revealed that, relative to the control condition, when the females' competence and achievement abilities were highlighted, they were objectified less, as well as perceived as more intelligent, responsible, and talented. Taken together, these results suggest that revealing less skin and highlighting capabilities can diminish the objectification of females, even female superheroes. The fact that references to Carol's appearance diminished over time is consistent with this interpretation, as is the fact that fans began to perceive her as opting for a practical costume over an overtly sexy or revealing one. A superheroine's femaleness need not be a liability; however, she needs to be placed in situations that allow her to effectively and creatively use her superpowers, while deemphasizing the salience of how she looks.

EXTENDING THE ANALYSIS OF THE SUPERHEROINE

There are several directions that might be taken in future research. Regarding plotlines, researchers could explore the ways in which gender is reinforced by the situations into which heroes are placed, as well the associations with gender stereotypes that those situations create. For example, both Captain America and Wonder Woman have recently been placed into story lines involving infants. After being transported to an alternate dimension ruled by his enemy Arnim Zola, Captain America rescued a male infant (i.e., Zola's "son") from Zola and set out to protect and raise him. Wonder Woman found herself caught up in the machinations of the Olympian gods as she sought to protect a young mother who was pregnant with, and eventually delivers, Zeus' child. What is interesting is that after Captain America rescues the child, the very next issue begins nine years in the future. Thus he goes from securing an infant to mentoring and raising an already autonomous nine-year-old. We may infer he did all the things necessary to care for an infant, but those activities are never depicted, and hence never directly associated with him. By contrast, Wonder Woman has been associated with pregnancy and infancy since September 2011 (when this story arc began), even though she herself is never shown changing diapers or mixing formula. The point being made here is not about specific depictions; rather, it involves the more subtle ways in which situations create and reinforce gender associations.

Several avenues offer themselves for research on fan reactions. A more in-depth analysis could be made of fan letters in the different volumes of Ms. Marvel. For example, a letter in volume 1, issue #4, by a female argued the general point that female superheroes are rarely treated as equals to their male counterparts. In volume 1, issues #7 and #8, letters from other women were printed specifically addressing those arguments. Although issues surrounding feminism and women's equality are not entirely lacking from the current set of letters, they certainly seem to be less prominent. That in itself may suggest how fans draw upon characters as resources for thinking about and debating current issues.

Comparative research could be undertaken to examine fan reactions to other characters' costume changes, particularly male characters. For example, in the wake of the Avengers vs. X-Men event, Tony Stark (aka Iron Man) decided to leave earth and explore the larger universe. He left behind a black and gold suit of armor to "stand in" for him with his various earth-bound teams while he adopted a new version of his traditional red and gold armor for his outer-space adventures. No uproar surrounded these changes, and in fact the few references, especially to the black and gold armor, were all positive.

Research might also be conducted on the characteristics of those who form parasocial relationships with female superheroes (including Captain Marvel). A study by Greenwood found that women who idealized female action heroes (e.g., Sarah Michelle Gellar as Buffy, Jennifer Garner as Sydney, etc.) reported more aggressive behaviors and feelings.[20] Identification with female action heroes, however, was not related to aggressiveness. Additionally, Greenwood noted that a number of open-ended descriptions referenced "more positive holistic impressions" (e.g., she's smart, powerful, sexy, witty).[21] The neglect of such positive characteristics in liking for super/action heroes coupled with a narrowed focus on aggression may itself reveal much about the bias of such research.

CONCLUSIONS: THE MEANING OF THE SUPERHEROINE

At the end of the day, we return to the issue of what it means to be a heroine. That is, should a heroine be different from a hero because she's female? In an article on Den of Geek, C. J. Wheeler and Jennie Whitwood ask, "Do all women have to look and act like blokes to be on an equal footing?"[22] Kelly Sue DeConnick, Captain Marvel's current writer, presented a counterpoint during an interview for *Hero Complex*, stating, "There's nothing inherently masculine about power fantasies. There's nothing inherently masculine about superhero comics."[23] A study by Johnson, Lurye, and Freeman sheds some light on this question.[24] The film *The Incredibles* allowed these researchers to compare gender, appearance, and behavior for the same characters in both superhero and nonsuperhero roles. Using still photos, they took the physical measurements of Bob and Helen Parr and compared them to their superhero alter egos, Mr. Incredible and Elastigirl. For Bob/Mr. Incredible, the transformation was mostly one of proportions. That is, Bob's chest-to-waist ratio (CWR) was close to the population average. When he became Mr. Incredible, his CWR was drastically altered, exaggerating the V-shaped physique of the masculine ideal, increasing "perceptions of strength, endurance, and masculinity."[25] For Helen, the relevant measure is the waist-to-hip ratio (WHR). Although Helen was within the normal range of the female population, Elastigirl's super-slim waist relative to her curvy hips creates a WHR that is "so extreme that it does not exist in nature."[26] Thus, the transformation from average person to superhero is marked by sexual dimorphism with respect to bodily appearance.

What about superhero behavior? Johnson, Lurye, and Freeman also had a group of participants evaluate the behaviors of Bob, Mr. Incredible, Helen, and Elastigirl using the Bem Sex Role Inventory.[27] Those results revealed that Bob and Helen engaged in sex-typed behavior: Bob's behavior was masculine and Helen's was rated as feminine. As one would expect, Mr. Incredible was rated as even more extremely masculine than Bob. By contrast, Elastigirl's behavior was cross sex typed; that is, Elastigirl's behavior was more masculine than Helen's behavior. Superhero behavior, then, seems to be defined as masculine, regardless of the gender of the hero performing it. Thus, in contrast to Kelly Sue DeConnick's statement, there may be something inherently masculine about superhero behavior. The authors conclude that, for female heroes, "her simultaneous embodiment of the ideal feminine physique and the ideal masculine/agentic attributes allows her not only to be adored and admired as a woman, but also respected and honored like a man."[28] A similar conclusion is reached by Tate in an analysis of Wonder Woman.[29] According to Tate, a person who exhibits gender-astereo-typical behavior may be subtyped—that is, perceived as an exception to a rule that is otherwise left intact. One result of this is that the person might be denigrated as a rule breaker; however, this can be avoided if the person can "balance" the "gender stereotype equation."[30] As Tate argues, "if women are too 'masculine' (e.g., strong) then they *must be* "feminine" (e.g., sexy) to 'balance out' the gender stereotype."[31]

The problem with this conclusion is that it simply reinforces the objectification of the superheroine's body: a superheroine can be strong, as long as she remains sexy. The results of the study by Johnson and Gurung suggest that objectification can be overcome if competence, rather than appearance, is emphasized. A superheroine needs to balance her masculine strength with a set of competencies that highlights her feminine qualities if she is to be accepted in a (fictional) world that may just be "inherently masculine." Is there such a set of values that can be used to balance the scales? One possibility is to explore the "ethics of care" advanced by Carol Gilligan. Gilligan argued that, for women, "identity is defined in a context of relationship and judged by a standard of responsibility and care."[32] A superheroine can be strong and she can be concerned with her relationships, exemplifying the competencies and practicalities of masculine and feminine values.[33] Kelly Sue DeConnick seems to be striving for something like this in Carol's recent adventures, as she is shown attending to the various relationships in her life without neglecting her position as a superhero.[34] And it seems that some fans are responding to DeConnick's efforts, as evidenced in the letter from Matt quoted above about Carol working things out with the Hulk, or Kelsey, the fan who wrote, "The importance of [Captain Marvel's] friendships with other women is fantastic, especially for a young woman like myself." Carol Danvers stands poised to truly take flight as a new model for the superheroine. And she may not have to punch anyone to do it.

NOTES

1. Sarah K. Donovan and Nicholas P. Richardson, "Women Are from Zamaron, Men Are from Oa," in *Green Lantern and Philosophy*, ed. Jane Dryden and Mark D. White (Hoboken, NJ: Wiley, 2011), 38.

2. Mike Madrid, *The Supergirls* (Minneapolis: Exterminating Angel Press, 2010), iv.

3. Madrid, *The Supergirls*, 175.

4. Carol actually debuted in 1968 in *Marvel Super Heroes* #13 as a supporting character and potential love interest of Mar-Vell (aka Captain Marvel), a Kree warrior who had infiltrated Earth.

5. *Essential Ms. Marvel* Vol. 1 collects *Ms. Marvel* #1–23, *Marvel Super-Heroes Magazine* #10–11, and *Avengers Annual* #10. References to early story lines are from this collection. Although an analysis of how Carol was portrayed by different writers and artists is beyond the scope of this chapter, it should be mentioned that Gerry Conway wrote the first three issues;

Chris Claremont took over starting in issue 4 and wrote the remainder of Carol's early adventures.

6. Captain Marvel is currently being written by Kelly Sue DeConnick.

7. Longtime fans of Ms. Marvel may note the omission of one of the most controversial story lines in comics: the abduction and rape of Carol Danvers by the extradimensional being called Marcus. It goes beyond the scope of this chapter to examine the issues raised by that event. Carol A. Strickland's article, "The Rape of Ms. Marvel," remains a definitive statement on the story line. Her article is available online at http://carolastrickland.com/comics/msmarvel/index.html.

8. Although Bruce Banner can be said to experience a loss of self when he transforms into the Hulk, the Hulk has always been an exaggerated manifestation of Banner's own inner personality, not an alien personality imposed externally.

9. For a thought-provoking discussion of Wolverine's frequent loss of identity, see Jason Southworth, "Amnesia, Personal Identity, and the Many Lives of Wolverine," in *X-Men and Philosophy*, ed. Rebecca Housel and J. Jeremy Wisnewski (Hoboken, NJ: Wiley, 2009), 21–23.

10. Briefly put, the Avengers vs. X-Men event was set in motion when the Phoenix Force was spotted making its way to Earth, presumably to inhabit the body of Hope Summers, the first mutant child to be born since M-Day, when the Scarlet Witch nearly eliminated the mutant population by uttering the words, "No more mutants." Captain America and the Avengers wanted to take Hope into their own custody, while Cyclops and his team of mutants wanted Hope to remain with them. When the Phoenix Force arrives at Earth, Iron Man devises a weapon that splinters its power so that it enters five mutants: Cyclops, Emma Frost, Magneto, Colossus, and his sister, Magik. Ultimately, Hope and the Scarlet Witch join forces and use the power of the Phoenix Force to "jump-start" the mutant population.

11. Madrid, *The Supergirls*, 176.

12. Ibid., 176.

13. Karen McGrath, "Gender, Race and Latina Identity: An Examination of Marvel Comics' *Amazing Fantasy* and *Araña*," *Atlantic Journal of Communication* 15 (2007): 275, doi: 10.1080/15456870701483599.

14. Barbara L. Fredrickson and Tomi-Ann Roberts, "Objectification Theory: Toward Understanding Women's Lived Experiences and Mental Health Risks," *Psychology of Women Quarterly* 21 (1997): 173–206, doi: 10.1111/j.1471-6402.1997.tb00108.x.

15. Jennifer Stevens Aubrey, Jayne R. Henson, K. Megan Hopper, and Siobahn E. Smith, "A Picture Is Worth Twenty Words (about the Self): Testing the Priming Influence of Visual Sexual Objectification on Women's Self-Objectification," *Communication Research Reports* 26 (2009): 271–84, doi: 10.1080/0882409093293551.

16. Eileen L. Zurbriggen, Laura R. Ramsey, and Beth K. Jaworski, "Self- and Partner-Objectification in Romantic Relationships: Associations with Media Consumption and Relationship Satisfaction," *Sex Roles* 64 (2011): 449–62, doi: 10.1007/s11199-011-9933-4.

17. See, for example, Anne Bartsch, "As Time Goes By: What Changes and What Remains the Same in Entertainment Experience over the Life Span?" *Journal of Communication* 62 (2012): 588–608, doi: 10.1111/j.1460-2466.2012.01657.x; Larua Fingerson, "Active Viewing," *Journal of Contemporary Ethnography* 28 (1999): 389–418, doi: 10.1177/089124199129023497.

18. Lawrence Grossberg, "Is There a Fan in the House?: The Affective Sensibility of Fandom," in *The Adoring Audience: Fan Culture and Popular Media*, ed. Lisa A. Lewis (London: Routledge, 1992), 50–65.

19. Valerie Johnson and Regan A. R. Gurung, "Defusing the Objectification of Women by Other Women: The Role of Competence," *Sex Roles* 65 (2011): 177–88, doi: 10.1007/s11199-011-0006-5.

20. Dara N. Greenwood, "Are Female Action Heroes Risky Role Models? Character Identification, Idealization, and Viewer Aggression," *Sex Roles* 57 (2007): 725–32, doi: 10.1007/s11199-007-9290-5.

21. Greenwood, "Are Female Action Heroes Risky Role Models?," 730.

22. C. J. Wheeler and Jennie Whitwood, "Carol Danvers: Just Another Captain Marvel?," *Den of Geek*, http://www.denofgeek.us/books-comics/11509/carol-danvers-just-another-captain-marvel (accessed December 7, 2012).

23. "Captain Marvel: DeConnick on Carol Danvers and the Comics Industry," *Hero Complex*, http://herocomplex.latimes.com/2012/08/16/captain-marvel-deconnick-on-carol-danvers-and-comics-industry, accessed December 7, 2012.

24. Kerri L. Johnson, Leah E. Lurye, and Jonathan B. Freeman, "Gender Typicality and Extremity in Popular Culture," in *The Psychology of Superheroes: An Unauthorized Exploration*, ed. Robin S. Rosenberg (Dallas: BenBella Books, 2008), 229–44.

25. Johnson, Lurye, and Freeman, "Gender Typicality," 236.

26. Ibid., 237.

27. See note 24.

28. Johnson, Lurye, and Freeman, "Gender Typicality," 242.

29. Chuck Tate, "The Stereotypical (Wonder) Woman," in *The Psychology of Superheroes: An Unauthorized Exploration*, ed. Robin S. Rosenberg (Dallas: BenBella Books, 2008), 147–62.

30. Tate, "The Stereotypical (Wonder) Woman," 155.

31. Ibid., 155–56.

32. Carol Gilligan, *In a Different Voice: Psychological Theory and Women's Development* (Cambridge, MA: Harvard University Press, 1982), 160.

33. The point is not to simply invert the hierarchy and make "feminine" strengths and values dominant over "masculine" ones. For the dangers of just such an approach in the superhero world, see Donovan and Richardson, note 1, above.

34. Since at least issue 9, Carol has been attending to her relationships with Jessica Drew (aka Spider-Woman), her new assistant Wendy, her friend Tracy who is dealing with cancer, an old woman she visits on a park bench named Rose, and a young girl named Kit who lives in her building, all this while attending to her typical duties as a superhero.

Chapter Fifteen

Jumping Rope Naked

John Byrne, Metafiction, and the Comics Code

Roy Cook

BYRNE, THE SHE-HULK, AND METAFICTION

Jennifer Walters, aka the Sensational She-Hulk, is one of the last superheroes created by the legendary Stan Lee (a fact that the self-aware She-Hulk proudly notes on more than one occasion[1]). As is often the case with female "versions" of male superheroes (Jennifer gained her powers via a blood transfusion from her more famous cousin—the Incredible Hulk), the She-Hulk was initially introduced in order to protect Marvel Comics' rights to a female version of the popular male character. Unsurprisingly, the She-Hulk's first solo title—*The Savage She-Hulk*—is, in retrospect, of little lasting interest to either fans or scholars of comics, since the She-Hulk is portrayed there as little more than an enraged, female clone of her cousin.

Things changed in 1989, however, when John Byrne began writing and drawing her second solo title—*The Sensational She-Hulk*. The comic is notable for portraying the She-Hulk in a more positive light—she is no longer merely a female copy of her cousin, but is instead able to balance roles as a successful lawyer and a member of both the Avengers and the Fantastic Four—all in her six-foot-plus, green-skinned She-Hulk persona. This more positive depiction of the She-Hulk in general, and of superheroines in particular, is already notable and worthy of attention by both fans and scholars, especially in the late 1980s and early 1990s, when depictions of females as anything other than scantily clad sexual objects for both their fictional superhero compatriots and their real-world fans were perhaps rarer than ever before or since. But the She-Hulk is notable not only for being Marvel Comics' premiere solo superheroine. She is also notable for being *aware* that she is Marvel Comics' premiere solo superheroine.

This is the twist that John Byrne introduced into the She-Hulk story: in the solo series, at least, the She-Hulk is aware that she is a character in a comic book, and aware of both the fact that she was created (and to some extent, at least, controlled—see the discussion in the concluding section) by Byrne and that she is constantly observed by beings outside official Marvel Comics continuity—that is, by us, the readers. In addition, she is able to take advantage of this awareness in a multitude of clever and creative ways—for example, traveling between dimensions by tearing a hole in the page of the comic, and by interacting with John Byrne directly (either by breaking the "fourth wall" and speaking to him, or by having him appear directly on the page in his trademark red flannel shirt).

In short, in John Byrne's hands *The Sensational She-Hulk* became metafiction. Patricia Waugh, in her seminal work *Metafiction: The Theory and Practice of Self-Conscious Fiction*, defines *metafiction* as follows:

> Metafiction is a term given to fictional writing which self-consciously and systematically draws attention to its status as an artefact in order to pose questions about the relationship between fiction and reality. In providing a critique of their own methods of construction, such writings . . . examine the fundamental structures of narrative fiction. [2]

Waugh clearly has metafictional novels in mind here, but the basic idea is this: metafictional works of art are works that are in some sense or another about the process, status, or mechanics of art in general, or that artwork in particular. Thus, for our purposes here, we can adopt the following somewhat looser definition of *metacomics*:

> A metacomic is a comic that is "about" comics in one sense or another, where this "meta" aspect of the narrative is intended not only to further the narrative, but also to comment on the nature of narrative itself.

Thus, a metacomic is a comic that is about comics (or about storytelling more generally, etc.).

John Byrne's run on *The Sensational She-Hulk* is one of the most overt, and most interesting, examples of a sustained metafictional narrative within mainstream superhero comics. [3] In addition to taking advantage of the formal conventions of comics as mentioned above, Byrne also uses the comic to parody, and to metafictionally interrogate, his own reputation as a "Good Girl Artist" (*Good Girl Art* is a technical term within comics fandom, and to a lesser extent comics scholarship, referring to artwork, particular titles, and particular artists that involve especially attractive or excessively sexualized depictions of female characters). [4]

It is with respect to Byrne's status as a Good Girl Artist, and his aware-ness of, and willingness to metafictionally address, this role, that *The Sensa-tional She-Hulk* #40—the notorious "jump rope" issue—becomes so interest-ing and, as an example of how metafiction can be used to simultaneously engage in conventional comic book tropes and critique those tropes, so im-portant. At first glance, this issue (or, at least, its cover and initial four pages) strikes the reader as little more than another example of the worst sort of gendered excess that was rampant in comics at the time. On closer analysis, however, it turns out that there is much more going on. The task undertaken in the remainder of this chapter is to explore what, exactly, Byrne was trying to achieve in *Sensational She-Hulk* #40, and to determine to what extent he was successful.

JUMPING ROPE NAKED: *THE SENSATIONAL SHE-HULK* #40

The cover to *The Sensational She-Hulk* #40 depicts the She-Hulk—apparent-ly naked—clutching a large piece of white paper close to her body in order to (barely) cover herself. An arm reaches in from the edge of the cover, offering a jump rope to the She-Hulk. This off-panel figure (clearly Byrne himself, as evidenced by the fact that the arm is sheathed in Byrne's trademark red flannel shirt) says, "Quit *stalling*, Shulkie! We've got twenty-two pages to fill!" to which the She-Hulk responds, "Hey . . . No! You're kidding, right?"[5]

Bad enough already. But the interior of the comic is (at least at first glance) even worse. The first four pages of the comic consist of four single-panel splash pages of the She-Hulk jumping rope (apparently) naked, with strategically placed motion lines obscuring (depending on the panel) one or more of her breasts, crotch, or derriere. The first panel provides a view from the front, the second panel a view from the side, the third a view from behind, and the fourth another view from the front, this time with the She-Hulk's arms placed behind her back to further emphasize her (partially ob-scured) breasts. Throughout these four pages, the She-Hulk speaks directly to the reader, expressing her disgust at her current predicament:

Page 1:
Can you believe this?
Page 2:
I know Marvel will do just about **anything** to make a sale . . .
. . . but this kinda goes **beyond the pale**, you know?
Page 3:
I mean, here I am, a successful **lawyer** . . .
. . . a member of the **Avengers** . . .
. . . a reserve member of the **Fantastic Four** no less . . .
Page 4:

> . . . and just because I happened to make a **joking** remark in the **letters page** . . .
> . . . I end up with all the **dignity** and **respect** I've worked so hard to **gain** . . .
> . . . **wiped away** in the name of **cheap thrills** and—**maybe**—higher sales![6]

At this point, a second voice comes in from off the page, shouting (as evidenced by the "burst" balloon), "Hey! What's going on here?"

At this point, *The Sensational She-Hulk* #40 does seem to consist in little more than the sort of cheap titillation that was unfortunately stock-in-trade for superhero comics of the 1990s. But, even on a superficial first reading, it is clear that Byrne intended something *more* than mere objectification here (even if it is also clear that Byrne, throughout his two runs on *The Sensational She-Hulk*, had no problem with sexualized depictions of female characters—the point is that, in many cases, objectification is not the *only* thing going on!). The evidence begins on the next page, where the mystery off-page speaker is revealed to be Renee Witterstaetter, the editor of *The Sensational She-Hulk* at the time (who also, like Byrne, often appeared within the comic). The following exchange takes place between Renee and the She-Hulk:

> Page 5, panel 1:
> Renee: She-Hulk!
> You stop that right this minute.
> Page 5, panel 2:
> She-Hulk: Oh, hi, Renee.
> Sorry, I know you're the **editor** of my book an' all . . .
> . . . but if I stop twirling this rope . . .
> Page 5, panel 3:
> She-Hulk: We're gonna end up in **bigger** trouble with the Keeper of the Comics Code than we probably **are** already!
> Renee: Oh, come off it, She-Hulk!
> Page 5, panel 4:
> Renee: You know **Tom DeFalco** wouldn't have **allowed** this in the first place . . . [7]

At this point, Renee whips the jump rope out of the She-Hulk's hands to reveal, at the top of the following page, that the She-Hulk was wearing a (skimpy) bikini all along. The relevant dialogue concludes as follows:

> Page 6, panel 1:
> Renee: . . . if you weren't actually **wearing** something behind those **blur lines**.
> Page 6, panel 2:
> She-Hulk: Oh great!
> Now you've **really** let the cat out of the bag!
> Now we stand about equal chance of getting in trouble with the **Legion of Decency** . . .

Page 6, panel 3:
She-Hulk: . . . and the **Better Business Bureau!**
The **cover did** imply I was **naked**, after all!
Renee: Let **me** be the one to worry about that, She-Hulk.
Page 6, panel 4:
Renee: Anybody who was **dopey** enough to think you could **really** be skipping rope in the nude . . .
. . . **deserves** to have **wasted** his money anyway![8]

At this point, the comic transitions into a standard (well, standard relative to the typical weirdness of Byrne's She-Hulk stories) superheroine adventure.

So, in a nutshell, we have a cover "advertising" the She-Hulk jumping rope nude, followed by four pages that (on their own) appear to show exactly that, followed by two pages of dialogue between the She-Hulk and Renee Witterstaetter humorously explaining why those pages couldn't have actually been what they appeared to be. This is certainly a cleverly humorous and self-aware way to insert overtly sexualized content into a mainstream superhero comic book (as well as a joking reference to the need to do so in order to boost flagging sales—a running joke within the entire run of *The Sensational She-Hulk*). But is anything else going on here? Is there any way to read this as anything other than another instance—regardless of how clever—of the sort of morally dubious depiction of females rampant within mainstream comics at the time (and, to be honest, still rampant twenty years later!)?

A closer reading of the cover and first few pages of *The Sensational She-Hulk #40* demonstrates that Byrne is not merely taking advantage of a clever opportunity to draw the She-Hulk (apparently) nude (although, as noted before, he is clearly doing that), but is also utilizing his ability to do so to construct a clever critique of the Comics Code Authority and the constraints on comic book depictions of women imposed by the Code. In order to develop this reading of *The Sensational She-Hulk #40*, we shall first have to review a bit of the history of the Comics Code itself, as well as Byrne's earlier references to the Code—a task we take up in the next section.

Before doing so, it is worth highlighting an issue that will become important in the conclusion of this chapter. I shall be showing that the jump-rope episode in *The Sensational She-Hulk #40* is not *merely* a piece of sexualized pinup art, and as a result should not be written off as being nothing more than morally dubious objectification of the female form. The fact that this content is not offensive *merely* in terms of its depiction of a respected female character jumping rope naked (since this content is being used to make a larger point, rather than merely for titillation), however, does not mean that it is not objectionable *at all*. As we shall see in the conclusion, there are additional aspects of this depiction that may still be offensive. Thus, the present chapter is not, and is not intended to be, a defense of the jump-rope incident depicted in the comic, but instead is meant to provide a more nuanced evaluation of this episode, resulting in a more ambiguous final assessment of the jump-rope incident than it typically receives.

1954, THE COMICS CODE, AND THE SHE-HULK

The year 1954 was a busy one for the comics industry, as well as for its opponents.[9] Just as video games are often blamed for the problems of today's youth, and Dungeons and Dragons received its share of the blame in the 1980s, comics were widely blamed for an apparent rise in juvenile delinquency and related problems in the 1950s. Parents and educators had begun worrying about the pernicious influence of comics on youth a number of years earlier, as is illustrated by *Time* magazine's rather matter-of-fact report on one of the many comic book burnings being organized by schools and churches at the time:

> In Binghamton, N.Y., students of St. Patrick's parochial school collected 2,000 objectionable comic books in a house-to-house canvass, burned them in the schoolyard.[10]

But the anticomics crusade really got going with the publication of Fredric Wertham's *Seduction of the Innocent*[11] in which he purported to demonstrate that comic books had a significant, and uniformly negative, impact on the youth that read them.[12] After the publication of *Seduction of the Innocent*, things really got going, and later in that same year a special meeting of the Congressional Subcommittee on Juvenile Delinquency was convened in order to determine the extent to which comics were a threat to America's youth. The comics industry fared badly in the hearings, and in the face of the resulting unfavorable public opinion and the very real threat of government regulation, the comics industry instituted the Comics Code.

The Comics Code was a set of regulations enforced by the Comics Code Authority (CCA)—an organization formed by comics publishers in the wake of the congressional hearings. The code consisted of a set of rules dictating what could and could not be depicted in comics bearing the CCA seal. Although participation was voluntary, it quickly became clear that many comics retailers would not carry, and many parents would not purchase (or allow their children to purchase), comics lacking the distinctive CCA seal. Only two publishers managed to successfully market comics lacking the CCA seal: Dell Comics and Gold Key Comics, both of which focused on wholesome-seeming comics such as Disney and Warner Brothers licenses. Other publishers either modified the content of their existing publications in order to meet the requirements of the code, or moved out of comic book publishing altogether.

Much of the content of the Comics Code focused on ensuring that authority was respected, crime was not glorified, the sanctity of heterosexual nuclear families was protected, and horrific and supernatural topics were avoided (leading the more cynical of its critics to conclude that the code was perhaps motivated more by a desire to rein in the crime and horror comics that were so successful at the time and less by a genuine desire to protect juveniles). But the code also had numerous provisions restricting the depiction of women. Most notable among these are the four provisions listed under the subsection of the code governing costume in comics:

1. Nudity in any form is prohibited, as is indecent or undue exposure.
2. Suggestive and salacious illustration or suggestive posture is unacceptable.
3. All characters shall be depicted in dress reasonably acceptable to society.
4. Females shall be drawn realistically without exaggeration of any physical qualities.

The code went through a number of revisions during its fifty-plus-year reign, and the original constraints had been relaxed somewhat by the time Byrne was working on *The Sensational She-Hulk*. For example, in the 1971 version only the fourth rule is retained in full—while nudity is still prohibited, indecent or undue exposure, suggestive posture, and dress that is unacceptable to society are no longer prohibited—and in the 1989 version the prohibition on nudity is replaced by the somewhat vaguer command that "primary human sexual characteristic will never be shown." Nevertheless, Byrne was working for Marvel Comics, and the comics produced by Marvel (with a very few exceptions) still carried the CCA seal in 1992 (Marvel would not abandon the code until 2001).

Thus, we need to interpret the cover and initial pages of *The Sensational She-Hulk* #40 with the Comics Code in mind, since Byrne is, if nothing else, quite consciously pushing the boundaries of what the code will allow on these pages. A close reading of the cover, however, suggests that much more is going on: It turns out that not one, but *two* copies of the CCA seal grace the cover of *The Sensational She-Hulk* #40. The first is the standard occurrence in the upper left corner, incorporated into the Marvel logo, and signifying that this comic passed the rigorous inspection of the CCA. The second, however, appears within the cover art itself: the large piece of paper that the She-Hulk is using on the cover to preserve her modesty is, in fact, a copy of the CCA seal. To put it bluntly, this copy of the code is *literally* preventing the She-Hulk from appearing nude on the cover!

Byrne continues this narrative play with the Comics Code in the interior pages of the comic. After the four pages depicting what appears—out of context, at least—to be the She-Hulk jumping rope stark naked, the joke is revealed when Renee rips away the rope, revealing the bikini that the She-Hulk must have been wearing all along. At the same time, she notes that Tom DeFalco—the editor-in-chief at Marvel Comics at the time—would not have allowed this to occur within the comic if the She-Hulk hadn't been "decent." The reference to DeFalco is critically important here: among other things, one of the duties of the editor-in-chief is to ensure that all of the comics published by Marvel meet the company's guidelines and policies, including adhering to the Comics Code. Renee is, in effect, noting that, since *The Sensational She-Hulk* carries the CCA code, it would have been obvious to the reader all along that the She-Hulk is not naked.

Byrne is fond of playing with visual tricks like this. For example, in *Alpha Flight* #6, a battle between two characters garbed in white—Snowbird and Kolomaq—occurs during a blizzard and is depicted as five pages that are completely blank other than panel borders, dialogue, and sound effects. Further, this is not the first time that Byrne poked fun at the Comics Code in his work. In *The Sensational She-Hulk* #4, the She-Hulk explains to another character that the reason her clothes don't tear inappropriately during battles is that they have the CCA seal sewn onto the label. But Byrne is doing more in *The Sensational She-Hulk* #40 than mere formal experimentation, or making wry observations regarding the role of the Comics Code. Instead, the jump-rope issue amounts to cleverly manipulating the Comics Code in such a way that it undermines itself. Along the way, Byrne forces the reader (at least, the reader open to and attentive to these sorts of metafictional commentary) to reassess the role, and the effectiveness, of the Comics Code itself.

Looking back at the four pages in question, something very interesting has occurred. The four pages Byrne drew depicting the She-Hulk jumping rope seem, when taken out of context, to depict her naked. In fact, it seems fair to say that these pages, on their own, *do*, in fact, depict the She-Hulk naked! If someone ignorant of the content of the pages to follow were shown one or more of the jump-rope pages on their own, it seems unlikely, if not impossible, that they would or could interpret the pages otherwise. He then framed these within the narrative of the issue in question in such a way as to force us to reinterpret them as depicting something else. Presumably, the drawings on the first four pages of this issue are exactly the sort of overt depiction of nudity, or at least "suggestive or salacious illustration," that the Comics Code was meant to police and eliminate. But, thanks to Byrne's clever setup, it is precisely the fact that the Comics Code seal appears on the cover that forces us to reinterpret these images in a manner consistent with the code itself. In short, Byrne has forced the Comics Code to undo itself: instead of preventing these drawings from appearing in the comic, the code is an essential part of the story regarding *why* these pictures are, in the end, acceptable and appropriate (according to the CCA's own guidelines!) for publication in a mainstream comic.

Of course, Byrne's point here—that the imposition of the sort of censorship embodied in the Comics Code (that is, the mindless enforcement of a set of moral proscriptions) rarely eliminates the supposedly objectionable content, but most often leads to the forbidden content being included in a hidden, coded, or metaphorical manner—is far from new. But Byrne's manner of making his point, and of turning the principles of the censoring institution in on themselves, is both novel and immensely effective. It also serves to remind us that such censorship, notwithstanding all the harm it does, often leads to extremely clever and formally innovative work as creators strive to overcome, subvert, or just flat out incorporate the resulting restrictions into the sort of stories they want to tell.

In addition to targeting the Comics Code as both ultimately ineffective and potentially hypocritical, however, this issue of *The Sensational She-Hulk* also continues Byrne's ongoing metafictional interrogation of his own role as a Good Girl Artist. As noted early in this chapter, Byrne is well known for his sexy, seductive depictions of female characters—often in skimpy clothes and suggestive poses—and his work on *The Sensational She-Hulk* is no exception. But within the pages of *The Sensational She-Hulk* he also frequently questions the role that these depictions play in mainstream comics: the She-Hulk often complains to Byrne about her outfits and poses, and in issue #45 Byrne fills the majority of the pages with non sequitur pinups (surrounded by much smaller panels telling the actual story), with Renee complaining about the inappropriateness and irrelevance of the art in overlaid narration boxes. In short, Byrne does not just draw scantily clothed, sexualized images of women, but does so in a way that self-consciously draws attention to the fact that he is doing so.

Along similar lines, the images of the She-Hulk jumping rope naked in issue 40 are characterized (jokingly) by Byrne, both on the cover and in the She-Hulk's dialogue, as not only something that he can deliver via clever manipulation of the Comics Code, but something *demanded* by the readers and thus something that it is his *responsibility* to deliver. Of course, for the reasons already outlined above, Byrne doesn't literally provide images of the She-Hulk naked, although he does provide images that can be interpreted as such out of context. As a result, in telling us, the readers, that this is what we wanted (and demonstrating that this is what we can receive, regardless of the supposed protections of the Comics Code), the story forces us to reflect on what mainstream comics readers really *do* want and what they *ought* to receive with respect to depictions of women. In short, it is impossible not to read this issue as a commentary on the depiction of women within mainstream comics, and on the increasing sexualization and objectification of women that became almost a defining feature of the medium during the

1990s. His implicit criticism of the fan who wants to see the She-Hulk naked, expressed through Renee's comments that such a reader is "dopey" and "deserves to have wasted his money," suggests that we need to reassess not only Byrne's cheesecake depictions of the She-Hulk jumping rope, but her depiction more generally throughout his run on the title (and, more broadly, the Good Girl Art he created throughout his comics career). Byrne might be willing to produce such sexualized work (and, it must be admitted, to do it well), but, in *The Sensational She-Hulk* at least, he doesn't seem willing to do so without forcing us to reflect on why such pinuppery exists, and whether we should be asking him to produce it in the first place.

So, the pages in issue 40 depicting the She-Hulk jumping rope (apparently) naked are not *merely* an exercise in sexual objectification. In addition, they present to us both a pointed critique of the Comics Code and a subtle interrogation of Good Girl Art in general, and Byrne's own work in this vein in particular. Thus, there is much of real interest in this particular episode. But does this excuse the apparent offensiveness of the images themselves? Perhaps, or perhaps not. There is one more aspect of *The Sensational She-Hulk* #40 that we need to examine.

COMICS AND METAFICTIONAL COERCION

The final problematic aspect of *The Sensational She-Hulk* #40 and its depiction of the She-Hulk concerns not so much the fact that she *is* jumping rope naked, but the fact that she is clearly being *forced* to jump rope naked. This aspect of coercion is quite explicit on the cover, where John Byrne's flannel-clad arm is holding the jump rope out to the She-Hulk, and he shouts "Quit *stalling*, Shulkie! We've got twenty-two pages to fill!" Coercion is less explicit in the interior pages, but nevertheless implicit when the She-Hulk states that Marvel Comics "will do just about *anything* to make a sale," suggesting that she is being forced to humiliate herself by Marvel Comics (and, presumably, by the creator employed by Marvel to write and draw the comic). Furthermore, the She-Hulk is depicted, on the cover, as frantically trying to cover herself with the outsized Comics Code seal, in a defensive position, with knees turned inward—in short, she is rendered on the cover as victim, with Byrne as victimizer. [13]

In assessing this aspect of the comic, we should be careful that we don't fall into one of two traps. First, we should make sure that we don't mischaracterize who, exactly, is potentially victimizing whom. John Byrne, as the creator who both wrote and drew the comic, clearly made it the case that the She-Hulk (fictionally) jumped rope naked for four pages (or at least appeared to do so). But John Byrne is a real person, and the She-Hulk is not, so there is no sense in which he harmed anyone (directly) in bringing these fictional events about—there is no one to be victimized, since the She-Hulk doesn't really exist. Now, it *is* fictionally the case that John Byrne's authorial avatar—the fictional comic book character depicted on the cover and in the interior pages of the comic—forces the She-Hulk to jump rope (apparently) naked. So this fictional character—Byrne's avatar—is fictionally guilty of a rather morally appalling act. But Byrne's avatar is not John Byrne. This authorial avatar is just another character that Byrne writes about in his stories. Such avatars are often used to provide testimony regarding the attitudes and motivations of the author, but it would be a mistake to conclude that every thought entertained, deed performed, or moral attitude held by the fictional surrogate is also a characteristic of the author himself. Byrne can have his fictional avatar force the She-Hulk to do all sorts of things, but we should not conclude from this that Byrne is the sort of person who would or even could do similar things in real life, if given the chance. In short, what we have here is a fictional depiction of a fictional character being forced, by a second fictional character, to do something objectionable, but no real person has actually been either victimizer or victim.

Second, we should not assume automatically that a fictional depiction of a morally objectionable act is itself automatically objectionable. Many great works of narrative art involve the depiction of morally repugnant actions, and in at least some cases it seems plausible that the greatness of these works hinges on aspects of the narrative that involve attempting to prevent, or reacting to, or overcoming such reprehensible events. In short, great works of art are often great, in part, because they fictionally depict awful things. The connections between the moral qualities of the characters and events depicted in an artwork and the aesthetic properties of that artwork are clearly not as simple as "if it depicts something evil, it is bad." Very good stories often require us to think about very bad things—arguably, this is one of the functions of storytelling.[14]

Nevertheless, there is something particularly distressing about the coercive aspects of *The Sensational She-Hulk* #40. Even after discussing this issue's metafictional commentary on the Comics Code, and its reflexive critique of the depiction of women within comics, many readers, including myself, still remain discomfited by the cover art in particular. This no doubt has to do with the gendered coercion depicted there. But it seems to me that it may also have to do with the fact that this aspect of the cover art is completely *unnecessary*. The critique so cleverly constructed in the interior pages of the comic could have been carried out in essentially the same manner had the cover depicted the She-Hulk autonomously deciding to jump rope naked. In fact, this would fit well with the theme of a number of other covers in Byrne's run on the title, where the She-Hulk is depicted doing all manner of other silly (although usually less sexually charged) things in order to boost sales. Given these precedents, Byrne had no reason to portray the She-Hulk as coerced on the cover, except, perhaps, that the She-Hulk's subordination might titillate a certain sort of reader.

It's too bad that Byrne made this particular narrative choice on the cover (regardless of what his actual reasons for doing so were), since this flaw mars an otherwise extremely clever self-referential examination of the depiction of women in comics and the role of the Comics Code. Thus, although the commentary and critique so cleverly encoded into this issue of the *Sensational She-Hulk* lifts it above the sort of shallow objectification of women of which it is often accused, this is not enough to excuse all of the initially problematic seeming aspects of its depiction of the She-Hulk. Marvel Comics' premiere solo superheroine deserves better. [15]

NOTES

1. See, for example, Peter David and Brian Reed, *She-Hulk Sensational* (Marvel Comics, 2010).

2. Patricia Waugh, *Metafiction* (New York: Methuen, 1984), 2. For further discussion of metafiction in comics, see M. Thomas Inge, *Anything Can Happen in a Comic Strip* (Columbus: Ohio State University Libraries, 1995); and Matthew T. Jones, "Reflexivity in Comic Art," *International Journal of Comic Art* 7, no. 1 (2005): 270–86.

3. Another, more recent example of metafiction within mainstream superhero comics can be found in comics featuring the sometimes X-Men associate Deadpool. For a discussion of metafiction and Deadpool, see Joseph J. Darowski, "When You Know You're Just a Comic Book Character," in *X-Men and Philosophy*, ed. Rebecca Housel and J. Jeremy Wisnewski (Hoboken, NJ: Wiley, 2009).

4. For a well-known "celebration" of Good Girl Art, see Ron Goulart, *Good Girl Art* (Neshannock, PA: Hermes Press, 2008).

5. A text balloon on the cover states "This is it! Because you demanded it!" referring to the fact that the idea behind the story stems from an ongoing joke in the letters column of the comic.

6. John Byrne, *The Sensational She-Hulk* #40, 1–4.

7. Ibid., 5.

8. Ibid., 6. Note the use of the male pronoun here!

9. For a much more detailed history of the Comics Code, see David Hajdu, *The Ten-Cent Plague* (New York: Farrar, Straus & Giroux, 2009).

10. *Time*, December 8, 1948, http://www.time.com/time/magazine/article/0,9171,799525,00.html.

11. Fredric Wertham, *Seduction of the Innocent* (New York: Rinehart, 1954).

12. It is worth mentioning that *Seduction of the Innocent* is, in actuality, a bit more balanced—sometimes even progressive—than it is given credit for by its most vocal detractors.

13. In my informal survey of initial impressions to the cover, responses ranged from "playfully covering" to "cowering," suggesting that the visual depiction on the cover might be ambiguous with respect to the power relations between Byrne's fictional, in-comic avatar and the She-Hulk. The dialogue, however, leaves no doubt that Byrne's avatar is commanding the She-Hulk. Also, although the She-Hulk does imply that Marvel Comics is compelling her to jump rope naked in the interior pages of the comic, her body language is much less submissive than on the cover.

14. For a good discussion of the connections (or possible lack thereof) between the aesthetic value of a work of art and the moral value of the actions depicted in that artwork, see Berys Gaut, *Art, Emotion, and Ethics* (Oxford: Oxford University Press, 2009).

15. An early version of this chapter was presented at a work-in-progress seminar at the University of Minnesota–Twin Cities and benefitted greatly from the collegial feedback received there. Additional thanks are due to Melanie Bowman, Patrick Laine, and Ken Waters.

Chapter Sixteen

Invisible, Tiny, and Distant

The Powers and Roles of Marvel's Early Female Superheroes

Joseph Darowski

"Groundbreaking."[1] "Innovative."[2] "A new age."[3] "A marked departure."[4] "Nothing like the other superhero titles."[5] "Radically different."[6] "Quite original."[7] "A new breed of superhero."[8] "One of the most popular cultural expressions of the twentieth century."[9]

These are some of the descriptions used by comic book scholars to describe the early superhero comic books published by Marvel Comics. Any thorough history or analysis of the comic book industry recognizes that Marvel Comics revolutionized the superhero genre with its output in the early 1960s. The subsequent rise in popularity of superhero comics, in turn, affected the entire comic book industry. The style of storytelling, the interactions of the characters, and the world in which the stories were told were all unlike what had come before. Stan Lee and his artistic collaborators, most notably Jack Kirby and Steve Ditko, are rightfully credited with transforming superhero comics and forever influencing American popular culture.

The first wave of American superhero comic books came just before and during America's involvement in World War II. DC Comics[10] published Superman, Batman, and Wonder Woman comic books, among many other superpowered adventurers. The publisher that would become Marvel Comics[11] produced comic books with superheroes such as Captain America, Namor, the Sub-Mariner, and the Human Torch. Other comic book publishers embraced the popularity of the superhero genre and had their own costumed crime fighters. Following the conclusion of World War II, interest in superheroes waned, and the majority of superhero comic books ceased publication. Publishers turned to other genres, including Western, romance, horror, sci-fi, humor, and crime comics, to satisfy evolving reader interests. For example, in 1951 DC Comics published the superhero-themed issue *All-Star Comics* #57, but the subsequent issue to hit the shelves was the cowboy-themed *All-Star Western* #58. Throughout the 1940s and 1950s, DC Comics continued to publish comic books featuring Superman, Batman, and Wonder Woman, but these characters were the exceptions.

Readers looking for enticing entertainment turned to crime and horror comics which were especially popular in the early 1950s. Worried parents, their concerns fanned to paranoid flames by critics such as Fredric Wertham, feared that reading these types of comic books might inspire their children to become criminals. The U.S. government became involved, holding hearings attempting to divine a connection between comic books and juvenile delinquency. In response to these public concerns and the threat of government censorship, comic book publishers formed their own self-censorship board called the Comics Code Authority that would monitor all comic book publications for inappropriate content. As a result of these regulations, publishers who had been profiting from crime and horror comics had to find safer, more wholesome stories to market to young readers. In 1956 DC Comics reintroduced the Flash, an attempt to rebuild interest in superheroes. Superheroes could fit into the Comics Code's strict moral guidelines much more easily than horror or crime comics, and this reimagining of an earlier Golden Age superhero worked well for DC Comics. Soon other Golden Age superheroes were reimagined by DC Comics' writers and artists. In 1960 a comic book featuring a team-up of these heroes, *The Justice League*, was published. The success of these superhero titles was noticed by other publishers. The comic book industry has always been filled with imitators, and if superhero comic books were selling well for DC Comics, other publishers would follow the trend sooner rather than later. But what came from Marvel wasn't a reimagining of Golden Age characters; it was a welcome evolution of the genre. Gerard Jones and Will Jacobs explain:

> The time was right for a revolution. Comic book sales were starting to pick up, buoyed by a burgeoning youth culture. In 1961 the baby boom was still going strong—its eldest members were only fifteen—and superheroes were seizing kids' imaginations. A desire for change was in the air. [12]

Beginning with *The Fantastic Four* #1 (November 1961), Marvel Comics introduced several new characters that have become icons of American popular culture. The Incredible Hulk, Iron Man, Spider-Man, Thor, the X-Men, the Avengers, and others were created in a matter of a few short years to supply the entertainment that paying customers were eagerly consuming.

Many aspects of Marvel's early superhero comic books were unique for the time. The stories were longer, sometimes continued in the next issue, sometimes having subplots that would run for several issues. The writing method, the so-called Marvel Method, in which a writer creates the dialogue to match the finished pencils rather than preparing a detailed script to guide the artist, changed the way comics were produced. The jovial tone of the editorial boxes in the comic books invited readers to feel part of a club, and soon Marvel did have an official club its fans could join. The writers and artists were all given nicknames to make them more personal for readers. And, as Bradford Wright explains, "the Marvel heroes resided in New York City rather than mythical locales like Metropolis or Gotham City. If not quite 'believable,' these stories at least took place in a world more relevant to the audience."[13] Additionally, the characters were more "realistic," though such a term must be taken with a grain of salt when talking about characters with fantastical powers and vibrant costumes. But, the Fantastic Four bickered when stressed, and Spider-Man worried about making ends meet, introducing a more human or flawed element to the superhero genre which had often been populated by paragons of humanity's ideals.

However, while the comics revolutionized aspects of comic book production and the superhero genre, these were not faultless tales. The universe building could be clunky and, even though there were fewer than a dozen titles being published, plagued with contradictions; the characterizations simplistic; the dialogue stilted; and the plots predictable (or at times surprising only because of illogical twists and turns). In terms of gender representation, Marvel's superhero comic books of the 1960s were less than revolutionary. Wright argues that "Marvel's comic books did little to advance feminism" and "Stan Lee missed an opportunity to broaden superhero audience across genders with appealing characters both powerful and feminine."[14] The company's publications were either male-solo titles or team books whose rosters were dominated by men. Between the first appearance of the Fantastic Four in 1961 and the release of the team titles the Avengers and the X-Men in 1963, Stan Lee and his collaborators created five times as many male superheroes as female crime fighters. Fifteen enduring male superheroes[15] were created in this two-year period, while only three superheroines appeared in Marvel comic books: the Invisible Girl of the Fantastic Four, the Wasp of the Avengers, and Marvel Girl of the X-Men. A consideration of the early portrayals of these three superheroines, the powers they possessed, and the roles they had on their respective teams in comic books from the early 1960s reveals the limiting, domesticated portrayals of women in early Marvel comics.

Marvel's portrayal of these three female characters aligns with several facets of female identity which Betty Friedan would critique in 1963's *The Feminine Mystique*. According to Friedan, society had created a problematic and narrow definition of womanhood which was propagated through the media, advertising, and cultural expectations. These comic books appear to be guilty of presenting this stereotypical feminine ideal that Friedan identifies as damaging to society as a whole.

SUSAN STORM: THE INVISIBLE GIRL

Susan Storm, the Invisible Girl, is the lone female member of the Fantastic Four and the first Marvel superheroine in this era of comic books. Sue Storm was created by Stan Lee and Jack Kirby, though who originated the general concept and then the specific aspects of the Fantastic Four remains a disputed topic.[16] Lee was the writer and Kirby the artist for the *Fantastic Four*, the first issue of which has a cover date of November 1961. The Fantastic Four were a team of adventurers who, in an effort to beat the Russians into space, fly in a rocket that is not properly shielded and are exposed to cosmic rays. The four passengers in the rocket ship develop strange powers as a result of this accident. Reed Richards, the scientist who designed the rocket, can stretch and contort his body and is called Mr. Fantastic. The pilot of the ship, Ben Grimm, develops a rocklike exterior to his skin and is called the Thing. Richard's fiancée, Susan Storm, can turn invisible and is code-named Invisible Girl. Susan's teenage brother, Johnny, can burst into flame and fly and is called the Human Torch.

Sue Storm's power to become invisible was not terribly original,[17] nor was it portrayed as terribly useful in a superhero fight. Quite literally, when the Fantastic Four face danger, the female is expected to disappear. Lee and Kirby recognized the limitations of this power, and in *Fantastic Four* #22[18] they increased her powers to allow her to create force fields and make others invisible. Lee admits that he did this both to make the character more involved, but also to help the visual dynamics of the comic book. He explains, "I wanted her to be more proactive. Being invisible is okay, but it's not very visual. I thought it would be fun for Jack to draw a force field."[19] Stan Lee expresses pride that he broke the mold in creating the Invisible Girl. He explains in his autobiography, "She was presented as an integral part of the FF's fighting team rather than as a token female who had to be rescued on every other page."[20] Nonetheless, there are stereotypes perpetuated in the portrayal of Sue Storm.

Despite Lee's claim that she does not need to be rescued every other page, she is portrayed as a damsel in distress with some frequency. Notably on the cover of the very first issue, Sue Storm is shown in the grasp of a monster rising up from the city streets. She is struggling to use her powers, stating, "I—I can't turn invisible fast enough," and asking, "How can we stop this creature?" While Sue Storm is offering her lament, the Human Torch aggres-

sively yells, "The Fantastic Four have only begun to fight"; the Thing declares, "It's time for the Thing to lend a hand"; and Mr. Fantastic is escaping
a coil of ropes, declaring, "It'll take more than ropes to keep Mister Fantastic
out of action."[21] On the cover introducing the Fantastic Four, and launching
the Marvel age of heroes, Sue Storm is trapped, struggling with her powers,
and questioning the team's ability to win while the men on the team are
confidently using their powers and preparing for a fight.

On the cover of the fourth issue, Sue is shown being kidnapped by the
Sub-Mariner, with the rest of the team charging to her rescue. In the comics
themselves, Sue is rescued by the Thing in the first issue, and in the third
issue she is hypnotized by the villain and leads the rest of the team into a trap
before being rescued by them. In the fourth issue Sue is claimed by Namor
for his bride, before being rescued by the rest of the team. In the fifth issue
Sue is taken captive by Dr. Doom and bound at his side, sitting out the
majority of the adventure until the rest of the Fantastic Four arrive. However
Lee envisioned the Invisible Girl, in practice she is often portrayed as a
damsel in distress, particularly in early issues of *The Fantastic Four*.

Readers noted this and wrote in to request that Sue do more during the
team's adventures. In a response in the letters column, Lee quoted Abraham
Lincoln's statement that "all that he was—all that he ever hoped to be—he
owed to [his mother]." In using this quote Lee makes clear that he saw Sue as
the mother of the Fantastic Four family. Robert Genter addressed this family
dynamic in the Fantastic Four, carrying the analysis beyond identifying Sue
Storm as a mother figure:

> It was of course not surprising that Lee appropriated the discourse surrounding
> the family to compose his new team. The nuclear family at the onset of the
> Cold War provided, as Elaine Tyler May has noted, "a secure nest from the
> dangers of the outside world." Using the domestic veil as an ideological tool to
> promote everything from rising consumption levels to traditional gender roles
> to Cold War foreign policy, experts connected economic and political stability
> to the family unit.[22]

Genter goes on to argue that Mr. Fantastic is the father, the Invisible Girl the
mother, the Human Torch the rebellious teenager, and the Thing the di-
apered, whiny baby of the "First Family of Comics." Laura Mattoon
D'Amore goes so far as to call Sue Storm "the superhero equivalent of the
suburban housewife," but notes that she is also a "caricature of feminine
ambiguity."[23]

Much of Sue Storm's characterization in these issues revolves around her
role as fiancée to Mr. Fantastic. While Reed Richards is a brilliant scientist
and leader of the team, Sue Storm is mostly portrayed as his adoring love
interest. Mr. Fantastic has a unique individual identity; the Invisible Girl's
sense of self is tied directly to her romantic relationship. Like Mr. Fantastic,

the Thing and Human Torch have clearly defined independent identities, even being well defined enough to be spun off into their own solo titles for a time. Invisible Girl's role is subordinate to that of the men around her; her identity is inextricably linked to them while they can operate in their own independent spheres. This is the cultural expectation that Betty Friedan would soon critique in *The Feminine Mystique*, but it is perpetuated in this popular-culture entertainment. The woman's role and identity are limited to being an appendage to a man, which is presented as inherently fulfilling.

However, if Sue is the surrogate adult mother of this family, her code name is perplexing: the Invisible Girl. Though she was an adult and engaged to the character Mr. Fantastic, she was given the diminutive title Invisible Girl. She would not change the name to Invisible Woman until almost three hundred issues into the series' run. The use of *Girl* rather than *Woman* carries implications of youth, naiveté, and frailty with it. Even if Sue is the mother of the team, her code name implies that she is the least among its members. While mother is a position of authority, true authority on the team resides with Mr. Fantastic, the patriarch of the family and established leader of the superhero team.

Sue Storm's power is used in such a way that makes her a less effective fighting member of the team. Her primary role is as a mother figure, particularly to the Thing and the Human Torch who are often brawling with each other, while Mr. Fantastic is a borderline absentee father figure, often tinkering in his lab when the team is not fighting a villain. The Invisible Girl is a problematic figure, a superpowered individual, but simultaneously a disappearing superhero whose primary identity is Mr. Fantastic's fiancée.

JANET VAN DYNE: THE WASP

However, at least the Invisible Girl is included prominently as a member of the Fantastic Four on the team's covers. On the cover of the Avengers' 1963 comic book debut, the names of the team members are splashed above the comic book's title: "thor! ant man! hulk! iron man!" The Wasp can be seen in the picture on the cover, shrunken to the size of an insect, as is her power, but she is not listed as a member of the team. Inside the comic itself on the title page, a listing of the team roster includes "Ant Man and the Wasp"—so she is listed, even if her name does not stand independent of her love interest.[24]

The Avengers comic was a team-up of several of Marvel's popular characters that had previously appeared in their own comic book titles. The Wasp had first appeared in *Tales to Astonish* #44 as a sidekick/love interest for Ant-Man. Janet Van Dyne's father, a successful scientist, is killed when an alien monster was unleashed during an experiment. Janet convinces Hank Pym, a previously established hero with the code name Ant-Man, to give her some of his "Pym Particles," which allow him to shrink, and she can now shrink as well. Additionally, she is subjected to an experiment that allows wings to sprout from her back when she shrinks, giving her the additional power of flight. Ant-Man and Wasp defeat the alien threat, and Wasp openly pines for Ant-Man and insists they remain a superhero team because she is in love with him.

The portrayal of the Wasp is less flattering than that of the Invisible Girl in the Fantastic Four. While the Invisible Woman was often captured by enemies and was frequently not involved in battles, she was shown as loyal to the team and her fiancée. The Wasp, in comparison, is openly flirtatious with other men despite being in what is presented as a long-term relationship with Hank Pym. While the Invisible Girl is a key figure in maintaining team unity on the Fantastic Four, the Wasp seems more interested in her makeup and in shopping than in helping her teammates.

When the Wasp, Janet Van Dyne, is first introduced, Ant-Man is berating her for taking time to powder her nose every time they have a mission. Despite being in a relationship with Ant-Man, she immediately swoons over Thor and asks Ant-Man, "How can I ever make him notice me?" And the Wasp is trapped and requires rescuing from Iron Man in the first issue. The high point of Wasp's contributions in the first issue is offering the name of the team, the Avengers. However, Ant-Man immediately takes credit, not letting her finish her thought and crying, "That's it, the Avengers!"[25] Hank Pym makes a habit of taking the glory; in a later issue, the Wasp will play a key role in obtaining equipment from Hank Pym's lab that is needed to defeat a villain, but Pym takes it from her and is the one to use it to vanquish the foe.

By the second issue, Ant-Man has reversed his size alterations to become Giant Man, while the Wasp retains her power to become tiny. In the same issue she swoons over Thor, daydreaming about him during a team meeting, and she also compliments Giant Man's dreamy blue eyes. And, as is becoming standard for females in comic books from this era, she is trapped by the villain and requires the team to come and rescue her. However, she does help the team by dismantling the villain's armor, allowing Thor to finally defeat him.[26] In the next issue the Wasp is incapacitated during a battle and vows to stay behind Giant Man for the duration of the fight.[27] In the fourth issue the Wasp is not seen at all during the main battle, and upon returning she explains, "I was doing what any girl would do in a moment of crisis—powdering my nose of course!"[28]

Over and over again the Wasp is shown to be a flirt who is primarily concerned with her appearance. She worries that her adventures take her to places "too dry for my delicate complexion" and declares, after a threatening situation, that she is "as all right as any girl could be who had her makeup all smudged up."[29] After proving helpful in a battle, Hank Pym compliments her timing, only for her to respond, "I'd rather you were impressed by my blushing beauty, but I guess any compliment is better than none."[30] While her Hank Pym is going to perform a scientific study, Janet says she's accompanying him solely for the shopping in the area.[31] Soon, besides flirting with the other men on the team and speculating about how dreamy the villains they're fighting are under their masks,[32] Janet begins to criticize and nag her steadiest love interest. In *The Avengers* #9, while Hank Pym is working to resolve a problem in his science lab, she sticks her head in to berate him, "You haven't taken me dancing in weeks." Later, in the same issue, she again appears in his lab to complain, "Well, I guess I know better than to expect you to take a hungry gal out for dinner tonight?"[33]

Like the Invisible Girl of the Fantastic Four, the Wasp is the member of the Avengers most likely to be captured and require saving at the hands of her benevolent male teammates. Wright describes the Wasp as "an annoying airhead who spent most of her time panicking, fainting, and worrying about smudging her makeup."[34]

While the men on the Avengers have their own individual roles to take, as scientists, leaders, soldiers, or tacticians, the Wasp is not given much to do besides pine for love and dote on her own looks. Her focus on appearance, fashion, and shopping are demonstrative of stereotypes about women popularized in the 1950s, many of which still endure to this day. Betty Friedan studied the advertisements of the 1950s and interviewed many of the men responsible for those ads. The concept behind these ads was that "the really important role women serve as housewives is to buy more things."[35] Additionally, because housewives have no identity or role, "American housewives can be given the sense of identity, purpose, creativity, the self-realization, even the sexual joy they lack—by the buying of things."[36] The Wasp has three primary roles: coy flirt, damsel in distress, and chief consumer of the Avengers. Her flirting can be seen as an attempt to gain an identity through her relationship with a male figure. Becoming a frequent damsel in distress is a failure in her role as a superheroine. And her consumption, in light of Friedan's analysis, is an effort to purchase and manufacture a meaningful identity.

JEAN GREY: MARVEL GIRL

While Invisible Girl was a mother figure who disappeared, and the Wasp was a flirt who shrunk, Marvel Girl of the X-Men was portrayed as a love interest who stayed in the background. Like the Fantastic Four and the Avengers, the X-Men were co-created by Stan Lee and Jack Kirby, and the first issue of the comic was published in September 1963. On the cover of the first issue the X-Men are attacking Magneto, and it is apparent what the powers are of all the members, except Marvel Girl. While Angel flies on wings, the Beast swings from a trapeze with obviously oversized hands and feet, Cyclops shoots lasers from his eyes, and Iceman appears as a snowman, Marvel stands in the background looking dainty.[37] Inside the comic, readers discover that Jean Grey, Marvel Girl's civilian identity, possesses telekinesis, or the power to move objects with her mind. Though this power seems more formidable than Sue Storm's invisibility or the Wasp's shrinking powers, the way the character is used falls into several of the same stereotypes. For example, in the second issue Marvel Girl is tricked during battle and knocked out, and the X-Men must rescue her before she is captured.[38]

Invisible Girl was paired off with Mr. Fantastic, the Wasp flirted with almost all the men she encountered, while Marvel Girl is an object of affection for all the men around her. As Marvel Girl is approaching the school in *The X-Men* #1 (September 1963), Professor Xavier calmly notes that she is a "most attractive young lady" while preparing the other students to meet her. The teenage boys on the team are less reserved in their appraisal. Cyclops, Angel, and Beast crowd to a window to watch her walk up the pathway to the school. Iceman, who is the youngest on the team, explains that he's glad he's not a "wolf" like the other members of the team. Iceman will fairly quickly develop "wolf"-like tendencies and demonstrate unreserved attraction for various female characters. Meanwhile, Cyclops proclaims that Jean Grey is "a real living doll" while Angel exclaims, "A redhead! Look at that face . . . and the rest of her." Angel later notes that "she has one very obvious power . . . the power to make a man's heart beat faster."[39] Marvel Girl is exclusively interested in Cyclops, but all the men take turns flirting with her. Even Professor X, a bald older man, confesses his love for the teenaged Jean Grey in one exceedingly creepy panel. This character development for Professor X is immediately dropped and rarely addressed ever again.

Besides being the love interest, Marvel Girl is also presented as a domestic homemaker. At the beginning of issue #6 we can see her homemaker side at its clearest. The scene is at the dinner table, and all of the X-Men are seated, eating, except Jean, who is in the kitchen doorway. Professor Xavier, the leader of the X-Men, thanks Jean for making the meal and "helping out on the cook's day off."[40] It is again evidenced in the eighth issue of the series, when the X-Men are training. While the males in the X-Men traditionally go through obstacle courses or battle simulations, Marvel Girl is asked to thread yarn through lace in order to train her powers. In later issues she will don a nurse's uniform to treat her wounded comrades and also sew the team's new outfits because she is looking for an outlet for her home economics skills (though she makes it clear that she had permission from Professor X before embarking on this endeavor).

As with Invisible Girl, attention must be drawn to Marvel Girl's name. In the initial roster of the X-Men, the code names generally are related to a specific aspect of the mutant power each member has. Cyclops wears a visor which makes him appear to have one eye, Angel has feathered wings, Iceman turns to ice, and Beast has inhumanly large hands and feet. Marvel Girl's code name is much more generic and could be applied to any character with superpowers. Indeed, Marvel Comics also feature the adventures of Ms. Marvel, Captain Marvel, and Marvel Boy. It should also be noted that Marvel Girl's code name does not identify her as a woman, but uses the younger, adolescent gender marker, *Girl*. This is contrasted by Iceman, who is not Iceboy. Making the inconsistency even more pronounced is the fact that in the first issue Iceman is identified as "a couple years younger" than the rest of the team. Marvel Girl's code name marks her as the youngest, most innocent, and perhaps weakest of the group, even though she is not in fact the youngest and her powers make her quite formidable (depending on the writer). In several of the adventures the X-Men have, though, she is shown to be the most frail member and to need the most care and protection.

THE THREE SUPERHEROINES

Having looked at how these superheroines were portrayed in the 1960s, it should be noted that the characters have evolved over the forty years their stories have been told. The Invisible Woman is now recognized to be one of the most powerful characters in the Marvel Universe. She is portrayed as a leader, wife, and mother and wields her powers in ways not demonstrated in the early Fantastic Four comics. Even after Lee and Kirby expanded her power set to include force fields, she largely used them defensively. However, other writers have shown her using her force fields in an offensive manner.

The Wasp often seemed to be an afterthought in the Avengers team, but she has become a team leader and is far more independent than her original interpretation. While Wasp's personal identity was initially intertwined with Ant-Man's, Wasp has become disentangled from that relationship. Marvel Girl also has advanced far beyond her original background status and become one of the most powerful figures in the universe, though in all these characters' progressions problematic story lines have emerged.

Kirby, who provided the art for all of these series, tended to draw fights with the supervillains as fistfights in these issues. The power to turn invisible, shrink to tiny size, and use telekinesis did not translate well to brawling fights, and the females were often lightly featured in the action scenes of the comic books. They were much more likely to be featured in the more domestic settings at the opening of the comics, in team headquarters and having conversations with their teammates, than during the more dynamic portions of an issue when good battled evil.

We can see that early Marvel superheroines fell into several stereotypes. They were often damsels in distress, and they were rarely involved in the main action of the comic books. Much more often than their male counterparts, they would be captured or faint in the midst of battle. While men on the team usually had clear identifying characteristics (the scientist, the leader, the hothead, the goofball, etc.), the women were all predominantly characterized through their romantic relationships. A romantic relationship is not an inherently bad or even problematic aspect of a character. In fact, romance is a key element of the long-running soap operatic narratives found in American comic books. But in this period, the portrayal of women is limited almost exclusively to that romantic element, while the men these women are in love with have several other roles. That was the key attribute Marvel's superheroines possessed as far as characterization: either they were in a relationship that occupied all their thought balloons, or their desires to be in a relationship occupied their thought balloons.

Superhero comic books have a long history in American culture, but in this period the stories and portrayals found in this popular entertainment propagated female stereotypes rather than challenging them. Just as it has been a long fight in American society, the quest for female empowerment and equality was not an instantaneous victory in comic books. The Marvel revolution changed popular culture, but in some ways it was still trapped in the past and lagged behind cultural movements.

NOTES

1. Shirrel Rhoades, *A Complete History of American Comic Books* (New York: Peter Lang, 2008), 78.
2. Matthew J. Costello, *Secret Identity Crisis: Comic Books and the Unmasking of Cold War America* (New York: Continuum, 2009), 9.
3. Gerard Jones and Will Jacobs, *The Comic Book Heroes: The First History of Modern Comics from the Silver Age to the Present* (Rocklin, CA: Prima Publishing, 1997), 74.
4. Randy Duncan and Matthew J. Smith, *The Power of Comics: History, Form & Culture* (New York: Continuum, 2009), 46.
5. Sean Howe, *Marvel Comics: The Untold Story* (New York: HarperCollins, 2012), 36.
6. Pierre Comtois, *Marvel Comics in the 1960s: An Issue by Issue Field Guide to a Pop Culture Phenomenon* (Raleigh, NC: TwoMorrows Publishing, 2009), 14.
7. Bradford W. Wright, *Comic Book Nation: The Transformation of Youth Culture in America* (Baltimore, MD: Johns Hopkins University Press, 2001), 204.
8. Larry Tye, *Superman: The High-Flying History of America's Most Enduring Hero* (New York: Random House, 2012), 167.
9. Robert Genter, "'With Great Power Comes Great Responsibility': Cold War Culture and the Birth of Marvel Comics," *Journal of Popular Culture* 40, no. 6 (December 2007): 953.
10. DC Comics began as part of National Allied Publications and was previously known as National Comics and National Periodical Publications. However, because the company has been popularly known as DC Comics even before the company legally adopted that name in 1977, it will be referred to as DC Comics throughout this chapter.

11. Similarly, the company that is now known as Marvel Comics previously went by the names Timely Publications and Atlas Comics, but for clarity it will be referred to consistently as Marvel Comics.

12. Jones and Jacobs, *The Comic Book Heroes*, 50.

13. Wright, *Comic Book Nation*, 207.

14. Ibid., 219–20.

15. These included Mr. Fantastic, the Human Torch, the Thing, the Incredible Hulk, Ant-Man, Spider-Man, Thor, Doctor Strange, Iron Man, Nick Fury, Professor X, Cyclops, Angel, Iceman, and the Beast.

16. Mark Evanier, *Kirby: King of Comics* (New York: Abrams, 2008), 122.

17. H. G. Welles' *The Invisible Man* was published in 1897, and there had been an American comic strip called *The Invisible Scarlet O'Neil* which ran from 1940 to 1956. Written and drawn by Russell Stamm, Scarlet O'Neil functions as a pseudo-superhero, using her power of invisibility to help others and the police.

18. Stan Lee (w) and Jack Kirby (a), "The Return of the Mole Man," *The Fantastic Four* #22 (New York: Marvel Comics, 1964).

19. Tom DeFalco, *Comic Creators on the Fantastic Four* (New York: Titan Books, 2005), 14.

20. Stan Lee and George Mair, *Excelsior: The Amazing Life of Stan Lee* (New York: Simon & Schuster, 2002), 116.

21. Stan Lee and Jack Kirby, "The Fantastic Four!" *The Fantastic Four* #1 (New York, Marvel Comics, 1961).

22. Genter, "'With Great Power,'" 957.

23. Laura Mattoon D'Amore, "Invisible Girl's Quest for Visibility: Early Second Wave Feminism and the Comic Book Superheroine," *Americana: The Journal of American Popular Culture* 7, no. 2 (Fall 2008): 1.

24. Stan Lee (w) and Jack Kirby (a), "The Coming of the Avengers!," *The Avengers* #1 (New York: Marvel Comics, 1963).

25. Ibid.

26. Stan Lee (w) and Jack Kirby (a), "The Avengers Battle . . . the Space Phantom!," *The Avengers* #2 (New York: Marvel Comics, 1963).

27. Stan Lee (w) and Jack Kirby (a), "The Avengers Meet . . . the Sub-Mariner!," *The Avengers* #3 (New York: Marvel Comics, 1964).

28. Stan Lee (w) and Jack Kirby (a), "Captain America Joins . . . the Avengers!," *The Avengers* #4 (New York: Marvel Comics, 1964).

29. Stan Lee (w) and Jack Kirby (a), "The Invasion of the Lava Men!," *The Avengers* #5 (New York: Marvel Comics, 1964).

30. Ibid.

31. Stan Lee (w) and Jack Kirby (a), "Their Darkest Hour!," *The Avengers* #7 (New York: Marvel Comics, 1964).

32. Stan Lee (w) and Jack Kirby (a), "Kang, the Conqueror!," *The Avengers* #8 (New York: Marvel Comics, 1963).

33. Stan Lee (w) and Jack Kirby (a), "The Coming of . . . the Wonder Man!," *The Avengers* #9 (New York: Marvel Comics, 1964).

34. Wright, *Comic Book Nation*, 219–20.

35. Betty Friedan, *The Feminine Mystique: A Norton Critical Edition* (New York: Norton, 2013), 173.

36. Ibid., 174.

37. Stan Lee (w) and Jack Kirby (a), "X-Men," *The X-Men* #1 (New York: Marvel Comics, 1963).

38. Stan Lee (w) and Jack Kirby (a), "No One Can Stop the Vanisher!," *The X-Men* #2 (New York: Marvel Comics, 1963).

39. Stan Lee (w) and Jack Kirby (a), "X-Men," *The X-Men* #1 (New York: Marvel Comics, 1963).

40. Stan Lee (w) and Jack Kirby (a), "Sub-Mariner Joins the Evil Mutants!," *The X-Men* #6 (New York: Marvel Comics, 1964).

Chapter Seventeen

Heroines Aplenty, but None My Mother Would Know

Marvel's Lack of an Iconic Superheroine

T. Keith Edmunds

In the world of superhero comic books, there are two companies that reign supreme—Marvel Comics and DC Comics. Between them, these two companies hold about two-thirds of the retail comic book market. In 2012, Marvel's share of this market was over 34 percent, while DC held slightly less than 32 percent. Image Comics, the next closest competitor, trailed a distant third with only just over 7 percent of the market.[1] Yet, despite the nearly equal share of the market, DC Comics can claim iconic superheroines that are recognizable to the general public—Wonder Woman, Cat Woman, Supergirl, and Batgirl—while Marvel cannot make this claim. Despite its catalog of over five thousand characters, Marvel Comics has no true iconic superpowered woman using her talents solely for good. The company has no female character immediately recognizable to the broader general public. In a 2011 interview, Marvel Comics' then editor-in-chief, Axel Alonso, acknowledged this lack of an iconic superheroine.[2]

Superpowered women appeared in comic books shortly after Superman's appearance in 1938. Wonder Woman, the most well-known superheroine, was created in 1941 as a role model for young women.[3] Although Wonder Woman was not the only heroine created during the Golden Age of comic books, she is certainly the longest lived. Following the establishment of the Comics Code Authority in 1954, gender roles adhered to a more conservative, traditional ideology.[4] With the rise of the feminist movement in the 1960s and 1970s, superheroines began to play a more prominent role in comic books. Through the 1970s and 1980s, more superpowered female

characters appeared—Ms. Marvel, Elektra, and She-Hulk, for example—
often more independent and purposeful than their predecessors.[5] The 1990s
and 2000s have seen an explosion of comic book properties spinning out of
the traditional comic book formats into television series, video games, generally immensely successful movies, and a billion dollar merchandising market. Yet, within this context of feminism and the development of comic book
properties into the wider popular culture, Marvel Comics has been unable to
develop a widely recognized heroine.

Despite the lack of an iconic female superhero, Marvel has developed
notable female characters that have done notable things. Marvel's first comic
book following its transition from Atlas Comics was *The Fantastic Four*,
published in 1961. One member of this superpowered team of heroes was
Susan Storm, also known as Invisible Girl. In 1965, Storm married Reed
Richards, Mr. Fantastic, making them the first married superpowered couple
in comics. Following this marriage, Storm became the first superheroine in
the twenty-five years since the development of the Comics Code to have a
baby. This development of Invisible Girl has been examined, particularly in a
feminist context, in some detail by D'Amore.[6]

The 1960s also saw the development of a number of other superheroines
in the Marvel catalog, most notably the Wasp and Marvel Girl. Each of these
characters was introduced through a team of heroes—the Avengers and the
X-Men, respectively. Although these characters were nominally full members of their teams, they initially functioned as love interests to other members on these teams, as the largest percentage of heroes at the time were
affluent, straight, white males. Just as the Invisible Girl was the romantic
interest of Mr. Fantastic, the Wasp was the love interest of Ant-Man (Henry
Pym's heroic identity of the time), and Marvel Girl was romantically linked
with Cyclops (Scott Summers).

The following decade and into the early 1980s, Marvel's writers developed stronger characters whose primary role was not that of a love interest.
Characters such as Ms. Marvel, She-Hulk, and the X-Men's Storm emerged
as more complex characters, following the company's aim of creating realistic individuals with whom readers could more readily identify.[7] Simultaneously, established characters were becoming more fully realized and independent[8]; even Sue Storm, the Invisible Girl since 1961 and despite having
married and birthed two children, finally changed her name in 1985 to the
Invisible Woman (in *Fantastic Four* #284). Despite these apparent gains,
Marvel's heroines tended to be clad in skimpy, highly sexualized outfits,
substituting their position of love interest for another character with that of
being a love interest for the reader, as it is widely assumed that males account
for between 80 and 95 percent of superhero comic readership. Unfortunately,
no reliable numbers exist in the public sphere, and the accuracy of this
assumption of male readership is a matter for debate. Though the sexualized

costuming trend has reversed itself to a degree (for example, Marvel no longer publishes a swimsuit issue), Marvel has not treated its heroines well.

Marvel heroines, since the first appearance of the Invisible Girl, have often been objectified, vilified, and marginalized, and it is not infrequent that female superheroes have been subjected to two or all three of these treatments. Closer examination of each of these mistreatments yields multiple notable examples.

Heroines with great power are often shown to be unable to wield it responsibly and eventually cause great damage to those they love most. This feminine weakness—whether mental or emotional—allows these heroines to either be easily exploited by outside forces or to personally wield their powers recklessly. Three of the most powerful female characters in the Marvel Universe have, at one point or another, been subject to such vilification.

The Scarlet Witch, a powerful mutant with reality-changing powers, in a story line in the mid-2000s went insane and depowered most of the mutant population, including a large number of major characters. This event is still the basis for ongoing story arcs as of this writing. Despite this major "unheroic" event, it is not the first vilification of this character, as she was originally introduced in 1964 as a member of the Brotherhood of Evil Mutants, foes of the X-Men.

In one of the longest-reaching story lines within Marvel Comics, Marvel Girl became Phoenix and, corrupted by the power, eventually became Dark Phoenix. This cosmically powerful and deeply evil character, for no other reason than her own twisted enjoyment, killed a billion alien creatures. In a moment of lucidity, Grey committed suicide. In the manner of superhero comics, however, Jean Grey has repeatedly been resurrected, only to die once again.

Even the maternal Invisible Girl has not been immune to vilification. Following the apparent death of her second child, Susan Storm fell victim to an entity named Malice. Using all of her powers, she attacked the rest of the Fantastic Four, placing her on the wrong side of good. Although Malice was eventually defeated and the Invisible Girl returned as a member of the Fantastic Four, her time as a villain was nonetheless damaging.

Less dramatic, but perhaps more important, are the female superheroes that struggle to overcome their poor choices and tragic events. For example, although both Wolverine and Spider-Woman have been brainwashed by evil forces and made to act against the forces of good, Wolverine was accepted back into the fold of multiple teams of superheroes relatively quickly, while Spider-Woman faced suspicion and mistrust for much longer.

Heroines, as evinced above, are often introduced as members of superhero teams and, as such, must struggle to create their own voice. The three heroines discussed above—Scarlet Witch, Marvel Girl, and the Invisible Girl—were all introduced as members of teams and, despite their powers, were unable to rise beyond the level of "teammate" to find their individual potentiality as an iconic heroine.

As expressed by Shugart, Marvel Girl's (or, in later years, Storm's) membership in the X-Men did little to change the overall white, masculine, and heterosexual attitudes of the group, with the only significant difference between the members being their superpowers.[9] In other words, the "femaleness" of the individual is lost in a collective masculinity. A superheroine, lost in such a sea, cannot rise to become an icon.

Similarly, those superpowered women that turn away from a life of fighting crime are often written out of story lines. Jessica Jones, at one time the superheroine Jewel, has made regular appearances despite her lack of costumed activity. The lead character in both the critically acclaimed series *Alias* and *The Pulse*, both of which were canceled, Jones has become the wife of Luke Cage of the Avengers and mother to his child.[10] From lead character in her own title to the regularly appearing role as a wife, Jessica Jones has been pushed off toward the margins.

Although female characters appear in the various Avengers titles, just as Susan Storm appears in *The Fantastic Four*, and although periodic attempts are made at individual female characters carrying their own title, as yet, none has found long-term success. An examination of the longest-running comic titles since the modern age of Marvel (often defined as beginning with the publication of *Fantastic Four* #1) reveals that the top ten longest-running titles, all with well over 250 issues, are male-character titled (such as *Amazing Spider-Man*, *Incredible Hulk*, and *Captain America*) or are team-titled comics (including the *Uncanny X-Men*, the *Fantastic Four*, and the *Avengers*). The *Uncanny X-Men* (volume 1) has the highest issue count of all Marvel Comics, totaling approximately 540 issues. A team-titled issue, the *Fantastic Four* also holds the second place with about 450 issues. The *Amazing Spider-Man* (volume 1), the highest count for a male-titled comic, is in third place with almost 450 issues. With only 100 issues, *Spider-Girl* has the highest issue count for a female-titled comic. *The Sensational She-Hulk* is in second place with 60 issues, and *Spider-Woman* is in third place with a mere 53. (Although the author has endeavored to provide an accurate issue count on these Marvel titles, the exact counts are open to debate due to the constant changes to series titles, volume numbers, and the use of special issues and one-offs.)

Perhaps the most telling point about the marginalization of superheroines, however, is the fact that in 2006, a comics scholar defined the superhero as male. According to this definition, the comic book superhero is, without exception, masculine. D'Amore, in response, notes that "superheroines have always been the aside, the marginalized, the coda."[11] Looking to superhero comics as a whole, this fact is substantiated by the fact that there are multiple female incarnations of male superheroes—Spider-Woman, She-Hulk, She-Thing—but no examples of male incarnations of female superheroes.

Finally, superheroines have, from almost the beginning, been objectified. With revealing costumes, eroticized body types, and overt sex appeal, most, if not all, female characters are primarily defined by their sexuality.[12] The sexual nature of these characters exists not only between characters within the pages of the comic but between the characters and the largely male readership. Susan Storm, for example, as early as 1962 was saving the human race from the wrath of the Sub-Mariner, not with her superpowers, but with her beauty and sexuality.[13] More overtly, the sex life of the She-Hulk has often been used as a comedic element, such as a court case where her breast size was established to be the largest in the Marvel Universe, or a separate court case where a list of her sexual partners was entered into evidence and contained hundreds of names.

More obvious, however, is the sexual dynamic and resultant objectification of superheroines between the page and the reader. Although these feminine superheroes are meant to be powerful individuals, often both physically and in regard to their superpowers, they must also be presented with a hyper-feminized body in order to avoid undermining the fantasy of the male readership.[14] It may be argued that artists seek to attract the reader's eye to the hero of the story. This is done for male characters, not through an exaggerated display of sexual features, but through imaginative costume design. With female characters, this costume design often involves skintight materials and generous displays of skin, as well as the amplified features of the female shape.[15]

This victimization aspect of superheroines may be classified as a subset of their objectification; by making them victims of insanity or torture or rape or murder in order to further a story line, they become no longer an important character but instead a prop, a plot device.[16] Much has been written about the brutal handling of female heroes and of the so-called Women in Refrigerators phenomenon—a term coined by Gail Simone to denote those superheroines who have been "depowered, raped, or cut up and stuck in the refrigerator."[17]

Marvel's superheroines have not been immune to such victimizations. Marvel Girl went insane and was killed (more than once due to the propensity of superhero comics not to let the dead remain in such a state). Ms. Marvel was raped, as was the Black Cat. In every case, the heroines were not just victimized; they were also submissive in the situation. Male heroes are often the victims of torture, too, but they tend to escape and, against all odds, save the day. Heroines tend not to be so powerful, stuck in their role as the submissive victim.

Despite the challenges facing Marvel's superheroines, the company does continue to attempt to find success with female-titled comics. For years, Marvel struggled to find a level of success for Dazzler even though the female-titled comic was canceled in 1986 after forty-two issues. Three attempts have been made at an ongoing She-Hulk title: *The Savage She-Hulk* ran from 1980 to 1982; *The Sensational She-Hulk*, the longest-running of the attempts, was published from 1989 to 1994; and *She-Hulk* saw print from 2004 to 2009. Many heroines have found some level of success with limited series. The Black Widow has carried over a dozen such series herself, yet has not achieved a level of awareness in the greater popular culture. However, with the recent release of *The Avengers* theatrical film and the character's appearance in the wildly popular *Iron Man* movies, there is a growing awareness of the character, but as of this date there are no plans for a Black Widow solo film despite many of the other characters in the Avengers—Iron Man, Thor, Captain America, and, to a lesser extent, the Hulk—having successful film franchises of their own.

Although the sum of all these difficulties carries no small weight, many of these issues facing Marvel's superheroines are not unique to them. The heroines at rival DC face many of the same concerns, yet have achieved iconic status. Why can the superheroines of Marvel not reach the same level of popular recognition?

Potentially it is a matter of readership. Though no current, reliable numbers regarding the readership of superhero comics exist, it is well accepted that the majority of readers are males. As such, the medium exists as a form of masculine wish fulfillment. Coupled with the fact that historically the bulk of individuals working within the industry were male, a situation arose where men were creating heroes for men. Along these lines, Ingalls illustrates how, from the standpoint of evolutionary psychology, the heroes developed for storytelling will all be extremely powerful, though the female heroes will be less powerful than the males.[18] Interestingly, the same theory predicts that heroes created by female creators will follow the same pattern, though all characters will tend to be on the whole less powerful than those developed by male creators.

This theory may go some distance toward explaining the disparity between male and female characters, but it does not explain the differences in the iconic status of characters between the companies of Marvel and DC. Wonder Woman, for example, the most iconic of superheroines, was created by a male, and every writer working on the Wonder Woman comic was a male until 1998.

Arguably, the two Marvel superheroines with the highest probability of becoming iconic due to their longevity, their high profile and importance within the Marvel Universe, and their appearances in media other than comic books are the Invisible Woman (Susan Storm) and Marvel Girl (Jean Grey). Why have these characters not achieved the level of recognition of Wonder Woman, Supergirl, or Batgirl? The difference in iconic status can, at this point, be boiled down to a matter of context.

Initially, the prototypical superheroine, the undisputed queen of comic book superheroes—Wonder Woman—must be explained away. Wholly unique, Wonder Woman was presented to the world with an independent backstory, powerful without the help of men, and, initially, realistically rendered. Introduced in the Golden Age of comic books, Wonder Woman has a history of feminism, so far as to have been adopted as a role model by the feminist movement in the 1970s—to illustrate, Wonder Woman graced the cover of the first issue of *Ms.* magazine in 1972. She is a character with a history that made her an iconic superheroine long before most other comic book heroines were created. Thus, using Wonder Woman as a basis for comparison is disingenuous. Supergirl, introduced in 1958, and Batgirl (1961) make for better comparisons for the Invisible Woman (1961) and Marvel Girl (1963).

There are two distinct differences between the Marvel and DC characters: their powers and their historical introduction and subsequent context. The Marvel superheroines, Invisible Woman and Marvel Girl, were both introduced to readers in a dual role. Initially, both characters were introduced as subservient love interests. The Invisible Woman (Invisible Girl at the time) was the girlfriend of Reed Richards. Despite having powers of her own, she was often the "damsel in distress" or, at best, a bit player in the adventures of the Fantastic Four. Similarly, Marvel Girl was the girlfriend of Scott Summers (aka Cyclops) and a member of the X-Men (and, in a hastily dropped and creepy subplot, the teenaged Marvel Girl was also an object of romantic interest for the X-Men's mentor and father-figure, Professor X). Reed Richards was the leader of the Fantastic Four, and Cyclops led the X-Men—their girlfriends, both of which are considered today to be among the most powerful characters in the Marvel Universe—deferred to their judgments. Both the Invisible Girl and Marvel Girl, therefore, developed in the context of their superhero team. Their characters have become too strongly embedded in the collective of the Fantastic Four and the X-Men, respectively. Iconic male superheroes from the Marvel catalog that have operated within team environments—Captain America and Iron Man, for example, are both Avengers—have also had the opportunity to develop an individual persona within their own self-titled comics with lengthy runs. Female Avengers such as the Wasp and the Black Widow have not had such an opportunity, nor have Invisible Woman or Marvel Girl.

It is possible that psychology here again plays a role. Male heroes are often seen as independent, capable of handling incredible odds on a "lone wolf" basis.[19] For example, Spider-Man and the Hulk both often operate alone, although teamwork is not unheard of. Females, however, are often seen as more social than their male counterparts, preferring the company of others to being alone. By inference, then, female superheroes should prefer to operate as part of a team rather than independently. Batgirl and Supergirl, on the other hand, are often (though not always) portrayed as working free of the constraints of a team of superheroes.

Finally, the iconic DC superheroines have taken a shortcut to achieving their public recognition that the Marvel heroines have not. Batgirl and Supergirl have taken their powers from the powerful and more widely recognizable heroes Batman and Superman. The heroines have the same powers as their male counterparts (although they are not as powerful), and differ only in the fact that they are female and have been clad in sexier costumes. This similarity may extend beyond psychology and overcome the social natures of females, leading to the more "lone wolf" status of Batgirl and Supergirl—reflecting the independent, though not adverse to teamwork, natures of their namesakes. The iconic status of these two heroines is only a natural extension of the prominence of the two most widely recognized superheroes in the world. Marvel Girl and the Invisible Girl have no iconic male counterparts from which to borrow such significance or recognition.

It remains to be seen if any Marvel superheroine will eventually enjoy a wider recognition in popular culture. With the current trend of successful, big-budget movies capitalizing on comic book properties, it is not beyond the realm of possibility for a female superhero to become the star of a successful franchise outside the bounds of comic book pages. However, with fragmenting audiences, such an achievement will be difficult to achieve.

NOTES

1. "Publisher Market Shares: 2012," *Diamond Comics*, http://www.diamondcomics.com/Home/1/1/3/237?articleID=129876 (accessed February 17, 2013).

2. Laura Hudson, "Marvel Editors Discuss Women in Comics and the Lack of Female-Led Titles," interview, *Comics Alliance*, last modified December 8, 2011, http://www.comicsalliance.com/2011/12/08/marvel-women-comics-editors.

3. Julie D. O'Reilly, "The Wonder Woman Precedent: Female (Super)Heroism on Trial," *Journal of American Culture* 28, no. 3 (2005).

4. Laura Mattoon D'Amore, "The Accidental Supermom: Superheroines and Maternal Performativity, 1963–1980," *Journal of Popular Culture* 45, no. 6 (2012).

5. Michael R. Lavin, "Women in Comic Books," *Serials Review* 24, no. 2 (1998).

6. D'Amore, "Accidental Supermom."

7. Lavin, "Women in Comic Books."

8. Christine Mains, Brad J. Ricca, Holly Hassel, and Linda Rucker, "Heroes or Sheroes," in *Women in Science Fiction and Fantasy*, ed. Robin Anne Reid (Westport, CT: Greenwood Press, 2009).

9. Helene Shugart, "Supermarginal," *Communication and Critical/Cultural Studies* 6, no. 1 (2009).

10. Jeffrey A. Brown, "Supermoms? Maternity and the Monstrous-Feminine in Superhero Comics," *Journal of Graphic Novels and Comics* 2, no. 1 (2011).

11. D'Amore, "Accidental Supermom."

12. Brown, "Supermoms."

13. Laura Mattoon D'Amore, "Invisible Girl's Quest for Visibility: Early Second Wave Feminism and the Comic Book Superheroine," *Americana: The Journal of American Popular*

Culture 7, no. 2 (2008), http://www.americanpopularculture.com/journal/articles/fall_2008/d'amore.htm.

14. Brown, "Supermoms."

15. Anita K. McDaniel, "Comics, 1960–2005," in *Women in Science Fiction and Fantasy*, ed. Robin Anne Reid (Westport, CT: Greenwood Press, 2009).

16. McDaniel, "Comics."

17. Gail Simone, "Women in Refrigerators," http://lby3.com/wir (accessed May 7, 2013).

18. Victoria Ingalls, "Sex Differences in the Creation of Fictional Heroes with Particular Emphasis on Female Heroes and Superheroes in Popular Culture: Insights from Evolutionary Psychology," *Review of General Psychology* 16, no. 2 (2012).

19. Ingalls, "Sex Differences."

Chapter Eighteen

Liminality and Capitalism in Spider-Woman and Wonder Woman

How to Make Stronger (i.e., Male)
Two Super Powerful Women

Fernando Gabriel Pagnoni Berns

On the official website of DC Comics, regarding issue #18 of Wonder Woman (March 2013), the following exchange between two users can be read in the comments section:

> Julio F Suarez G: The Original mythos of WW was a convoluted mess. Almost no one could work well with it. I'm glad they changed it. It feels fresh and more in tune with what [*sic*] its own direction.

> Jasmin Hernandez: But the reason it was convoluted was because writers kept changing her and now Azarello [*sic*] did it again?[1]

The reason why this chapter begins with this exchange is that it perfectly sums up the problems that Wonder Woman suffers since the classic miniseries *Crisis in Infinite Earths* (1985), in which the different worlds and parallel universes which composed the DC Universe as a whole were erased, to leave in its place just one version of planet Earth. In this new version, all of DC's characters restarted their biographies, some almost unchanged (Batman), others with several changes (Superman), and others from zero (Wonder Woman). George Pérez takes the Amazon princess,[2] changes her relationship with Steve Trevor, creates new supporting characters, and inserts the heroine in the world of Greek mythology.

Pérez's years were successful both in sales as well as critically,[3] and when he left the series, his place was taken by William Messner-Loebs, who came from triumphing with *The Flash*. The problem was that Messner-Loebs tried to do with the character of Wonder Woman what he did so successfully with Wally West, creating a series of mundane/suburban stories which highlighted the role of Wonder Woman as a superhero in the city while getting her away from her mythological roots, even making her work as a waitress in order to solve economic problems. Regardless of whether this strategy was a good one or not (not), the fact is that this decision to virtually ignore all her previous life and characteristics without an "official" reboot was just the initial kick of the biggest problem that would plague the most iconic female character of DC Comics. Almost all the creative teams which followed Pérez took the decision to make a kind of tabula rasa with the character's previous stories and instead start from scratch, thus establishing a structural weakness in the adventures and biography of the Amazon princess.

Even as official reboot to the series took place with the saga of fourteen episodes, *Odyssey* (2011), created by Michael Straczynski, which aimed to change the status of Wonder Woman in the DC Universe, plans were cut by a new reboot, this time around the whole DC Universe (the New 52).

Currently, in the Brian Azzarello age, Wonder Woman myths have suffered structural changes that have readers divided. If for many reviewers this new incarnation makes the character appealing,[4] too many fans loyal to this new character's tradition, prone to fight and less reflective, said it is a travesty that has betrayed everything that made the character something special. Martin Gray, reviewer of the online site *Too Dangerous for a Girl* and self-confessed enthusiast of the character, recognizes his inability to connect with the current incarnation and just decides to step aside while Azzarello remains in charge of the series since "the DC new Wonder Woman is what it is, but it ain't for me."[5] Even more radically, the amazonarchives.com site (dedicated to the *real* Wonder Woman),[6] which aims to file all about the Amazon, decided to shelve all that goes on with the new incarnation of Wonder Woman that Azzarello and DC "have left beyond recognition."[7] Therefore, the site is a "DC New 52 Free Zone."

Is this a problem for Wonder Woman only? Not really. Another superheroine with her own monthly series has had the same problems. Spider-Woman (Marvel) got her own series in April 1978, with the first eight issues written by Marv Wolfman. By the end at issue #50, the series had become a "muddled mess"[8] because the different writers that took the character ignored the previous arguments, the character's personality, and her secondary cast to begin from zero. This is a problem that we have heard already before, so is it possible to deduce that the difficult thing is not to maintain a coherent series relating the adventures of a superhero, but *maintaining consistency in a series starring a superheroine*. Not coincidentally, "muddled mess" is the term that Tyler Weaver chose to refer to the character of Wonder Woman in the 1990s.[9] Clearly, writing for a superheroine is difficult.

Now, why is it so difficult to write for a female superhero? Maybe it is possible to find an answer taking into account four eras of the mentioned heroines. This chapter will work with George Pérez and Messner-Loebs on *Wonder Woman*[10] and the years of Marv Wolfman and Michael Fleisher in *Spider-Woman* as runs denouncing the tensions and problems that appear when defining the image and personality of a female superhero who carries her own monthly series.

SUPER WOMEN AS LIMINALITY

To George Pérez, Wonder Woman "is not Supergirl. She's not a superhero, she's a fantasy character who gets involved with super-heroes."[11] Thus, Pérez's decisions are understandable when he faced the reboot of the character in the 1980s. Diana was a young woman completely innocent about the specifics of the patriarchal world. Upon her arrival, there are two women who will guide her: Julia Kapatelis, an expert on Greek mythology, and Vanessa, her teenage daughter. The first will help Diana understand the way of thinking in the patriarchal world. The second, with her teenage idolatry, will help her understand the reactions that her presence and image cause in the Western world. A third woman, Mindy Mayer, an unscrupulous agent who will try to exploit Wonder Woman, will show her the small human miseries (for the large ones, of course, are the supervillains). Mindy represents unbridled capitalism always ready to exploit anything from which she can extract some profit, this time Wonder Woman as an icon. It is clear that each woman represents a face (and a generation) of Western women with which Wonder Woman must learn to live. This sum of facets mirrors the instability of postmodern identity, which is built on many complex discursive practices. In her culture shock, in her need to fit in and understand, Diana reflects the lack of "solidity, continuity, and structure"[12] of postmodern identities, and therefore her character is more labile, more polysemous, and more open to interpretation and reinterpretations. Diana doubts herself and her decisions many times, wondering about the best course of action when facing a problem. This does not mean that she is unsure. Rather, it is her capacity for reflection and self-questioning that gives her power and takes her away from being a generic hero, because it prevents crystallization in a legible identity. For example, when Diana is summoned before Zeus, it is because he requires total dedication, a carnal worship more than a spiritual one.[13] Diana refuses, angering the god and endangering the other Amazons. Diana questions the wisdom of her actions and believes that perhaps she should have accepted the proposal.[14] Pérez also inserted between story arcs single issues without any physical action that present reflections about Diana's life in the patriarchal world and how she adapts to her new life.[15] Those were thought-provoking issues inviting readers to interrupt the narrative built on a series of violent battles to question the reason for this violence and how it affects people.

This approach to the character was new in the world of comics, always prone to action, but gave Diana fleshiness. However, with time, many fans went away (especially when Pérez left the drawing), and by the 1990s, Diana was considered "*too* nice, too much of a Pollyanna"[16] to be a superhero (perhaps not understanding that, as stated, Pérez never considered Diana a superhero to begin with). The "Pérezian" Wonder Woman "was too goody-goody to crack a joke or play a trick,"[17] and the adventures "a little too slow-moving and often concentrated more in the book's supporting cast."[18]

When Pérez left the series, DC decided to "fix" this nest of errors. After all, Pérez had been able to place Wonder Woman on the radar again. Now she had to be kept there. The decisions were clear: move Wonder Woman away from the mythical realm and make her interact more with the superhero world. Reformulate Diana so she becomes "a little more involved in the more mundane crime-fighting type of activity."[19] To do this, she must leave behind her "complexities generated by George."[20] And she should be tougher, more confident, even at the risk of masculinizing her.

This is where she is intertwined with the Spider-Woman of the 1970s.[21] Like Diana, Jessica Drew is a woman for whom the patriarchal world is new. Jessica and her parents, Jonathan and Merriam Drew, lived in Mount Wundagore to work on scientific projects. There, Jessica fell seriously ill from exposure to uranium, and her father decides to inject her with an experimental serum based on irradiated spiders' blood. Since the serum required a month's incubation, Wyndham placed her in a genetic accelerator. Shortly afterward, her mother died, and her father left for the United States, leaving Wyndham to care for her. While in the accelerator, she aged at a decelerated rate. When she was finally released, decades later, Drew was only seventeen years old.

Ignoring the world outside Mount Wundagore, Jessica is manipulated by the criminal association Hydra and becomes Spider-Woman. When she learns the true nature of Hydra, Jessica confronts them and escapes their domain. Alone in the world of men, she must learn to live and move in society while trying desperately to know herself and establish a concrete identity, which fluctuates between being a nocturnal and anonymous super-being, a threatening menace, or a justice seeker. Her integration will not be easy because Jessica has in her blood a hormonal imbalance that makes women feel anger toward her, while men feel a mixture of sexual attraction and distrust.[22]

Like Diana, Jessica constantly questions herself and reflects about her place in this new world. Both women's heroic actions do not have as a motor a normative or universal ideal of justice, but an ethic of care that leads them to try to help others, transcending any normative rules, which puts them in a marginal situation in society. This way they distance themselves from pre-conceived universal ideas of justice. And in the Occident, universal equals male and "the female has value only in her specificity."[23] Following Robyn Ryle,

> while traditional ideas of justice assume that right and wrong must be deter-mined by an objective devaluation of empathy and compassion, a more femi-nine sense of justice is deeply entwined with the idea of being able to take the position of others. Masculine ideas of justice are blind and assume that one can only determine what is just by ignoring the particulars of a person's situation. Feminine justice assumes that the unique set of particulars must be consid-ered.[24]

It will be useful to bring up the concept of liminality as described and defined by Victor Turner. In modern Western society, discursive and symbolic prac-tices are constructed mainly on a dichotomous basis, male/female, white/black, good/evil, savage/civilized, and so on. Any term will be framed in one pole. So stereotypes are built and a deep analysis avoided, through which we can observe that discursive practices are actually a construct of a social and historical nature. Liminality presents a third term that cannot be framed on any pole. *Liminality* comes from Latin and means "threshold."[25] It is not inside or out; it is right at the threshold, in the middle. It is neither one nor the other. This concept allows critiquing the binary axis. The liminal is some-thing that is presented as an alternative to the hegemonic, to the known and labeled. So it is dangerous, because it questions the naturalness of certain practices. They are, as defined by Turner, ambiguous characters since they "slip through the network of classifications that normally locate states and positions in cultural spaces. Liminal entities are neither here nor there."[26] Wonder Woman and Spider-Woman are such characters. Both women are liminal by their condition of being not superheroes, not criminals, not civil-ians. They, as liminal beings, have no status[27] because they are unclassifiable since they do not belong to any specific place.

Victor Turner distinguished between societas and communitas. Societas is based on hierarchical structures of power. Every term is in relation to another, below or above, and well separated in terms of whether something or someone is "more" or "less" than someone else.[28] It is our actual capitalist society, for example. In contrast, communitas is characterized by "equality, immediacy, and the lack of social ranks and roles."[29] This intimacy and equality between members of the community results in a process that causes "the dissolution of structure, the absence of social distinctions, a homogenization of roles, the disappearance of political allegiance, the breakdown of regular borders and barriers. With the suspension of status distinctions, human beings recognize the core humanity they share. Relationships are immediate and spontaneous."[30] The latter is interesting. The relationships between individuals are spontaneous, emotional, and characterized by empathy. Here Diana and Jessica would be inserted. Both women are neither heroines nor vigilantes. They are not above people. They do not exert power over people, since justice is a standard that is above individuals. Both women, as liminal characters, belong to the scope of communitas, recognizing, first of all, the essential human bond, without which "there could be *no* society."[31] Both are women from the communitas lost in the societas.

Diana and Jessica, lost in the patriarchal world, act "concerned about the situation a given person is in," and their focus "is on the individual herself rather than on any abstract or general moral principles."[32] Spider-Woman, in the first issue, contemplates the possibilities of stealing food. Although she understands that this action is bad, in no way she decants for its opposite: not to steal. Being a hero is an idea that is not in her plans. It is the circumstances that push her to act on behalf of those who are in distress. Wonder Woman does not reach the patriarchal world as an emissary of justice. In her first adventure, her purpose is to stop Ares' war plans, which would cause the destruction of the gods, and with them, the Amazons. Later she stays in the world of men not as an emissary of justice, but of peace. These women do not regard themselves as "superheroes" whose mission is to do good, differentiating without doubt what is right from what is wrong. It is hence that both women, before beginning a battle with an unknown enemy, always open a possibility of dialogue to meet their adversaries and learn their motivations. This fact moves them away from the universe of male heroes, always predisposed to fight first and ask later. This attempt at dialogue could be understood as an attitude of weakness in the female characters. Wonder Woman in the Pérez years continually interpellates her enemies on their purposes to try to understand what makes them behave aggressively. For example, when Silver Swan attacks for the first time,[33] Diana attempts before anything to reason with her, and only when innocent lives are at risk does Wonder Woman engage in battle. When Spider-Woman first sees the villain Gypsy Moth flying above the city, she decides to go after her with the intention of meeting her more than looking for a fight.[34] Jessica even thinks that maybe Gypsy Moth could be a soul mate since both women are half-human, half-insect.

Being half-human, half-animal is an internal difference which constructs Jessica as a liminal character. She's not just a woman in a costume that replicates certain insectoid forms. Jessica has human and insect genes, and she is both and neither at the same time. It is neither one thing nor the other, and therefore it does not exactly fit in society. As defined by Hortense Spillers, this difference within is a new model of identity in our culture: "neither/nor."[35] Diana, too, has this difference within. Raised as a perfect machine for war, she is the messenger of peace in the patriarchal world. A warrior with a message of peace. An embodied contradiction. She, like Jessica, is neither one thing nor the other. There was even an attempt to integrate Wonder Woman in the Justice League Europe, but it was unsuccessful. The character could not seamlessly integrate in the heroic universe because of her liminal nature.

WONDER WOMAN AND SPIDER-WOMAN WORK HARD FOR THEIR MONEY

Both characters get a reboot when the original writers leave the series. Actually, Marv Wolfman leaves *Spider-Woman* at issue #8, but Mark Gruenwald follows Wolfman stories and style closely. It is only with the third writer, Michael Fleisher, that the first reboot of the series is made (*Spider-Woman* #21), while William Messner-Loebs takes over Wonder Woman after Pérez in issue #63. Both new writers have the intention of creating new bases: make Diana/Jessica tougher, confident. To do this, probably without realizing it, they masculinize both women and resume the idea that a female hero is "really a man,"[36] a woman with masculine behavior and ideology whose only difference from the male superheroes is a biological one. Erased are what made these women unique: precisely their "default" of constant self-reflection, the ongoing quest to build a place of their own, the need for dialogue, for understanding more than fighting. Any traits of liminality are gone now. Being a "superhero," even a female one, is a fixed place in society that does not allow ambiguities. Instead, in their early adventures, Wonder Woman and Spider-Woman were deviants of the patriarchal order, since they do not have a social role that fits normative patterns.

In the first issue of Fleisher, while Spider-Woman flies over the city, one panel reads, "For years now, she has been a being tormented, rootless, her relationships agonizingly ephemeral, her life tossed constantly, hither and thither, by fickle winds of capricious change. She longs for constancy this Spider-Woman, and yet in the past few weeks her entire life has changed again."[37] This text serves as metatext that recognizes the character's liminal status, the lack of some concrete focus in her adventure. Obviously, this lack of specifically defined personality was seen as a weakness, a real "sin" in the world of superheroes, always prone to aggression. Fleisher in this panel tacitly apologizes to readers for so grave a mistake and promises that Spider-Woman would be the heroine that she always meant to be, fully integrated into the Western world, aggressive, and confident. Any female differentiation is blurred now, and any doubt about herself is obliterated.

So the first decision when the creative teams change was to integrate their heroines to the heroic universe, and the second and more controversial was to turn Diana and Jessica into bounty-hunters or do-gooders for money.

In the Messner-Loebs run, Diana agrees to work with Micah Rains (a low-end private detective) in an agency which protects people for money, while Spider-Woman is associated with Scotty McDowell and becomes a bounty hunter (again, for money). Thus, both women suffer a double conversion. On the one hand, they are now fully integrated into a heroic universe where the notion of justice is clear. This does not mean that justice for money has no ambiguous facets or that the idea is not controversial, but it should be mentioned that both women work with people associated with institutions of justice: Wonder Woman with a private detective, a figure considered inside the law, and Spider-Woman with a criminologist (Scotty) and in collaboration with the police department of the city. On the other hand, both women are integrated into the capitalist system. Thus, it is possible to understand that both women are masculinized, especially if we keep in mind that jobs such as physical protection and bounty hunters have been associated with masculinity, conservatism, and even Caucasians.[38] They are now fully integrated into societas, and therefore belong to a hierarchical system that separates them from the rest. No longer shall they operate by human empathy, but now for money, and above all, because it is right. Both women now differentiate good from bad actions because they are in a system of justice that understands these differences for them.

Of course, this intention was disguised under the idea of giving both Diana and Jessica more security in themselves. Even Wonder Woman readers noted these changes and praised Diana's "new assertiveness"[39] and her new confidence.[40] But there were many who noted that "Diana's much vaunted confidence is being pushed a little too soon, too fast. There's been no established reason for this sudden leap of assurance,"[41] allowing a reflection that "turning Diana into a female Rambo in order to increase sales would be a sad thing indeed,"[42] to the point that in *Wonder Woman* #71, Ruben Diaz, who was in charge of answering correspondence, agreed in the mail section that there is a "strong disapproval over the direction" of the series and that "some of our readers feel that she has been cast as a stereotypical female super-hero." In Spider-Woman, the reactions were similar: though many were happy that the character had found her identity, many noticed that the series editors chose the easy way.[43] "She was a sensitive woman,"[44] but now Jessica had replaced her tendency to "think a lot"[45] in favor of "action."

This mail from both series shows that readers noticed the sudden change in direction of the main character and that this direction was intended to give more confidence to their heroines in exchange for making them lose what made them unique: a sense of justice in terms of caring, of comprehension, "a female ethic of care and empathy, in contrast to a fundamental and universal male ethic of justice,"[46] as proposed by Carol Gilligan in her book *In a Different Voice*, published in 1982, between the publications of Spider-Woman and the Pérezian Wonder Woman.

That the female power and their ability to form empathic relationships with others as alternative to violence can be seen as a threat to the all-action approach of today's comic books is clearly delineated already in the first issue of George Pérez's *Wonder Woman*. In just the first two pages framed in the prehistory of mankind, a caveman who has just been outcast by his tribe cruelly kills a pregnant woman only because he felt that her sympathy for his pain was a threat to his masculinity. Women can be an alternative for the universal/male justice based in violence and coercion. One could argue that this is a way of essentialized women, but both Wolfman and Pérez wanted to find features that make their heroines alternative to the male model of justice, rather than fixed models based on sex differences. Liminal creatures cannot be essentialized because they have no concrete, fixed personality. This is what is lost when the two women decide to join the system and charge money for doing justice. It is no coincidence that both women associate with men while working in these new professions. It is no coincidence that this change occurs in *Wonder Woman* with the arrival of Mike Deodato in the drawing, and his hypersexualized female figures. Furthermore, both women are no longer operating outside of everyday life: prior to the change, neither is fully integrated into the heroic universe (they are not part of any vigilante/superhero group), nor to the system (they don't work, as Wonder Woman, or they are not able to maintain employment, as Spider-Woman), but now both play their role in society, probably even contributing taxes. A Messner-Loebs obsession was to find a job for Diana, making her work in a burger joint. Then she was completely assimilated.

Of the two women, it is clearly Spider-Woman who comes out better for the situation, and this is because in spite of working as a bounty hunter for a man, at least she is always disobeying him to save people who are not customers, to Scotty's regret, who does not see with good eyes Spider-Woman's insistence on keeping some autonomy of action, which is an act of rebellion in a woman who never wanted to be a heroine in the first place. At least not before Fleisher, because Scotty mentioned in *Spider-Woman* #23 that she approached him and asked him to turn her into a superheroine, thus losing the marginal nature of the character, who is now fully integrated into society. Not innocently, Fleisher decides to wipe out the issue of Jessica's pheromonal disorder, which prevented her from assimilating, from passing for "normal." Of course Wonder Woman will continue to protect innocent people without getting paid for it, but her new skintight black suit and her sexy poses (Deodato's drawings) fail to characterize her as more than a sex-pot, a sex fantasy for men, the cliché of the buxom vixen tougher than nails.

There is not much that Messner-Loebs and Michael Fleisher made with the new status of their two now-capitalist heroines. The issue is quickly abandoned, either because Fleisher left the series after only nine issues, or because Diana is busy recovering the name of Wonder Woman lost to Artemis. It is not that surprising. The idea was just a gimmick to transpose the heroines into a male frame in the editorial needs to make both women more action driven and thus more palatable to the taste of readers. In other words, make them more *generic*. This process of masculinization occurs not only by the muscling of the body and the use of huge weapons,[47] but also when heroines take ideological male attributes, such as a concept of justice and capitalist practices, based more in the impersonal (get paid to act good) than in empathy with some other.

While male heroes handle themselves according to how the world works, the heroines try to understand *how the world of their opponents works*. This is the basic difference. If the characters do not have traits culturally associated with the masculinity as violence trope and the need for action, readers will appreciate it, but many will ask for action. And when the publishing house tries to give the characters new traits that are more action driven, almost invariably the characters will fall into a masculinization which makes of a very special heroine a generic (male) hero, which will lead to them being granted new features that distinguish them, which will be discussed/resisted by readers, thus leading to infinite reboots.

NOTES

1. Retrieved from DCComics.com, March, 29, 2013, http://www.dccomics.com/comics/wonder-woman-2011/wonder-woman-18.

2. *Wonder Woman* (Vol. 2), nos. 1–62, plus two annuals.

3. Chris Lawrence, *George Pérez: Storyteller* (Dynamite Entertainment, 2006), 79.

4. Especially from reviewers who acknowledge not having been fans of her previous incarnations.

5. http://dangermart.blogspot.com.ar/2012/12/wonder-woman-15-review.html.

6. The word *real* is in italics, thus marking a sharp distinction between a correct and an apocryphal version of Wonder Woman.

7. http://www.amazonarchives.com/index2.htm.

8. Gina Misiroglu, *The Superhero Book: The Ultimate Encyclopedia of Comic-Book Icons and Hollywood Heroes* (Canton, MI: Visible Ink Press, 2004), 465.

9. Tyler Weaver, *Comics for Films, Games, and Animation: Using Comics to Construct Your Transmedia Storyworld* (Burlington, MA: Focal Press, 2013), 199.

10. This chapter will work with *Wonder Woman* Vol. 2, and the numbering of each issue mentioned is from this volume.

11. Lawrence, *George Pérez*, 79.

12. Anthony Elliot, *Concepts of the Self* (Cambridge, UK: Polity Press, 2008), 54.

13. *Wonder Woman*, vol. 2, no. 10 (November 1987).

14. Ibid., 11.

15. For example, *Wonder Woman* #8, *Wonder Woman* #22, *Wonder Woman* #27, *Wonder Woman* #41, *Wonder Woman* #46, and more.

16. Letter of Kevin Carrier in the postal section of *Wonder Woman* #13.

17. User Sean T in the blog *Too Dangerous for a Girl*, http://dangermart.blogspot.com.ar/2012/05/wonder-woman-9-review.html (accessed April 2, 2013).

18. User Edmund Lau Kok Ming in an Amazon review, http://www.amazon.com/Wonder-Woman-Gods-Goddesses-Novel/dp/0761517138 (accessed April 2, 2013).

19. Letter of Bob Clinton in the mail section of *Wonder Woman* #68.

20. Letter of Chris Khalaf in the mail section of *Wonder Woman* #66.

21. This is the decade that marks a social turning point with the appearance of the second and more radicalized wave of feminism. Eyes were alert to any strong female character.

22. Maybe this fear mirrored the real fear that conservative sectors of society felt about the new and empowered woman of radicalized feminism.

23. Danielle Haase-Dubose et al., "Introduction," in *French Feminism*, ed. Danielle Haase-Dubose et al. (Thousand Oaks, CA: Sage, 2003), 195.

24. Robyn Ryle, *Questioning Gender: A Sociological Exploration* (Los Angeles: Pine Forge Press, 2012), 137.

25. Victor Turner, *The Ritual Process: Structure and Anti-Structure* (Chicago: Aldine Transaction, 2008), 94.

26. Ibid., 95.

27. Ibid.

28. Ibid., 96.

29. Jeffrey Rubenstein, "Purim, Liminality, and Communitas," *AJS Review* 17, no. 2 (Autumn 1992): 251.

30. Ibid.

31. Turner, *The Ritual Process*, 97. Emphasis in the original.

32. Michael Slote, *The Ethics of Care and Empathy* (New York: Routledge, 2007), 10.

33. *Wonder Woman* #15.

34. *Spider-Woman* #10.

35. Hortense Spillers, "Notes on an Alternative Model—Neither/Nor," in *The Difference Within: Feminism and Critical Theory*, ed. Elizabeth Meese and Alice Parker (Philadelphia: John Benjamins, 1989).

36. Yvonne Tasker, *Spectacular Bodies: Gender, Genre and the Action Cinema* (New York: Routledge, 1993), 132.

37. *Spider-Woman* #21, 1.

38. Matt DeLisi and Peter Johns Conis, *American Corrections: Theory, Research, Policy, and Practice* (Burlington, MA: Jones and Bertlett Learning, 2013), 141.

39. Letter of Nancy Champion in the mail section of *Wonder Woman* #66.

40. Letter of Gary Hellen in the mail section of *Wonder Woman* #66.

41. Letter of Nancy Champion in the mail section of *Wonder Woman* #70.

42. Letter of Paul Girard in the mail section of *Wonder Woman* #69.

43. Letter of Joel Jaffer in the mail section of *Spider-Woman* #27.

44. Letter of Brian Nelson in the mail section of *Spider-Woman* #27.

45. Letter of Deborah Lipp in the mail section of *Spider-Woman* #25.

46. Ute Gerhard, *Debating Women's Equality: Toward a Feminist Theory of Law from a European Perspective* (New Brunswick, NJ: Rutgers University Press, 2001), 157.

47. Jeffrey Brown, *Dangerous Curves: Action Heroines, Gender, Fetishism, and Popular Culture* (Jackson: University of Mississippi Press, 2011), 30.

Chapter Nineteen

Empowerment as Transgression

The Rise and Fall of the Black Cat in Kevin Smith's
The Evil That Men Do

Michael R. Kramer

The Black Cat (aka Felicia Hardy) has been a recurring character in Marvel's Spider-Man comic books since 1979. During that time, the character's role in the Spider-Man mythos has evolved from cat burglar villainess, to romantic partner, to trusted friend/confidante. Because of her alluring appearance and strong, bantering chemistry with Spider-Man, Black Cat's popularity has endured much longer than many fans expected—to the point where many longtime readers place Felicia in the "Big Three" of Peter Parker's love interests (along with the iconic Mary Jane Watson and Gwen Stacy). However, the character also remains a paradox in terms of her role as a heroine. Felicia is confident, assertive, fiercely independent, and possesses admirable physical prowess and fighting skills, all of which make her a symbol of empowerment. On the other hand, she's often frivolous, objectified, and at times mentally unstable. Her sexuality both empowers and marginalizes her in the Marvel Universe.

This paradox is reflected and reinforced in the high-profile miniseries, *Spider-Man and the Black Cat: The Evil That Men Do*, written by Kevin Smith and illustrated by Terry Dodson. The involvement of Smith, the successful screenwriter, film director, and actor, garnered the series much attention. In this chapter, I will analyze *The Evil That Men Do* from a feminist rhetorical perspective, arguing that the book reinforces the no-win situation faced by many comic book heroines. Even as they possess empowering elements, comic book heroines are often punished for their power. Such depictions strengthen the status quo and further undermine the heroine's

233

ability to deliver positive gender messages to society. This chapter first provides background on the character of the Black Cat and the development of Smith's miniseries. Then the concept of *gender transgression* is explained and applied to *The Evil That Men Do*. Finally, implications of the analysis are discussed.

BACKGROUND

The Black Cat, aka Felicia Hardy, was introduced in *Amazing Spider-Man* #194 and made an immediate splash with fans. First, the title boasted few female villains at the time, so the Black Cat filled a noticeable void among the web-spinner's testosterone-heavy rogue's gallery of the Green Goblin, Doctor Octopus, Venom, and many others. Second, the comic immediately injected elements of physical attraction and sexual tension into the Spider-Man/Black Cat relationship. In the pantheon of Marvel characters, the Black Cat's skills and powers were unremarkable. At first, she possessed no superpowers but relied on excellent gymnastics and hand-to-hand fighting skills. Skintight cat suit and flowing platinum hair aside, Felicia was no "blond bimbo." Her "bad luck" powers, in which opponents experienced seemingly random accidents, stumbles, and other physical mishaps, were the product of cleverly coordinated booby traps set at the location in advance of combat. Although probably an intellectual inferior to Tony Stark and Reed Richards, the Black Cat certainly possessed a keen knowledge of physics, engineering, and kinetics. Her penchant for witty banter and wordplay also suggested an intelligence and assertiveness that few women characters were permitted in the late 1970s Marvel Universe.

Having no plans for world domination, Felicia Hardy aimed only to live the high life and honor her father's legacy as a cat burglar. Her thievery often led her into conflict with Spider-Man, his attempts to thwart her crimes punctuated with (and often distracted by) the near-constant flirtation between the characters. After a few years of this back-and-forth, the Black Cat gave up heisting for crime fighting, and the two became lovers. The relationship was rocky throughout, with Spider-Man doubting Felicia's ability to "go straight" and the Black Cat disdaining Peter Parker's conventional life out of costume. They eventually broke up; Peter married his true love, Mary Jane Watson; and Felicia reappeared from time to time as a somewhat unpredictable ally and friend.

In 2002, Marvel announced that actor, writer, and director Kevin Smith (*Clerks*, *Chasing Amy*) would pen a Black Cat/Spider-Man miniseries as part of a multiyear exclusive pact with the comic book company.[1] The miniseries was touted as a significant, high-profile event for Marvel. A hip, pop-culture multitasker, Smith brought with him an aura of irreverence and freshness to the forty-year-old company, and the filmmaker rejected any notion that comic book work was a "step down." In fact, Smith once stated, "I'm as proud of my work in comics as I am of anything I've done on film."[2] Marvel editor-in-chief Joe Quesada trumpeted Smith as the "perfect ambassador" to "take the world of comics to the masses."[3] When *The Tonight Show* booked Smith to appear on June 24, 2002, apparently for the unprecedented purpose of promoting a comic book, Marvel executives dubbed the appearance a "giant step" for the comics industry that would generate high demand for the Black Cat/Spider-Man miniseries.[4] To add to the stakes, the six-part miniseries was also eyed as a launchpad for a new Smith-scribed Black Cat solo series. Needless to say, Marvel and comic book fans everywhere held high hopes for *Spider-Man and the Black Cat: The Evil That Men Do* (*ETMD*).

Smith wrote and Marvel published the first three issues of *ETMD* in 2002, and then something unusual happened. It just stopped. Frustrated fans waited month after month for another installment of the story, but nothing came. Finally, after three years, Smith completed issues #4 through #6 of *ETMD*. He blamed the delay on laziness, joking (apparently) that he only resolved to finish the miniseries to end harassment from teenage fanboys.[5] Nevertheless, Marvel editor Axel Alonso still expressed optimism for the story's conclusion, predicting that the final issue was "bound to be the buzz of the internet for months to come."[6]

The reaction to *ETMD* was mixed. Critics' reviews were generally middling to negative. *Spider-Man Crawl Space*, a prominent website devoted solely to the web-slinger, found Smith's work quite uneven but enjoyed the ending nonetheless,[7] while the *Comics Alliance* blog placed the miniseries on its list of "The 15 Worst Comics of the Decade," finding the story "weird and totally creepy."[8] The surrounding hype did generate strong initial sales; readers bought more than 126,000 copies, making it the second best selling comic book of June 2002.[9] In 2007, Marvel published *ETMD* as a trade paperback graphic novel, which has received overall positive reader ratings on Amazon.com (4.0/5.0)[10] and goodreads.com (3.64).[11] Clearly, Smith's miniseries fell short of being the game changer Marvel envisioned, but the story still provokes debate among comic book fans today. Much of that conversation revolves around Smith's portrayal and treatment of Black Cat. In this chapter, I argue that *ETMD*, rather than celebrating the elevation of Black Cat to potential lead character status, consistently undermines its heroine in ways that reinforce patriarchy and traditional gender roles.

GENDER TRANSGRESSION

Scholars for years have studied the cultural impact of mass media gender portrayals. Meredith Li-Vollmer and Mark E. LaPointe point out that "as reflectors and creators of culture and cultural values, media are clearly implicated in the ways in which we understand and react to the concepts of gender."[12] That understanding then shapes our sense of "how gender has been performed, is performed, and should be performed."[13] For example, Li-Vollmer and LaPointe remind us that "television shows for children have a history of presenting characters that perform gender according to narrow behavioral stereotypes, with men in more active, aggressive, and leadership roles; women are shown as more deferential, nurturing, and passive."[14] Of particular interest to critics are those popular-culture texts often viewed as less important and that therefore escape academic attention despite their gender messages. Children's cartoons, comic books, and graphic novels fall into that category.

In addition to concerns about stereotyped characterizations of women, critics have also studied the treatment of female characters who challenge or violate traditional gender roles. While some texts celebrate the character's efforts to resist patriarchy, others treat the behavior as *gender transgression* deserving of castigation and punishment. For example, a female character displaying aggression (a traditionally male attribute) may be portrayed as deviant, thereby undermining her resistance and discouraging similar resistance in the audience.[15] This point is particularly salient for women villains in popular culture. Drawing from Bell, Haas, and Sell's work on gender in animated film, Li-Vollmer and LaPointe argue that "transgressive female villains . . . are always brought under control and destroyed to restore the natural social order, removing any possibility for these characters to truly subvert heterogender norms."[16] Although women villains appear powerful and independent, stories often punish their transgressions and ultimately send the message that empowerment is undesirable, even dangerous. In the next section, the concept of gender transgression is applied to demonstrate how Kevin Smith's comic arc *The Evil That Men Do* undermines Black Cat as a heroine and complicates the audience's reading of her as an empowering character.

ANALYSIS

Plot Synopsis

Spider-Man and Black Cat are conducting independent investigations into the death of honor student Donald Phillips and the disappearance of a young woman named Tricia Lane. The former lovers are reunited by the discovery that both incidents are linked to a man known as "Mr. Brownstone." Peter and Felicia suspect that Mr. Brownstone, a drug kingpin who can make people overdose against their will, is actually Garrison Klum, a respected Manhattan philanthropist. Though they are working together, Peter and Felicia spend a lot of time arguing about both their past relationship and their investigation strategy. Black Cat goes off to confront Brownstone in his apartment. Brownstone reveals that he possesses the ability to teleport small amounts of liquid, an ability he parlayed into the business of distributing drugs to wealthy users wishing to avoid visible track marks. Brownstone easily subdues Black Cat and is about to rape her when the issue ends. It is at this point in the story when Kevin Smith's three-year hiatus begins.

When the story resumes, Felicia is in jail on charges of murdering Garrison Klum. She denies both killing Klum and being raped. Spider-Man and Matt Murdock—Felicia's attorney and masked crime fighter Daredevil—attempt to break her out of prison. However, Francis Klum, Mr. Brownstone's brother, arrives first and teleports himself and Black Cat away from the scene. Francis informs Felicia that Garrison sexually assaulted him throughout his life, so when he happened upon Garrison about to rape Felicia, he killed him. Black Cat then reveals that she was the victim of date rape in college. As Felicia and Francis commiserate about the past, Spider-Man and Daredevil arrive on the scene and attack Francis, incorrectly believing he was about to murder Black Cat. When Francis wounds Peter, Felicia goes to his aid. Infuriated by this perceived betrayal, Francis attempts to shoot Black Cat but is thwarted by Spider-Man.

Gender Transgression in *The Evil That Men Do*

Once Peter and Felicia suspect that Garrison Klum is the murderous drug lord Mr. Brownstone, the two heroes argue about the tactics of their investigation. The former recommends gathering more evidence before moving on Klum, while Black Cat wants to immediately confront and interrogate the suspect, using force if necessary to extract a confession.

The spirited and well-articulated dispute centers on a critical tension for costumed crime fighters—the obligations and opportunities of vigilantism. Felicia insists that they exploit the advantages of extrajudicial action and trust their experience and instincts to apprehend Brownstone quickly. Placing his hands on her shoulders, Spider-Man suggests that Black Cat's judgment is clouded by her emotional concern for Tricia Lane. When he ends this lecture with a condescending question ("You see what I'm saying here?"), Felicia breaks his hold and explodes:

Felicia: Yes! I do! You're saying what you always say . . . that you're better at this than I am! That if we're not playing the game by your rules, then we're not playing at all!

Peter: You've gotta listen to me on this!

Felicia: To hell with that! I'm not a kid anymore, Peter! I came to New York looking for answers about Tricia, and Klum's my best lead! And as my best lead, I'm gonna grill him like a side of beef! And if he so much as twitches, I'll bludgeon the sick bastard 'til he's passing blood in his stool!

Peter: *(forcefully grabbing her wrist)* I can't let you do this, Felicia. [17]

This scene offers a strong depiction of the Black Cat as a determined woman of action and conviction who brooks none of Peter's condescension and intimidation. She openly confronts him about his past domination of their relationship, a domination based on a dynamic of his superiority and her immaturity. It was Peter who dictated the "rules" of their partnership while Felicia was just "a kid." As she rejects that past dynamic, Felicia is assertive in principle and aggressive in language. At the end of the above passage, her description of what she may have to do to extract Klum's confession evokes the hypermasculinity of Wolverine or the Punisher rather than the more reserved and passive discourse of many comic book heroines. Spider-Man clearly views Felicia's behavior as a gender transgression, a threat in need of control as he attempts a second, more aggressive attempt to physically restrain her body followed by the proclamation that he cannot "let" her go after Brownstone.

What follows is what should be a critical turning point for both the miniseries and the Black Cat/Spider-Man relationship. Felicia breaks Peter's grip and attacks him, using her agility and fighting acumen to land multiple blows on the surprised web-slinger. She then seizes *his* wrists to pin him to the ground and, in a move that is rarely (if ever) executed successfully against Spider-Man, turns his own web-shooters against him, webbing the stunned hero to the rooftop. The significance of Black Cat besting the more experienced Peter in physical combat cannot be overstated. It appears to be a giant step forward for the character. There is nothing nurturing, passive, or deferential about Black Cat in this scene, despite Spider-Man's efforts to hold her back. A subtext of sexual empowerment also emerges, with Felicia ending the battle literally on top of her former lover, who finds himself trapped in his own sticky, hand-delivered fluid. [18]

What should be a glorious moment of empowerment for Black Cat is quickly diluted. Peter immediately retreats to paternalism, warning Felicia, "You can't confront this guy . . . *alone* . . . Felicia. He could be dangerous" (italics added). His own defeat at her hands apparently is insufficient evidence to establish Black Cat as a heroine who can succeed alone. She responds, "And I'm a woman with father issues who's pushing thirty, crammed into wet leather, and nursing a mean case of PMS. Who the hell's more dangerous than that?" [19] With that, she swings off to face Mr. Brownstone. This page lends itself to a mixed interpretation. On the one hand, Felicia's line suggests both another man's influence over her (in this case, her father) and a continued fixation on her female body with its unique physicality and physiology. More troubling is the implication that Felicia herself believes that her anger and aggression stem from "PMS" and not Peter's attempts to marginalize and control her, thus reinforcing negative stereotypes about women. Alternatively, the dialogue could be read as an empowering description of the experiences and challenges unique to comic book heroines. Moreover, artist Terry Dodson's splash page here depicts Black Cat, with her sinewy limbs, gritting teeth, and clinched fist, as a woman of undeniable strength, agility, and resolve. Where Smith's story goes next, however, is much less ambiguous.

After leaving Peter, Black Cat sneaks into Garrison Klum's suite and begins questioning the suspect. Klum uses his teleporting power to transfer heroin directly into Felicia's system, incapacitating her. Shoving her onto his bed, Klum admits that he is Mr. Brownstone and leaves no doubt that he is about to rape Felicia as the issue ends. In a scene with profound ramifications for the character, Smith puts Black Cat in a situation where she is unable, despite all of her fighting skill and experience, to offer even the slightest resistance to her attacker. The writer devotes four pages to Brownstone standing over Felicia's powerless body as he explains his powers to her. Her assault is presented as a logical consequence of her aggressiveness and independence. As Klum begins to disrobe, he states, "Mister Brownstone can't have you meddling with his business, or his place in the community, just because a few junkies died, can he? So Mister Brownstone's going to teach you not to stick your nose where it doesn't belong . . . in the most effective way he can imagine."[20] The rape is designed to punish Felicia's commitment to bringing criminals to justice, and, in doing so, crush her identity as a heroine. Also, the scene shows that Klum *is* too much for Felicia alone, just as Peter had predicted not long before. In the seconds before the rape, Brownstone asks Felicia, "I take it your friend won't be joining us?" reminding the reader of Spider-Man's absence and his earlier admonition.[21] Heroines who work alone remain relatively rare; they usually operate within male-dominated teams. Black Cat's resistance to that norm brings with it horrible ramifications. All of Felicia's gender transgressions—her strongly articulated opinions, her refusal to abide Peter's orders, her defeat of Spider-Man in battle, and her willingness to face Mr. Brownstone alone—which should be celebrated as empowering, instead are punished to the most severe degree.

Sexual assault occurs rarely as a plotline in mainstream superhero comic books, so Smith's decision to have such a fate befall a popular heroine is extraordinary to begin with. However, his decision to leave the story hanging at this point for an extended period intensifies the meaning and impact of that finale scene. While creative types who bounce among different media no doubt have busy calendars, Smith cited laziness as the reason for delaying the final three issues of *ETMD*. Therefore, Smith chose to leave Felicia trapped as a victim in sex crime limbo *for three years* with little apparent regard for the feelings of readers invested in the story or characters. It should not have been overly onerous for Smith, if he had recognized the magnitude of the situation, to pen one more issue resolving the Black Cat–Brownstone encounter. Instead, the punishment for Felicia's gender transgression lingers for years, and a heroine on the brink of empowerment is, as Li-Vollmer and LaPointe argued, "brought under control and destroyed to restore the natural social order, removing any possibility . . . to truly subvert heterogender norms."

Once Smith resumed writing *ETMD*, he revealed that, despite the clear impression given at the end of the miniseries' third issue, Garrison Klum/Mr. Brownstone did not rape Felicia but was mysteriously killed before the assault began. However, this development also bore negative consequences for Felicia. Therefore, Black Cat's sanction for her gender transgression now took the form of her false imprisonment for Brownstone's murder. Once again, Smith presents Felicia as helpless, her fate totally in the hands of men. Spider-Man enlists the help of male superhero Daredevil, both to serve as Felicia's defense attorney and to help her break out of jail. However, the heroes arrive to find that Francis Klum, Mr. Brownstone's younger brother, has already freed a teary-eyed Black Cat, and they can only watch as Felicia and her rescuer teleport to a new location. Peter and Daredevil then turn to yet another male superhero, Nightcrawler, to work on the case. At this point, Felicia has fallen far from the assertive, independent crime fighter who dominated the first half of the miniseries. Now, no fewer than four men had seized control of her destiny—and of Smith's narrative.

Although free from jail and back in costume, Black Cat remains a passive figure in the story. For an extended scene, she listens to Francis recount how his brother sexually abused him for much of his life. At this point, the reader also discovers that it was Francis who killed Brownstone to prevent the latter's rape of Felicia. Felicia reciprocates by telling Francis about her own experience as a victim of date rape in college and tries to convince him to turn himself in. When Spider-Man arrives on the scene and overpowers Francis in a climactic battle, the latter uses his telekinetic powers to teleport Felicia's mask into Peter's neck, nearly severing his carotid artery. This odd form of attack represents yet another example of retribution against Felicia's heroine status. The mask is an iconic symbol of the comic book superhero. Smith's decision—to let a villain take control of Black Cat's mask and wield it as a weapon against her ally—further erodes her credibility as a competent crime fighter. The sequence also reads as a corrective to Felicia earlier using Peter's web-shooters against him to escape his control and confront Brownstone.

The entire structure of *ETMD* works in a way that offers Black Cat the opportunity to break free of traditional comic book gender roles in the arc's first half and then, in the final three installments, sanctions her for seizing that opportunity. In issues #1 through #3, through her defeat of Spider-Man and encounter with Brownstone, Felicia is featured in fifty-four of seventy-four total pages. She is depicted as independent, witty, strong, and actively involved in the investigation of Brownstone's crimes. She offers articulate opinions about the case and acquits herself well in combat (until her meeting with Brownstone at the end of issue 3). In issues #4 through #6, when the reader would expect a main character's prominence to build, Black Cat appears in only thirty-nine of sixty-nine total pages. Moreover, in the pages where she is featured, Felicia is completely passive. She sits in prison, is rescued from prison, listens to Francis' story, tells her own story, and finally is rescued from Francis. Felicia does deliver a powerful monologue about rape, works hard to convince Francis to surrender to the police, and gains therapeutic benefit from talking about what happened to her. It is stunning, however, that Black Cat spends half of her own miniseries engaged in literally no fighting or other physical activity. The "natural" social order of the superhero universe is restored as Spider-Man, Daredevil, Nightcrawler, and even Francis Klum assume total control of the story's action while the recently empowered Black Cat is penalized and made to watch from the sidelines.

CONCLUSION

Comic book superheroes remain a potent force in popular culture. As new generations become familiar with these characters through film adaptations, trade paperbacks, fan websites, and the comics themselves, the representations of these superheroes grow in breadth and influence, and critics should pay close attention. In particular, superhero comic books often present problematic messages on issues of gender, reinforcing traditional gender roles, stereotypes, and the objectification of women. Nevertheless, the superhero genre consists of characteristics (strength, toughness, action) that offer opportunities for writers and artists to populate their stories with empowered heroines who can then empower female readers. Those stories and their creators should be celebrated.

Creating heroines that empower women and challenge gender roles alone is not enough. Once developed, those characters cannot be undermined in ways that negate their positive impact. When empowerment is treated as gender transgression that demands scorn and punishment, the reader is left with confusion, dashed hopes, and the status quo. Therefore, when a writer presents a heroine as strong and independent, and then takes away that strength and independence, the symbolic power of that heroine is thwarted and traditional gender roles are reinforced. Kevin Smith's miniseries *Spider-Man and the Black Cat: The Evil That Men Do* suffers from this problem. Despite strong interest in the project and plans to launch a Black Cat solo series (which never materialized), Smith is unable to present Felicia as a superhero in her own right. As demonstrated in the analysis above, he at first entices the reader with a strong, dynamic heroine who directly challenges the superhero patriarchy, only to have her later retreat into victimhood, dependence, and passivity. *ETMD*'s potential to offer a transformative heroine and positively influence comic book culture could not be denied. The story received unprecedented promotion, enjoyed brisk sales for a time, and remains available in trade paperback or back issues. It is unfortunate that the story could not get out of its heroine's way.

In addition to helping better understand *ETMD*, this chapter also expands upon and extends the work of Li-Vollmer and LaPointe by applying the concept of gender transgression beyond villainy to an established superheroine and by further identifying the different ways in which gender transgression can be punished or corrected through words, images, and structure. Additional studies are needed to identify and analyze other examples of heroines undermined for their perceived gender transgressions.

NOTES

1. Jonah Weiland, "Silent Bob Speaks! An Evening with Kevin Smith," *Comic Book Resources*, 2002, accessed July 22, 2013.

2. Jonah Weiland, "Kevin Smith Hits the *Tonight Show* to promote *Spider-Man/Black Cat*," *Comic Book Resources*, 2002, accessed July 22, 2013.

3. Weiland, "Kevin Smith Hits."

4. Weiland, "Kevin Smith Hits."

5. David Moran, "New York Comic Con, Day Two: Kevin Smith Answers Your Questions," *Comic Book Resources*, 2002, accessed July 22, 2013.

6. Jonah Weiland, "Preview: *Spider-Man/Black Cat: The Evil That Men Do* #4," *Comic Book Resources*, 2005, accessed July 22, 2013.

7. *Spider-Man and the Black Cat: The Evil That Men Do*, review, *Spider-Man Crawl Space*, n.d., accessed July 24, 2013.

8. Laura Hudson, "The 15 Worst Comics of the Decade, Part 2," *Comics Alliance*, 2009, accessed July 22, 2013.

9. "June 2002 Comic Book Sales Figures," *Comichron*, 2002, accessed July 24, 2013.

10. *Spider-Man/Black Cat: The Evil That Men Do*, paperback, Amazon.com, n.d., accessed July 24, 2013.

11. *Spider-Man/Black Cat: The Evil That Men Do*, Goodreads, n.d., accessed July 24, 2013.

12. Meredith Li-Vollmer and Mark E. LaPointe, "Gender Transgression and Villainy in Animated Films," *Popular Communication* 1, no. 2 (2003): 90.

13. Ibid., 90.

14. Ibid., 94.

15. Ibid., 95.

16. Ibid., 95.

17. Kevin Smith and Terry Dodson, *Spider-Man and the Black Cat: The Evil That Men Do* (New York: Marvel, 2007), 60–61.

18. Ibid., 61–62.
19. Ibid., 62–63.
20. Ibid., 73.
21. Ibid., 64–72.

Index

Abu Ghraib, 69
abuse, 3, 69, 73, 156, 240
aging, 3, 9, 10
Amazons [mythical race], xiii, 134, 139,
    145, 146, 148, 149, 150, 161, 221, 222,
    223, 226
ambiguous, 6, 11, 190, 225, 227, 228, 239
androgyny, 157–158
Angel [character], 108, 110, 111, 207
Araña [character], 82, 90, 91
archetype, 30, 34, 76n18; heroic, 155;
    heroine, 31, 33, 34; lesbian heroic, 155,
    157, 160; witch, 29, 30, 31, 37
assigned space, xiii, 122, 123, 126, 127,
    130
assimilation, 91, 161, 229
authenticity, 32, 66–67, 69, 71, 72, 74, 120,
    122
authorship, 66, 69
Aztec [culture], 81, 86, 87, 89

Baba Yaga [character], 5, 6, 9, 10, 11,
    15n56
Batman [character], 99, 103, 121, 133, 145,
    154, 157, 163, 199, 218, 221
"battle buddy", 70–71
Batwoman [character], 155, 159, 162,
    163–164
beauty, 4, 25, 46, 50, 57, 58, 59, 123, 125,
    137, 177, 205, 215; physical, 121, 122,
    124, 129, 140

Bechdel, Alison, 155, 159–160, 164
Benedict, Helen, 65–66, 69, 70, 73, 74
Black Cat [character], 233, 234, 236, 237,
    238, 239, 240, 241
Black Panther [character], 119, 120, 121,
    123, 128, 129, 130
Black Panther [comic book], 119, 120,
    126, 127, 128, 129, 130
Black Widow [character], 216, 217
Blair, Jane, 66, 69, 70, 72, 74
"blond bimbo", 234
borderland, xii, 81–82, 86, 89, 91
bounty hunter, 228, 229
Brown, Jeffrey, 154, 218n10, 231n47
Brownstone [character], 236, 237, 238,
    239, 241
Buffy The Vampire Slayer [television
    show], 30, 133, 179
Burke, Kenneth, 35, 37, 40n28
Byrne, John, 185–186, 186, 187, 188, 189,
    191, 192, 193, 194, 196

Campbell, Joseph, 3, 8, 9, 13n1, 19, 23
Captain Marvel [character]. *See* Danvers,
    Carol
censorship, 193, 200
Chicana, 82; ethnicity, 91; feminist
    identity, 87, 88, 89; movement, 86, 87,
    92n22
Clasen, Tricia, xii, 255
class, 3, 4, 5, 6, 74, 81, 82, 85, 91, 135

245

today, 208
Superman [character], 88, 133, 136, 138, 139, 141, 146, 154, 199, 211, 218, 221
Swan, Bella [character], 17, 18, 20
symbolism, 66

T'Challa [character]. *See* Black Panther
tales, 3, 4, 5, 6, 8, 9, 10, 11, 12, 18, 21, 45, 121, 138, 139, 141, 201, 204
teamwork, 217, 218
Tolon, Selma [character], 96, 99, 100, 101, 102, 103. *See also* Janissary
Tonight Show, The , 235
transformation, 4, 23, 24, 25, 26, 74, 180, 208
Turkey, Republic of, 95–97, 98, 99, 100, 100–101, 102, 103, 104
Turner, Victor, 225
Twilight [novel], xii, 6, 17, 18, 20, 21, 22

Uncanny X-Men [comic book], 107, 108, 110–111, 112, 115, 116, 123, 124, 125, 127, 214

vampire, 6, 7, 8, 17, 21–22, 22, 23, 24, 25, 26, 30, 34, 36, 38, 133
Van Dyne, Janet [character], 204, 205. *See also* Wasp, The
victim, 29, 55, 59, 86, 100, 172, 173, 194, 213, 215, 237, 239, 240
victimization, 68, 70, 75, 87, 138, 194, 215
vilification, 213

Wagenheim, Christopher Paul, xiii, 260
Walter, Jennifer [character], 185. *See also* She-Hulk

War in Iraq, 65, 67, 69, 70
warrior, 74, 89, 161, 172, 226; heroes, 47, 68, 69, 74; women, 74, 77n46, 89, 103
Wasp, The [character], xiii, 201, 204, 204–206, 206, 207, 208, 212, 217
Wertham, Dr. Frederic, xiii, 145, 149, 190, 200
wicca, 30, 31, 37
wife, 8, 22, 25, 43, 45, 119, 123, 127, 128, 129, 130, 140, 208, 214. *See also* marriage, mother
Williams, Kayla, 66, 73
witchcraft, 29, 30, 31, 33, 34, 35, 38, 39, 39n2
womanhood, 21, 23, 45, 60, 68, 201
women soldiers, 65, 68, 73, 75
women in Turkey traditional, 97
Wonder Woman [character], xiii, 102, 133–134, 137, 138, 139, 148, 161, 217, 222, 223, 228; as male version of Superman, 138, 139; as male, 227
Wonder Woman [comic book], 133, 138, 139, 145, 147, 148, 225, 227, 229

X-Men [characters], 107, 109, 110, 111, 112, 113, 114, 115–116, 119, 122, 124, 125, 127, 172, 173, 174, 175, 179, 200, 201, 206, 207, 212, 213, 214, 217
X-Men [comic book], xiii, 110, 112, 119
X-Men: First Class [comic book], 107, 108, 112, 113, 115, 116
xenophobia, 107, 108

Zechowski, Sharon, xiii, 260

About the Editors

Maja Bajac-Carter is a doctoral student in the College of Communication and Information at Kent State University. She is interested in gender, identity, and media studies. Her research is focused on cultural studies and mass media regarding circulation of gender, racial, and stereotype images and their co-creation between the media and viewers/society at large. Furthermore, Maja is interested in critically examining how portrayals of female characters in popular media influence individual and collective identities within a culture. She has contributed to *We Are What We Sell: How Advertising Shapes American Life . . . and Always Has.* She serves as an assistant editor for the *Popular Culture Studies Journal*. Bajac-Carter received her master's degree from the University of North Texas in communication studies with a focus on constitutive rhetoric and social movements in Serbia. She has received her bachelor's degree in fine arts, also from the University of North Texas.

Norma Jones is a David B. Smith Fellowship recipient and doctoral candidate in the College of Communication and Information at Kent State University. Her research interests include popular culture, identity, and narrative. Specifically, she is interested in critically examining heroic narratives as related to cultural identities and representations of various groups in society. Additionally, she has contributed to the *Asian and Pacific Islander Americans* edition in the Great Lives from History series, *American History through American Sports* volumes, as well as popular press books regarding business management strategies and nontraditional student experiences. Recently, she was named an associate editor for *The Popular Culture Studies Journal*, the official journal of the Midwest Popular Culture Association. Earlier in her career, Norma spent over a decade working in the media as well as consulting for international companies in a variety of fields, including public relations, marketing, sales, high-end jewelry, and international tele-communications. Jones received her master's degree from the University of North Texas in communication studies, focusing on gender, race, and the mass media. Her bachelor's degree is also in communication studies, from the University of California, Santa Barbara.

Bob Batchelor is James Pedas Professor of Communication and executive director of the James Pedas Communication Center at Thiel College. A noted cultural historian and biographer, Bob is the author or editor of twenty-four books, including *John Updike: A Critical Biography* and *Gatsby: A Cultural History of the Great American Novel*. He edits the "Contemporary American Literature" book series for Rowman & Littlefield. Bob is the founding editor of the *Popular Culture Studies Journal*, published by the Midwest Popular Culture/American Culture Association. He is a member of the editorial advisory boards of the *Journal of Popular Culture* and the *International Journal for the Scholarship of Teaching & Learning*. Bob also serves as director of marketing and media for the John Updike Childhood Home Museum in Reading, Pennsylvania. Visit him on the web at http://www.bobbatchelor.com.

About the Contributors

Tricia Clasen (PhD, University of Nebraska) is an associate professor of communication at University of Wisconsin–Rock County. Her primary research interests revolve around gender constructions in popular media as well as power and pedagogy. She previously published "Taking a Bite out of Love: The Myth of Romantic Love in the Twilight Series" in the *Bitten by Twilight* anthology. She lives with her husband and two daughters, and she spends her free time serving as a dance mom and writing middle-grade fiction.

Roy T. Cook is an associate professor in the department of philosophy at the University of Minnesota, and an associate fellow at the Northern Institute of Philosophy at the University of Aberdeen. He specializes in logic, the philosophy of mathematics, and the aesthetics of popular art (especially comics). He has published papers on comics and related issues in the *Journal of Aesthetics and Art Criticism* and other venues, and is co-editor, with Aaron Meskin, of *The Aesthetics of Comics: A Philosophical Approach* (2012). He is a co-founder (with Qiana Whitted and Frank Bramlett) of the comics theory blog *Pencil Panel Page*, online at http://www.pencilpanelpage. wordpress.com.

Joseph Darowski received his PhD from Michigan State University. He is a faculty member at Brigham Young University in Idaho. Darowski is a popular culture scholar, with emphases on comic book theory, literature, and twentieth century American literature.

Itir Erhart studied philosophy and Western languages and literatures at Bogazici University, Istanbul, where she also completed her MA in philosophy. She got her MPhil at the University of Cambridge. In 2006 she earned her PhD from Bogazici University in philosophy. She has been teaching at Istanbul Bilgi University, Department of Media and Communication Systems, since 2001. She is the author of the book *What Am I?* (2008) and several articles on gender, sports, human rights, and media. Her most recent publication is "Ladies of Besiktas: A Dismantling of Male Hegemony at Inonu Stadium" (2013). She is also a long-distance runner and the co-founder of Adim Adim (Step by Step), Turkey's first charity running group. In 2009 she was featured on CNN Turk's "Turkey's Changemakers," which is sponsored by the Sabanci Foundation. She was awarded the Ten Outstanding Young Persons (TOYP) award in 2010.

Hande Eslen-Ziya received her doctorate degree at the Polish Academy of Sciences IFIS PAN, Warsaw. She also received a PhD specialization on gender studies at the Central European University in Budapest in 2002. Her research is theoretically informed by social psychology, feminist psychology, and sociology, as well as gender role strain, conceptions of femininity and masculinity, and gendered migration. Since 2011, Dr. Eslen-Ziya is the project coordinator of a two-year project titled "Construction of Femininity and Masculinity in Friday Prayers in Turkey." Her most recent publication is "Domestic Work, Gender and Migration in Turkey: Legal Framework Enabling Social Reality," in *The Discourse of Politics of Migration in Europe*, edited by U. Korkut (2013). Her other articles include "The Role of Women's Activism in the Amendments of the Turkish Penal Code: A Success Story," *Journal of Sociological Research* 15, no. 1 (Spring 2012): 119–49; "The Impact of Social Conservatism on Population Politics in Poland and Turkey," *Social Politics: International Studies in Gender, State & Society* 18, no. 3 (2011): 387–418; and "Political Religion and Politicized Women in Turkey: Hegemonic Republicanism Revisited," *Totalitarian Movements and Political Religions* 11, nos. 3–4 (2010): 311–26.

Mauricio Espinoza is a PhD candidate in Latin American and Latino/a studies at the Ohio State University. His scholarship focuses on literature, popular culture, and cultural studies, with an emphasis on Central America and U.S. Latino/a communities. He has published book chapters and essays on Latino/a advertising, comics, Costa Rican film, and folklore. He is co-translator of *The Fire's Journey* (2013), a translation of Costa Rican poet Eunice Odio's *El tránsito de fuego*. His poetry translations have appeared in several U.S. and British journals. He holds a bachelor of arts in journalism from Ashland University and a master of arts in Latin American studies from Ohio State.

T. Keith Edmunds is a PhD candidate at the University of Guelph. He is employed as an instructor in the School of Business at Assiniboine Community College.

Michael R. Kramer (PhD, University of Minnesota) is associate professor of communication studies and chair of the Department of Communication Studies, Dance, & Theatre at Saint Mary's College, a women's college in northern Indiana. His research interests include political rhetoric, media and cultural criticism, and image restoration. He also writes *Club Apologia*, a blog analyzing how public figures respond to controversy and scandal.

K. A. Laity is a tenured faculty member at the College of Saint Rose in Albany, New York, where she teaches medieval literature, popular culture, gender, film, and digital humanities. She was a Fulbright Fellow as well as the award-winning author of *Lush Situation, Owl Stretching, Unquiet Dreams, À la Mort Subite, The Claddagh Icon, Chastity Flame, Pelzmantel and Other Medieval Tales of Magic*, and *Unikirja*, as well as editor of *Weird Noir* and *Noir Carnival*. You can find her online at her website, http://www.kalaity.com, and on Facebook and Twitter. She divides her time between New York and Dundee, Scotland.

Lauren Lemley is an assistant professor of communication and director of the Speaking Center at Abilene Christian University. She received her PhD in communication with an emphasis in rhetoric and public affairs from Texas A&M University. Her dissertation focused on understanding and analyzing the rhetoric of the Salem witchcraft crisis, and her current research and teaching fall primarily in the fields of argumentation, public address, and public memory studies.

Sandra J. Lindow lives on a hilltop in Menomonie, Wisconsin, where she teaches, writes, edits, and competes with vermin for the plenitude of her vegetables and flowers. Her critical book *Dancing the Tao: Le Guin and Moral Development* was published in summer 2012. Other critical work can be found in "Addiction, Morality and Marriage in Geoff Ryman's *Lust*," *Foundation* 40, no. 113 (Spring 2011); *On Joanna Russ* (2009); and *Lois McMaster Bujold: Essays on a Modern Master of Science Fiction and Fantasy* (2013). Her seventh poetry collection, *The Hedge Witch's Upgrade*, was published in summer 2012.

Anita K. McDaniel is an associate professor at the University of North Carolina, Wilmington, where she teaches in the Department of Communication Studies. She received her BA degree in speech communication from Texas A&M University, her MA in interpersonal and organizational communication from the University of Houston, and her PhD in interpersonal communication from the University of Texas at Austin. She has presented papers at national conferences and published in international journals on the intertextual play between the visual and written texts represented in comic books. Her most recent publications include "Obama-man: The Fanboy Ideograph for 'Hope and Change'" and encyclopedia entries titled "[Women in] Comics: 1960–2005" and "Hip Hop Comics."

Nathan Miczo (PhD, University of Arizona, 2004) is a professor in the Department of Communication at Western Illinois University, where he teaches courses in interpersonal communication, health communication, research methods, and message production. He has published articles in the *Journal of Family Communication, Communication Studies, Health Communication, Human Studies,* the *Journal of Communication Studies,* the *Journal of Intercultural Communication Research, Communication Reports,* and *Qualitative Health Research,* as well as several book chapters.

AprilJo Murphy grew up in Malone, New York, a place that has given her a fondness for crossing borders and Laura Ingalls Wilder novels. Her first job was spiritual cleaning at the Ursuline Convent; she followed this up with secular employment at the Wead Library. For a time, she worked for Encyclopedia Britannica in Chicago, creating, editing, organizing, and secretly trying to memorize everything. AprilJo graduated from SUNY Fredonia in 2008 with a BA in English. Before graduation, she was an intern for Academic Affairs and wrote several chapters of *Beyond Normal: How to Make Your Writing Devilishly Good,* a project whose title is more clever than you'd think. In her heart of hearts, AprilJo's ventricles are powered by grammar and linguistic structures. Shortly after leaving Fredonia, AprilJo began her PhD in English at the University of North Texas, where she is currently a doctoral candidate in creative nonfiction writing and serves as the web editor for *American Literary Review.* She has worked various technical and professional communication jobs for deans' offices, university marketing, etc., while pursuing this generally-considered-worthless degree, and they have given her basic practical experience. A finalist for the 2012 Richard J. Margolis Award, AprilJo writes about bodies and what it means to have one in different kinds of culture. She doesn't think bodies are much different from grammar and encyclopedias, if you look at them just right. Her nonfiction has been published in *Mason's Road* and *Hippocampus* magazine, and her fiction is forthcoming in *Sinister Wisdom.* She is currently working on a radical project that reimagines the possibilities of memoir—a project that's secretly not very revolutionary at all. You can follow her at http://www.AprilJoMurphy.com.

Caryn E. Neumann is a lecturer in integrative studies and an affiliate in history at Miami University, Middletown. She earned a PhD in U.S. women's history from the Ohio State University. The author of three books, she serves as an area chair for the Midwest Popular Culture/American Culture Association.

Fernando Gabriel Pagnoni Berns currently works at the Universidad de Buenos Aires (UBA) – Facultad de Filosofía y Letras (Argentina) as graduate teaching assistant of estética del cine y teorías cinematográficas. He is a member of the research groups Investea (theatre) and Art-Kiné (cinema) and has published articles on Argentinean and international cinema and drama in the following publications: *Imagofagia, Cinedocumental, Telondefondo.org, Stichomythia, Ol3media, Anagnórisis-Theatrical Research Magazine, Lindes,* and *UpStage Journal.* He has published articles in the books *Undead in the West,* edited by Cynthia Miller and A. Bowdoin Van Riper, published by Scarecrow Press; *Horrofílmico: Aproximaciones al Cine de Terror en Latinoamerica y el Caribe,* edited by Rosana Diaz Sambrana and Patricia Tomé; *Lessons in Blood: Essays on the Saw Franchise,* edited by John Wallis and James Aston (forthcoming); and *The Culture & Philosophy of Ridley Scott,* edited by Nancy Kang and Ashley and Adam Barkman (forthcoming).

Trina Robbins, writer and herstorian, has been writing and drawing comics since before she produced the first all-woman comic book, *It Ain't Me, Babe,* in 1970. She also writes award-winning graphic novels for young readers and books about women: women who draw comics, women who kill, women from Ireland, women who happen to be goddesses. She lives in a 108-year-old house in San Francisco, California. In 2013 Trina Robbins was elected into the Will Eisner Comic Book Hall of Fame.

Adina Schneeweis teaches journalism and media communication at Oakland University. Dr. Schneeweis specializes in international mass communication, race and ethnicity communication, cultural studies, postcolonial studies, and visual communication. Her main research focus is on the Roma communities, commonly known as the Gypsies, as they are represented in a variety of discourses, ranging from the press, to popular culture, to advocacy for Roma rights. Her work is published in internationally renowned journals including *Women's Studies in Communication,* the *Journal of Communication Inquiry,* the *International Communication Gazette,* the *Journal of Visual Literacy, Intercultural Communication Studies, Ecquid Novi,* and the *Journalism & Mass Communication Quarterly.* A native of Romania, Dr. Schneeweis was a documentary writer, reporter, and editor, creating fifty-three documentaries for a national public television station.

Christina M. Smith received her MA in communication from San Diego State University and her PhD in communication from Arizona State University. She is currently an assistant professor of communication at California State University Channel Islands where she teaches courses in research methods, persuasion, and media campaigns. Her research interests are in visual rhetoric and digital culture as they relate to war and conflict, including studies of the Abu Ghraib images, soldier-produced videos from Iraq, and documentary films from soldiers and embedded journalists.

Christopher Paul Wagenheim is currently a third-year doctoral student in the American Culture Studies Department at Bowling Green State University in Bowling Green, Ohio. In addition to his doctoral studies, Wagenheim teaches for many departments on campus including telecommunications, ethnic studies, theatre and film, and American studies. He holds a master's degree in American studies from the University of South Florida in Tampa. His undergraduate work is in creative writing, also earned at the University of South Florida. Wagenheim's research primarily focuses on the representations of race and gender in popular culture, particularly those present in contemporary American film. He is also actively researching and writing on the genealogy of film scholarship in the United States.

Sharon Zechowski is a visiting assistant professor of communication at Miami University, Middletown. She teaches a wide variety of courses in the area of media criticism, history, and policy. Her research interests include critical cultural theory; mediated representations of social class, race, and gender; and the political economy of corporate media. She is currently writing an article about the end of shock radio and the mainstreaming of pornographic culture.